Further education today
A critical review

Further education today
A critical review

Leonard M. Cantor
and
I. F. Roberts

Routledge & Kegan Paul
London, Boston and Henley

First published in 1979
by Routledge & Kegan Paul Ltd
39 Store Street, London WC1E 7DD,
Broadway House, Newtown Road,
Henley-on-Thames, Oxon RG9 1EN and
8 Park Street, Boston, Mass. 02108, USA
Set in Press Roman 10/11pt by Columns
and printed in Great Britain by
Unwin Bros. Ltd

British Library Cataloguing in Publication Data

Cantor, Leonard Martin

Further education today
1 Adult education – England
2 Vocational education – England
3 Education, Higher – England
I Title II Roberts, Iolo Francis
374.9'42   LC5256.G7   79-41024

ISBN 0 7100 0412 5
ISBN 0 7100 0413 3 Pbk

Contents

Illustrations

Figures

Tables

Introduction

In this book, we use the term 'Further Education' generically to cover all forms of post-school education, except that provided by the universities. Clearly, further education so defined is a highly developed sector of our educational system covering a field of great diversity and embracing a wide variety of institutions. In November 1975, for example, there were over 3,920,000 students in more than 7,000 grant-aided establishments of further education made up of 30 polytechnics, about 600 major establishments and some 6,500 evening institutes. Of these students, over 1,212,000 were on courses leading to recognized qualifications, the rest attending recreational and cultural courses in further education colleges and evening institutes. Thus, while further education provision is broadly vocational in purpose, it also includes a great deal of general education, in the form of courses such as the General Certificate of Education, and also education for cultural and leisure activities which can broadly be defined as 'adult education'. We are concerned in this book almost exclusively with the provision of vocational and general education. In terms of standards, further education embraces the whole spectrum from lower-level courses for unqualified school-leavers right through to post-graduate courses. For the purposes of convenience, courses are generally classified as non-advanced, that is up to and including GCE A Level and TEC/BEC Certificates and Diplomas, and advanced. The latter provision, which makes up higher education within further education, has grown very considerably in recent years. As will readily be seen, further education therefore has a wider remit than any other sector of our educational system.

In writing this book, we have adopted a somewhat different approach from that in the two editions of our previous book on the subject, *Further Education in England and Wales*, Routledge & Kegan Paul, 1969 and 1972. The latter dealt with the whole of the post-war period from 1945 and included detailed descriptions of the various aspects of the further education sector, together with a critical analysis of its major features. In this book, we are concerned with a shorter time span, that is the 1970s, and have endeavoured to build on the previous book by assuming that the reader is familiar with the general landscape of further education, thereby enabling us to concentrate on providing, in the words of the title, a critical review of further education today. Although the title of the book no longer includes the words 'in England and Wales', these are the countries with whose system of further education we are concerned in this book, though from time to time reference will be made to other countries in order to illumine our own practices.

We hope this book will be of interest to students who are studying Education, irrespective of the field of educational practice they may later choose to enter; to industrialists who have special interests in this field; to the makers of educational policy, including politicians and administrators; and also to interested laymen.

Finally, although the conclusions we draw and any errors and omissions we have made are our own, we wish to express our appreciation to the following who have allowed us to make use of their knowledge and who have, in a variety of ways, helped us to write this book: Tom Driver, formerly General Secretary of NATFHE; Frank Fidgeon, Deputy Chief Officer of TEC; Janet Elliott, Deputy Chief Officer of BEC; Dr J.F. Dickenson, Director, North Staffordshire Polytechnic; E. Clements, Head of the Faculty of Art and Design, Wolverhampton Polytechnic; F.D. Say, Principal, Staffordshire College of Agriculture; J.H. Davies, Further Education Officer, WJEC; Professor J.R. Webster, Head of Education Department, University College, Aberystwyth; Geoffrey Melling, Director, FEU; Alistair Campbell, Librarian, Institute of Education, University of Keele and his staff for their help in obtaining source material; Geoffrey Barber who drew the maps and diagrams; others too numerous to mention who have responded willingly to requests for information and materials; and, above all, our wives who have been an unfailing source of encouragement and support.

Leonard M. Cantor
Iolo Roberts

1 Further education in the 1970s

In the second edition of our book, *Further Education in England and Wales*, we began by describing the phenomenal post-war growth in further education by which the number of students doubled from 1,595,000 in 1946 to 3,174,000 in 1970 and the number of teaching staff increased even more dramatically during that period from under 5,000 to 50,000. In the 1970s, the figures reveal a continuing growth so that by 1976, for example, further education establishments contained almost 4,000,000 students taught by over 76,000 teachers. However, as we shall see, this growth is partly due to the movement of the former colleges of education into the further education sector. The optimism and expectancy of continued expansion, particularly in regard to higher education, which infused education as recently as 1972 has, at the time of writing, been replaced by a more realistic appreciation of the situation. Two main factors are responsible for this radically changed position: the economic recession resulting in large part from the oil crisis following the 1973 Middle East war and the sharply declining birth rate of the late 1960s and early 1970s.

The first years of the 1970s were marked by a public debate on the nature and content of teacher education and training, a debate which had rumbled on for many years but which came to a head at this time. Public concern led to the setting up of the James Committee, which issued its report, 'Teacher Education and Training', in January 1972. Although the Report proposed no major institutional changes in the colleges of education sector, it did recommend that the colleges themselves should cease to be monotechnics providing only courses in teacher-training and should diversify their provision in the form of a two-year course of general education to be known as the Diploma of Higher Education (Dip.HE).

In December of the same year, the Conservative Government of the day issued its White Paper, 'Education: A Framework for Expansion', which, as its title indicates, still envisaged a period of continued growth, especially in higher education. Accordingly, it recommended that student places in higher education should be increased from under

1

500,000 in 1972 to 750,000 in 1981, the places to be shared equally between the universities and the further education sector. In other words, the public sector colleges should accommodate 375,000 students by 1981. This was to be accomplished partly by merging the great majority of the colleges of education, hitherto a separate sector of higher education, with polytechnics and other further education colleges. The White Paper, recognizing that there was some decline in the birth rate and that this would require a cut-back in the output of trained teachers, announced that the number of teacher-training places in the public sector colleges would be reduced from a maximum of 114,000 in 1972 to between 75,000 and 85,000 initial and in-service places by 1981. Finally, it strongly advocated the introduction of the Dip.HE as recommended by the James Report.

In the following March, the DES issued Circular 7/73, 'The Development of Higher Education in the Non-University Sector', asking local authorities and voluntary bodies to put forward detailed plans for the re-organization of the colleges of education which for the most part would be expected to move into the public sector. Clearly, at that time it was not envisaged that very drastic surgery would be required as the planned increase in student numbers would more than compensate for the reduction in teacher-training places. However, as the full impact of the steep decline in the birth rate, 832,000 live births in 1967 to just over 600,000 in 1975, began belatedly to be recognized by the DES, so it felt it necessary successively to reduce the number of teacher-training places in the colleges. The final target figures, announced at the end of 1977, are 45,000 places by 1981, including some 9,000 for in-service courses for practising teachers. The fall-out from these decisions has had far-reaching effects: the college of education sector has virtually disappeared; a number of colleges of education have closed altogether; the merger of the remaining colleges with further education colleges has created a new group of institutions known generally as Colleges or Institutes of Higher Education; and the further education sector has now acquired a substantial stake in teacher training, albeit considerably smaller than that envisaged in the 1972 White Paper. As a result, the institutional structure of further education has changed substantially in recent years (Figure 1).

Closely linked with these developments has been the growth of the Diploma of Higher Education. From the introduction of the first two courses in September 1974, student numbers have gradually increased to about 5,000 in 1977 on some 50 courses. However, these numbers are very tiny when compared to those of students on degree courses in further education who number more than 100,000 and, in any case, many of the Dip.HE programmes are, in effect, the first two years of an integrated degree course. It is therefore still too early to tell whether the Dip.HE has firmly taken root.

The growth of higher education in the further education sector has inevitably focused attention on the management of those institutions, notably the polytechnics, which are very largely concerned with the provision of advanced courses. Not surprisingly, they measure themselves against the universities and envy them their powers of self-validation of courses and, more especially, their relative freedom of financial management within agreed budgetary limits. By contrast, the polytechnics are constrained by the necessity of advanced course approval through the Regional Advisory Councils and by complex financial procedures exercised by the parent local education authorities and through the 'pool' (see p.99). These problems have been further complicated by the arrival on the scene of the Colleges and Institutes of Higher Education and their public airing has culminated in the 1978 Oakes Report, 'The Management of Higher Education in the Maintained Sector'. The Oakes Report recommended the establishment of a national body for England to oversee the development of maintained higher education, a recommendation that was taken up by the Labour Government which decided to press for the establishment of two national bodies, to be known as Advanced Further Education Councils (AFECs), one for England and one for Wales. This proposition was incorporated in an Education Bill which, by Spring 1979, had reached the Committee stage of the House of Commons when the general election intervened. At the time of writing (April 1979), it is uncertain whether the recommendations of the Oakes Report will be given legislative effect; should this occur, it will remain to be seen how far they succeed in resolving the management problems of the polytechnics and colleges of higher education.

The 1970s have also witnessed far-reaching changes in the field of industrial training. The structure created by the Industrial Training Act of 1964, based upon the creation of industrial training boards, was coming under increasing criticism by the beginning of the decade on the grounds that the boards had had only limited success in increasing the quantity and improving the quality of training. Consequently, the Government conducted a review of their work resulting in the publication in 1972 of a consultative document, 'Training for the Future'. It recommended the establishment of a National Training Agency to co-ordinate the work of the industrial training boards and to develop a national training advisory service, and it adumbrated the possibility of creating a general council on manpower services. These recommendations soon bore fruit with the passing in 1973 of the Employment and Training Act which declared the Government's intention of establishing a Manpower Services Commission (MSC) under the aegis of the Department of Employment. The MSC would

3

have as its main responsibility the promotion of more and better industrial training and for this purpose two executive bodies would be
created, to be known as the Training Services Agency (TSA) and the
Employment Services Agency (ESA). The Government moved rapidly
towards these objectives and the MSC was established in January 1974
and the TSA and the ESA in April 1974.

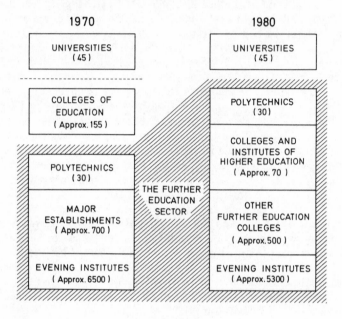

Figure 1   *The pattern of further and higher education in the 1970s*

In May 1975, the TSA (renamed the Training Services Division of
the MSC in April 1978) issued a discussion document, 'Vocational
Preparation of Young People', underlining the serious deficiencies in
the existing provision and suggesting appropriate action. This, in turn,
led to a joint initiative by the TSA and the Department of Education
and Science, namely the establishment of a limited number of schemes
of Unified Vocational Preparation (UVP) which came into being in
1977. Although they cater for relatively small numbers of young
people, these schemes are of considerable significance in that they
represent a joint venture by the major forces in industrial training
and education respectively.

Of considerably greater scope and significance in this respect is the
Youth Opportunities Programme (YOP), operated by the Special

4

Programmes Division (SPD) of the MSC. Set up in April 1978 to provide a comprehensive national scheme for over 200,000 unemployed school-leavers and stemming from the Holland Report, 'Young People and Work', published in May 1977, YOP is essentially an endeavour to prepare young people for work by means of Job Creation projects, work experience schemes and specially prepared programmes of further education. It is of great significance for the colleges in that it is introducing to further education a group of young people for whom they have scarcely catered before. This thrusts upon teachers in the colleges a considerable challenge, namely that of working out the most suitable provision for a group of youngsters many of whom have few or no qualifications and who in the course of their schooling were apathetic or even hostile towards education.

Another group of school-leavers who have been entering further education in increasing numbers in recent years are those between the age of 16 and 19 enrolled on full-time courses in the colleges. Relatively highly motivated, they are mainly undertaking courses leading to GCE awards, both at O and A levels, Ordinary National Diplomas, and CGLI awards. Many could have remained at school to continue their GCE studies; instead, for a variety of reasons, they have opted for the further education college. In some areas of the country, however, all provision for the 16 to 19 age group is made in one institution, known as the Tertiary or Junior College. As the effects of the sharp decline in the birth rate in the late 1960s and the first half of the 1970s begin to work their way through the education system, so it will become increasingly necessary to co-ordinate post-16 provision, presently made in school and further education colleges. In such circumstances, some local education authorities may well turn to the tertiary college as an attractive solution to their problem.

Another major area of further education which came under the microscope of public opinion in the late 1960s was technician education. The Haslegrave Committee issued its Report on Technician Courses and Examinations in 1969, advocating the introduction of a unified pattern of courses of technical education for technicians in industry and in the field of business and office studies. The Report recommended the establishment of two new councils, the Technician Education Council (TEC) and the Business Education Council (BEC), to devise and approve an entirely new pattern of courses spanning both advanced and non-advanced further education. Although these recommendations were accepted by the Government, there was a long delay before the new councils were created, so that it was not until March 1973 that TEC came into existence and May 1974 before BEC appeared upon the scene. Since then, however, as a result of the activities of the two councils, a completely new pattern of technician training is emerging, embracing not only education for technicians in industry and business but also some aspects of art and design education. In addition, it seems likely that the lower-level courses in agriculture will shortly be brought within the remit of TEC.

A belated and encouraging development in recent years has been the increase in teacher-training and staff development for further education, partly stimulated by curriculum changes wrought by bodies such as TEC and BEC and the CNAA. With the recommendations of the 1975 Haycocks Report on the training of full-time teachers of further education having been accepted by the Government, we may well be on the eve of a very considerable expansion of provision.

Wales, like England, has been subject to all these changes but events there have been given an added dimension both by the transfer to the Welsh Office of responsibility for all post-school education other than the university and also by the debate which preceded the referendum on devolution. Had the people of Wales voted in favour of devolution, it would have resulted in the creation of a Welsh Assembly with ultimate responsibility for all further education provision in Wales.

Finally, the present decade has witnessed an encouraging growth in research and curriculum development in further education. The number of research projects currently in operation is considerably larger than it was at the beginning of the 1970s. However, in terms of volume, it still lags far behind the amount of educational research sponsored by the university and school sectors. Curriculum development has been given a fillip by the work of TEC and BEC and by the need to cater for youngsters undertaking YOP and unified vocational preparation courses. The setting up, in January 1977, of the Further Education Curriculum Review and Development Unit (FEU) is a most welcome development and, if first indications are anything to go by, it should contribute greatly to much-needed curriculum development in the further education colleges.

Thus, during the 1970s, the further education sector has been, and indeed still is, undergoing a major transformation whose full effects have yet to be felt. The past decade has witnessed substantial changes in higher education within further education, like the creation of the new Colleges and Institutes of Higher Education and the introduction of the Diploma of Higher Education; major curricular developments are taking place in technician education as a result of the work of TEC and BEC; teaching-training and staff development in further education are increasing; and the growing problem of unemployment has stimulated the provision by the MSC of industrial training and associated further education and highlighted the need properly to integrate education and training. Above all, perhaps, increasing public concern over these issues has been the stimulus which has led government, industry and the education service to take remedial and long-overdue action. How effective this will turn out to be only time will tell.

2 The administrative framework

The educational system of England and Wales is commonly described as a 'national system, locally administered', with the Department of Education and Science as a major operational partner rather than its sole controller.[1] The other partner is, of course, the local educational authorities (LEAs). The legal basis for this partnership is supplied by the 1944 Education Act, together with various amending acts, and within the legal framework which these provide the Secretary of State for Education and Science is given overall responsibility for all education in England, whilst the Secretary of State for Wales has, since April 1978, had a similar responsibility for Wales. The day-to-day running of the education service is, however, the responsibility of the local education authorities upon whom the 1944 Education Act placed, for the first time, a statutory duty to provide 'adequate facilities' for further education in their areas, further education being defined as full-time education and leisure-time occupation for persons over compulsory school-leaving age.

One major feature of further education which distinguishes it from both the school sector and the universities is the existence of regional machinery, primarily in the form of Regional Advisory Councils (RACs). Thus, in broad terms, further education is administered at three levels: national, regional and local (Figure 2). At the national level, the most important agency is, of course, the DES. However, there is also a number of other interested parties of varying degrees of influence ranging from government departments such as the Department of Employment, operating principally through the Manpower Services Commission, and the Ministry of Agriculture, Fisheries and Food; through bodies representing industry, business and trade unions like the Confederation of British Industry, the British Association for Commercial and Industrial Education (BACIE), the Industrial Training Boards and the National Association of Teachers in Further and Higher Education (NATFHE); to validating and/or examining bodies such as the Council for National Academic Awards (CNAA), the Technician and Business Education Councils (TEC and BEC), the City and Guilds of London

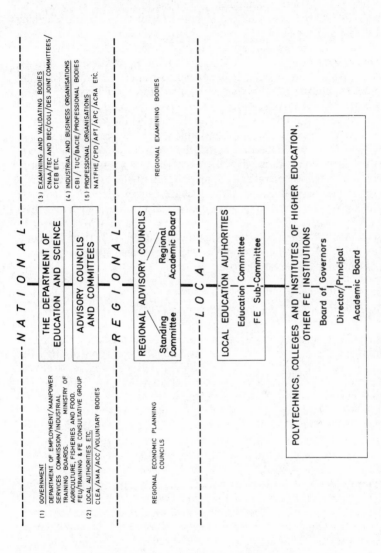

Figure 2 *The administrative framework of further education*

NATIONAL

(1) GOVERNMENT
DEPARTMENT OF EMPLOYMENT/MANPOWER
SERVICES COMMISSION/INDUSTRIAL
TRAINING BOARDS.   MINISTRY OF
AGRICULTURE, FISHERIES AND FOOD.
FEU/TRAINING & FE CONSULTATIVE GROUP
(2) LOCAL AUTHORITIES ETC.
CLEA/AMA/ACC/VOLUNTARY BODIES

THE DEPARTMENT OF
EDUCATION AND SCIENCE

ADVISORY COUNCILS
AND COMMITTEES

(3) EXAMINING AND VALIDATING BODIES
CNAA/TEC AND BEC/CGLI/DES JOINT COMMITTEES/
CTEB ETC.
(4) INDUSTRIAL AND BUSINESS ORGANISATIONS
CBI/ TUC/BACIE/PROFESSIONAL BODIES
(5) PROFESSIONAL ORGANISATIONS
NATFHE/CPD/APT/APC/ACRA ETC.

REGIONAL

REGIONAL ECONOMIC PLANNING
COUNCILS

REGIONAL ADVISORY COUNCILS

Standing   Regional
Committee   Academic Board

REGIONAL EXAMINING BODIES

LOCAL

LOCAL EDUCATION AUTHORITIES

Education Committee

FE Sub-Committee

POLYTECHNICS, COLLEGES AND INSTITUTES OF HIGHER EDUCATION,
OTHER FE INSTITUTIONS

Board of Governors

Director/Principal

Academic Board

Institute (CGLI) and a wide range of professional bodies. At the regional level, in addition to the RACs, both Regional Economic Planning Councils and Regional Examining Boards have an interest in and an influence on further education. Finally, at the local level, the prime agencies are, of course, the local education authorities and through them their establishments, together with a number of colleges run by voluntary bodies, all of which seek to meet the needs of and, to an extent, reflect the wishes of local industry and business.

However, this tripartite division is merely a convenient way of expressing a complex relationship which, in many cases, transgresses the boundaries we have drawn: one has only to think of the average polytechnic which although run by a local education authority is, in terms of its full-time student population, essentially a national institution; or the local education authorities themselves which seek to exert a collective influence through the Council of Local Education Authorities (CLEA), a national body which represents them all. Thus, bearing in mind that the administrative structure of further education is a complex matrix, we shall endeavour to describe the main agencies operating at the national, regional and local levels.

The Department of Education and Science (DES)

The DES is relatively small, as government departments go, and almost wholly concerned with policy. In addition to operating through the performance of certain statutory duties, it relies to a large extent on the influence which it exerts on the local education authorities and the teaching profession.[2] The Department is headed by the Secretary of State, who is a member of the Cabinet, supported by two Ministers of State, one of whom is Minister for the Arts, and a hierarchy of permanent civil servants. The work of the department is divided into four broad areas: schools and educational building; higher and further education; civil science, arts and libraries; and educational planning, each of which is further subdivided, as appropriate. Thus, within higher and further education there are four separate policy branches. The first is concerned with planning the development of higher education in the non-university sector, including policy on the Dip.HE. The second branch deals with the building programme for the whole of non-advanced further education, advanced further education including polytechnics, a wide range of subject areas including art and design, agriculture, paramedical training and social work, and adult education. The third branch deals with further education for industry, including the work of TEC and BEC and the industrial training boards, and the Youth Service. The fourth branch is primarily concerned with policy matters relating to the universities but also deals with policy relating to financial support for all students in higher education.

Her Majesty's Inspectors (HMIs), servants of the Department in fact if not in name, act as a field force for the DES in the oversight of all aspects of education, including further education. Of the six Chief Inspectors who are based at Elizabeth House, the DES headquarters in London, one is specifically concerned with further education and thus acts as a major link on matters of policy and planning between the DES and the inspectors who are in the field. These work both as members of territorial teams, England being divided into eight territorial divisions, and as subject specialists. Since responsibility for all non-university education in Wales was devolved upon the Welsh Office in Cardiff in April 1978, Wales now has its own inspectorate. Nationally, HMIs act as assessors on such bodies as the CNAA and the industrial training boards, and include in their ranks the Regional Staff Inspectors (RSIs) who advise the RACs and make recommendations to the DES on such matters as the viability and location of advanced courses. At the local level, inspectors act as consultants who help and advise colleges on a wide range of subjects and contribute to the solution of specific problems within the institutions. The inspectorate also engages selectively in the in-service training of further education teachers in the regions and mounts an annual programme of short courses for serving teachers.

Thus, the DES exercises control and direction over the further education sector in a variety of ways. Through its Finance Branch it negotiates with the Department of the Environment which pays the Rate Support Grant (RSG) annually to local authorities as the government's contribution to the cost of local services including education. As central government funds averaged about 61 per cent of local authority net approved expenditure in 1977-8, the rest coming from local rates, this clearly represents a substantial degree of influence. In addition, the Department is responsible for controlling the rate, nature and distribution of educational building and its approval must be obtained before a local authority can borrow money to undertake a major scheme of capital building. The DES also disburses direct grants to a few specialist colleges and a small number of independent further education colleges.

Through its Circulars and Administrative Memoranda it advises and instructs local authorities on a wide range of topics including the development of higher education in the non-university sector, the government of technical colleges, and the setting up of vocational preparation schemes. It has recently extended its interest into the field of further education curriculum development by establishing, in January 1977, the Further Education Curriculum Review and Development Unit (FEU) whose remit is to act as a focal point for curricular matters in further education. It also collaborates with the Department of

11

Employment in the work of the Training and Further Education Consultative Group which provides a forum for the discussion of matters of common interest to the education and training services.

In these various ways, the DES exerts a considerable degree of control and direction over the whole spectrum of further education and its future development. However, it is difficult to detect a clear-cut DES policy for the further education sector as, indeed, for the educational system as a whole. Although, as we have seen, the DES does undertake a good deal of long-term planning, it has been subject to considerable criticism that its concept of planning is too limited. In 1975, for example, the Organization for Economic Co-operation and Development (OECD) issued a highly critical report based on a study of the Department's activities.[3] It made three main criticisms of the DES's planning activities: that too many of them take place in secret; that the Department takes too passive a role by merely reacting to events instead of identifying new goals and influencing trends and demands accordingly; and that its attitude to planning is too purely educationally oriented and is not sufficiently concerned with the role of education in meeting the needs of a modern industrial society. These criticisms were, interestingly enough, in large part publicly endorsed by Lord Crowther-Hunt, himself a former Minister of State at the DES.[4] They were then picked up by the education sub-committee of the House of Commons Expenditure Committee which issued a report on the subject towards the end of 1976.[5] Dismissing some of the complaints made about the DES by the OECD and others – it considers, for example, that the Department did all it reasonably could to publicize its policy on the re-organization of the colleges of education, though Hencke, for one, would disagree[6] – it none the less concludes that it is too secretive at times and does not involve outside interest groups in long-term planning. Among its recommendations are that the Department should make many more documents open to the public and should encourage wider public debate about policy; that a Standing Education Commission, of employers, trade unionists and others, should be set up to bring more outsiders into the education debate; and that DES planners should spend more time considering broad educational objectives, and not just the allocation of resources.

The root of the problem, as identified by Lord Crowther-Hunt and others, is that the DES is ill-organized to assume an effective planning role. Certainly, the DES is working under very considerable difficulties and, inevitably, given an annual budget of the order of £1,500 million, much of its time is bound to be taken up with resource allocation. The pressures of its workload are enormous, it lacks sufficient staff expert in further education, the demands made upon the inspectorate are inordinately heavy, and the Department's complex, internal structure inhibits the development of a coherent policy. It might be possible, however, to shed some of the existing responsibilities by, for example, dispensing with some of the detailed control — like the requirement that local authorities submit schemes for further education — presently exercised by the Secretary of State.[7] Certainly, the DES is not unaware of its own shortcomings and, as a consequence, has been undergoing, at the hands of a committee of senior civil servants, a thorough review of its changing role and its relationship with the rest of Whitehall and with the local authorities, in a period of economic austerity and public concern about educational provision. The review is taking into account the criticisms made by OECD in 1975 and by the sub-committee of the House of Commons Expenditure Committee in 1976. As, however, it assumes a continuation of the existing machinery of government and as its chairman is Sir James Hamilton, permanent secretary to the Department who has already been responsible for strengthening the planning side of the DES, it is unlikely to recommend radical changes.

What seems undeniable, however, is that in recent years the DES has indeed reacted to events rather than tried to shape them. This would certainly seem to be true of its policy of re-organizing the colleges of education sector. Similarly, until very recently, it has done little to provide for the further education of the less well-educated school-leaver and appears almost to have been drawn into this important area by the activities of the Manpower Services Commission, which admittedly, unlike the DES, has obtained from the government large sums of money for this purpose. In the field of technician education, too, the DES has appeared to drag its feet: as we have seen, four years elapsed between the recommendations of the Haslegrave Committee in 1969 and the setting up of TEC and BEC in 1973 and 1974 and, since then, the Department appears to have contributed little in the way of constructive criticism in public to the work of the two councils. Nor is the position any better in the field of art and design education: it was back in April 1974 that the Gann Report on Vocational Courses in Art and Design recommended the establishment of a national validating body, but it was not until February 1977 that responsibility for validating these courses was passed to TEC. In broad terms, the Department seems to have been unable or unwilling to think of further education provision in its totality and to formulate a clear-cut policy which, among other things, accords priorities and endeavours to bridge the divide between advanced and non-advanced further education. The resulting lack of firm leadership, which can only come from the DES, inevitably leaves the further education sector somewhat bereft of a sense of direction.

13

National Advisory Councils

In formulating policy, the Secretary of State relies on a number of National Advisory Councils, of which the most influential in further education has been, until recently, the *National Advisory Council on Education for Industry and Commerce (NACEIC)*. Set up by the Minister of Education in 1948, it had as its chief function, 'to keep under continuous review and to advise the Secretary of State by means of reports and in other ways on the national policy necessary for the full development of education in relation to industry and commerce'. Membership of NACEIC, mostly nominees of the Regional Advisory Councils, consisted of representatives of local authorities, teaching staffs of establishments of further education, universities, and industry and commerce. Abolished by the DES at the end of 1977 and not replaced, it provided a unique forum for the expression of a collective view on the further education sector by both educational and industrial interests. During its lifetime, and more particularly during recent years under the chairmanship of Sir Lionel Russell, it made a very substantial contribution to the development of the further education sector. In the past decade, for example, it sponsored both the Haslegrave Report on technician education and the Hudson Report on agricultural education and, in the last few years, it has greatly helped to increase awareness of the need to provide adequately for the education and training of the 16 to 19 age group.

Although it was agreed by both the DES and the NACEIC itself that it had become necessary to change the Council's structure and mode of operation, the unilateral decision by the Secretary of State to do away with it altogether came as a surprise, especially since it had been expected that it would be replaced by a smaller, streamlined body, whose terms of reference would be 'to keep under review and tender advice upon all aspects of further education and its development'.[8] As the NACEIC was unique in being the only national body representing both education in the public and university sectors and also industry and commerce, and in spanning the whole provision of further education, both advanced and non-advanced, its demise has left a vacuum which will in no way be filled even if the National Body recommended by the Oakes Report comes into existence.

Another important national body established by the DES is the *Advisory Committee on the Supply and Training of Teachers* (ACSTT), whose membership includes representatives of further education teaching staffs, local education authorities, school headmasters, universities and the CNAA. It has in turn established a Sub-Committee on the Training of Teachers in Further Education which in the last few years has produced three influential reports, one on the training of full-time

14

education teachers, one on part-time teachers and the third on training for education management. Another important body whose remit extends into further education is the *Advisory Council for Adult and Continuing Education* which was set up in the autumn of 1977 under the chairmanship of Dr Richard Hoggart, Warden of Goldsmiths' College, London. There is also a *National Advisory Committee for Printing Education*, which has recently put forward proposals for re-organizing printing education. Finally, if the recommendation of the Oakes Report is accepted, we shall have new national bodies, somewhat analogous to the Universities Grants Committee, with responsibility for advising on the total provision to be made for higher education in the public sector.

The Regional Advisory Councils

The responsibility for co-ordinating further education provision in different areas of England and Wales rests with the Regional Advisory Councils (RACs), which were established in 1947-8 by voluntary co-operation between local education authorities and are financed by them. There are ten RACs in all, nine in England and one, the Welsh Joint Education Committee (WJEC), for Wales. However, they have strange areas of jurisdiction in so far as these do not coincide with any other regional units such as regional economic planning councils or regional divisions of Her Majesty's Inspectorate.[9] Moreover, they do not always coincide with local authority boundaries, in some instances no precise boundary has been determined and, strangest of all, they occasionally have overlapping jurisdiction as in the case of Wiltshire and Dorset which fall both within the Southern and South-Western RACs. In addition, the functions of the RACs vary somewhat one from the other. However, they have in common their chief purpose which is to advise the constituent LEAs and the further education colleges in the region on the needs which have to be met in relation to all aspects of further education and to seek to co-ordinate provision in the region. Accordingly, they fulfil a number of important functions which generally include: a regular review of further education provision to identify deficiencies and to avoid unnecessary duplication; the provision of a forum for the exchange of ideas among the further education institutions and between them and industry, business, government agencies such as the Manpower Services Commission, and the universities in the region; and making known the facilities available in the region by publishing Directories, Bulletins, Reports and the like. RACs also commonly organize short courses, conferences and seminars and encourage the training and staff development of further education teachers. In addition, some RACs organize and make arrangements for examinations.

The structure of a typical Council is complex but, broadly speaking, each is administered by a permanent secretary and a small supporting staff and delegates its responsibilities to its main committees, a Regional Academic Board and a Standing Committee. In addition, much of the detailed work is done by a lower layer of committees which fall broadly into two categories: the first is concerned with general considerations such as fees and other matters affecting local authority financial resources, examinations and teacher education and training and the second consists of advisory committees in specific subject areas.

A very important element in the work of any RAC is the part it plays in the complex procedures of course approval which apply to the further education sector. Under current DES regulations, all institutions within an RAC have to submit proposals for advanced courses, previously approved by the LEA. These fall into two categories: full-time courses, other than teaching-training proposals, which once approved by the RAC have then to be submitted to the Secretary of State for approval; and all wholly part-time courses, other than post-graduate Dip.HE, and initial teacher-training courses, for which the RACs themselves have powers of approval under general authority from the Secretary of State. In both cases, approval is based upon the provision of appropriate support and facilities and viable numbers of students and not upon academic validation. The way in which the system works is that proposals for advanced full-time courses go simultaneously to the RAC and the DES's Regional Staff Inspector (RSI). Once the RAC has approved the application, usually in consultation with the RSI, it is then looked at again by the RSI and the DES against overall national provision and the support being obtained for similar courses elsewhere. The final decision is then made by the DES in this context. The rationale behind this procedure is clear: it is to try to ensure that expensive, full-time advanced courses should be provided only if there is a demonstrable need and sufficient students and facilities to make them viable.

Inevitably, however, this complex procedure has caused a great deal of dissatisfaction and criticism within the colleges. The polytechnics in particular argue, with a good deal of justice, that many of their proposed courses will draw their students from the country as a whole and should not therefore be judged by regional criteria; and that the bureaucratic procedures involved are unnecessarily convoluted and impose undue delays on the development of new courses. At the RAC level, it is contended that the procedures cause friction between local authorities and colleges and, as a result, local and individual interest occasionally predominate over academic judgments. Moreover, since the basic concept of resource provision is extremely nebulous at the outset of the procedures, it is very doubtful whether they can operate effectively. Finally, there are those who believe that as a result of the powers given by the system to the RSI, his role is 'inconsistent with democracy'.[10] However, at the time of writing, the future of these arrangements is uncertain. If the recommendations of the Oakes Report are implemented, individual course approval will be replaced by a procedure which allows colleges offering a substantial programme of advanced work to obtain approval from a national body for a programme of work for a period of three to five years. Thus, in this respect, the role of the RACs will inevitably be somewhat diminished. However, the Oakes Report has also recommended that nine new RACs be established for England and that their remit should be extended to include courses of initial teacher-training in public sector institutions.

When considering the future of the RACs, it should be borne in mind that despite the criticism to which they have been subjected they have made a number of positive contributions to the development of further education in recent years. Although clearly there are considerable differences between one RAC and another in respect of their modes of operation and general effectiveness, nonetheless they have made useful contributions to the work of TEC and BEC and of the Training Services Division of the MSC by stimulating regional discussions of their proposals. In the same way, they are providing a forum for an airing of the work of the Further Education Curriculum Review and Development Unit. With the abolition of the University Area Training Organisations, they have provided an administrative structure for the provision of initial teacher training in the public sector colleges. At least one of them, the Welsh Joint Education Committee, has had an important function as an examining body and, recently, the West Midlands RAC has taken on a similar role by absorbing the Union of Educational Institutions, the Regional Examining Body offering examinations for operatives, craftsmen and technicians in the region.

In these various ways, the RACs perform useful administrative and advisory functions. However, they are faced with a number of fundamental problems, not least that, having only a small permanent secretariat, they have to rely heavily on the voluntary services of the chairmen and members of their committees. The burden of work on the permanent staff is heavy and has grown considerably in recent years as, for example, the re-organization of the colleges of education has given the RACs new responsibilities. It is for this reason that one RAC has recently commissioned an expert inquiry into the working of its Secretariat to determine the most effective and efficient organization and structure to meet present and future regional needs. Another problem is that any body of this kind which provides a forum for the airing of the views of the further education sector inevitably exposes itself to the tensions which are endemic to it: the rivalry between local education authorities; the conflicting aspirations of one institution and another; and the competition for resources between advanced and non-advanced provision. Moreover, in so far as the RACs are financed by the local education authorities, it is inevitable that to a considerable extent they reflect their views and are the forum for compromises between constituent LEAs. In the words of a strongly critical review of the RACs, 'Horse-trading between authorities is no way to encourage rationality, innovation or economy'.[11] The fundamental issue therefore is 'What is the precise role of a regional body such as a Regional Advisory Council?'. The Oakes Report answers this question somewhat obliquely by recommending that, although they are still to be financed by the LEAs, the RACs should be established by trust deeds and should have governing bodies with two main sub-committees: the first to concern itself with higher education including initial teacher-training and the second with the induction and in-service training of teachers. The Report also considers that it would probably be convenient if the RACs extended their functions to include non-advanced further education but does not develop this argument since it lies outside the Committee's terms of reference. However, the Oakes' recommendations have marked shortcomings: they do not clarify the relationship between the RACs and the proposed national body; while indicating the need for co-operation between the RACs and the universities, they, perhaps understandably, give no firm suggestions how this might be accomplished; in respect of teacher-training, they make no clear recommendations for the co-ordination of provision between the public sector colleges and the universities; they do nothing to bridge the gap between advanced and non-advanced course provision; and, given that the effectiveness of the RACs depends in large part upon the appointment of an appropriate secretariat, the Report perpetuates the arrangements whereby the funds to appoint staff to run the RACs are derived from the member LEAs.

All in all, therefore, while the implementation of the Oakes Report, should it come about, will make for a more rational structure in some respects, in others it will leave the fundamental problems unresolved. It should certainly ease the burden of advanced course approval both on the colleges and on the RACs and, provided university interests can be accommodated, it should also rationalize the present *ad hoc* arrangements for teacher-training by officially including them within the remit of the RACs. On the other hand, it will do little or nothing to still the two fundamental criticisms which have been levelled at the RACs in the thirty years of their existence: that, as the virtual servants of the LEAs, they do not control objectively the regional allocation of resources; and that largely because of their inadequate secretariats, they have not paid sufficient attention to forward planning.

A more radical solution is that proposed by Regan:[12] that, ideally, they should become units of administration and absorbed into a regional tier of government, as and when it is created. Should devolution come about in Scotland and perhaps eventually in Wales, the next step may be regional devolution in England, in which case Regan's proposal becomes a real possibility. In the meantime, the boundaries of the RACs should be redrawn so that they are unambiguous and coincide with those of Her Majesty's Inspectorate divisions and they should co-ordinate non-advanced as well as advanced course provision. Although it seems unlikely that any of these reforms will come about in the near future, the need for a strong regional presence in the administrative framework of further education remains. Unlike the school sector, further education transcends local authority boundaries, particularly in the case of vocational course provision. Moreover, since the demise of the NACEIC, the RACs are the only forum reflecting a wide range of interests including the education service and industry and business.

Certainly, the local authorities are anxious to press ahead with the establishment of successors to the RACs. In January 1979, the Council of Local Education Authorities (CLEA) issued a draft circular and guidelines on regional machinery for Further Education in England to all LEAs in England. In it, the Council suggested to LEAs that they make a start on the process of establishing what it calls Regional Advisory and Consultative Councils for Further Education (RACCsFE), a suggestion with which the DES concurred. These bodies will assume the functions of the present RACs and will also assume new ones, notably in connection with the training and education of teachers. They will shed some functions, however, notably the approval of advanced courses. CLEA suggests that a suitable description of their new functions might be: to consider, promote, monitor and advise LEAs and institutions in the region and the Advanced Further Education Councils on the planning, co-ordination and development in the regions of (a) advanced further education outside the universities, including the initial, induction and in-service education and training of teachers and (b), at the discretion of the constituent LEAs, non-advanced further education.

The proposed RACCsFE will, therefore, have only an advisory role as far as advanced further education is concerned. However, this presupposes that the AFECs will come into existence and, as we have seen, this is, at the time of writing, uncertain. As far as non-advanced further education is concerned, the role of the existing RACs varies considerably; the new bodies, if they come about in the form suggested by CLEA, will exercise the functions outlined above, unless the circumstances in any region preclude it.

In conclusion, mention must be made of the Standing Conference of Regional Advisory Councils (SCRAC), a national body which was set up by the RACs to provide a forum for the exchange of views between them and to represent their collective views on matters falling within their competence. SCRAC sees itself as an advisory and consultative body providing a national forum for a wide range of education and training interests and with the demise of the NACEIC its role has become more important. However, it is less widely representative than the NACEIC and, as it essentially reflects the views of the LEAs and the secretariats of the RAC, it cannot be considered an adequate substitute for it. Moreover, it is at present in something of a limbo as the secretariats of the RACs, rather low in morale and fearful of the future, await the outcome of the Oakes Report.

The Local Education Authorities (LEAs)

As we have seen, the responsibility for providing further education rests very largely with the local education authorities, the cost being met from the central government's Rate Support Grant and from local rates.* As a result of the Local Government Act of 1972, local government boundaries were reoganized, substantially reducing the number of authorities and, for the most part, enlarging their areas. Since April 1974, when the new act came into operation, there have been 105 LEAs, consisting of the Inner London Education Authority, the 20 outer London Boroughs, 30 English shire counties, 36 metropolitan districts in England, the 8 Welsh counties, and the Isles of Scilly. As previously indicated, the LEAs are required by the 1944 Education Act to provide adequate facilities for further education in their areas and, for this purpose, their education committees set up from their members a sub-committee with special responsibility for further education. The day-to-day administration of education is in the hands of a Chief Education Officer who is assisted by senior administrative staff, one of whom usually has special responsibility for further education. In addition, LEAs employ a number of advisors, organizers or local inspectors who give advice to teachers, including those in the colleges, and to the authority itself concerning its further education provision.

Within the local authority structure, therefore, further education

*In addition, there is a small number of independent colleges of further education which do not operate under any form of local government control and are owned by a proprietor-principal, by a Trust, or by a company. Self-financed from fees received from their students, they are for the most part located in London and the southern half of England and are small, having 150 students or fewer. The best known of these colleges are members of the Conference of Independent Further Education.

is treated separately from the schools in so far as it is dealt with by a separate committee structure. To a large extent, this reflects not only the fact that the number of institutions is relatively small but also that public interest is concentrated more upon the schools which in many cases are regarded as more important. While this fact of life may or may not work to the disadvantage of the further education colleges, it has undoubtedly made it more difficult to co-ordinate provision for the 16 to 19 age group as a whole. Attitudes among authorities are, however, beginning to change as is evidenced by the growing number of authorities like Staffordshire which has appointed an advisor with special responsibility under a newly-established steering committee for provision for the 16 to 19 year-olds. However, policy towards this particular educational issue, as towards local government in general, varies considerably from authority to authority, depending much on the political views of the council and the predilections of individual influential councillors.

Although the LEAs' main concerns are centred around provision within the boundaries of their own areas, their interests also extend beyond them to the regional and national levels. As we have seen, the authorities are much involved, through the Regional Advisory Councils, with provision throughout their regions and with such matters as inter-authority payments to students who live in one local authority area but study in another authority's college. Commonly, within the RAC there is a very influential sub-committee made up of the Chief Education Officers of the constituent LEAs. In addition, the CEOs or their nominees attend all the RAC's main committees. Above all, since the LEAs directly control the purse strings of the RACs, they, to say the least, strongly influence their decisions.

At the national level, the local authorities express their views on local government as a whole through two major bodies, the Association of County Councils (ACC) and the Association of Metropolitan Authorities (AMA). To represent their educational interests, they have established the Council of Local Education Authorities (CLEA) which is, in effect, an amalgam of the two wider bodies. CLEA has taken an active part in discussions concerning the future of further education, particularly in respect of higher education since the publication of the 1972 White Paper, and in 1975, for example, put forward proposals that new, larger RACs be established, to be known as Further Education Advisory Councils in the Regions (FEACRs), with a remit embracing the whole of further education including teacher-training.[13] Thus, they would have three main areas of responsibility: initial teacher training; in-service teacher-training, including induction courses and the provision of professional centres; and the provision of non-advanced further education and advanced courses in the public sector. Not surprisingly, these proposals attracted strong opposition, primarily from the Committee of Directors of Polytechnics who advocated the creation of a national body, and from teacher-training interests in the universities who objected to their inclusion in the regional framework. Having failed, therefore, to command general acceptance, CLEA's proposals were dropped.

Following the appearance of the Oakes Report, the ACC and AMA considered its major recommendations and agreed in principle with them. However, the LEAs were unhappy about a number of unresolved issues[14] and have been pressing for more representatives on the AFECs and for the removal of the clause enabling individual polytechnics to transfer to national control. It was for these reasons that the Education Bill, first placed before parliament at the end of 1978, proposing the establishment of the two AFECs, left these contentious issues unresolved. In January 1979, as we have seen, CLEA put forward proposals for the establishment of Regional Advisory and Consultative Councils for Further Education as successor bodies to the RACs. However, these bodies assumed the creation of AFECs which would have come into being had the Education Bill not become a casualty of the forthcoming general election. At the time of writing (April 1979), it is not easy to forecast the future of the Education Bill. If the Labour government is returned to office, it will probably be resubmitted quite quickly to parliament; if, on the other hand, a Conservative government comes to power, its future is much more problematical. But whatever happens to the proposed AFECs, existing regional machinery will, sooner or later, have to be reshaped, if only to embrace teacher training. When that happens, it is quite likely that the new RACs will assume a form not unlike that suggested by CLEA.

As far as relationships between local authorities and their further education colleges are concerned, these inevitably vary a great deal from authority to authority and, indeed, between the authorities and individual colleges. However, it is generally the case that the Principals and Governing Bodies of the colleges are given more freedom of manoeuvre than the schools. In the case of a particular establishment, such as a technical college, for example, the Principal is the chief executive, being responsible for the organization, management, conduct and discipline of the college. Traditionally, he has tended to be 'all powerful' within his college; in recent years, however, his role has changed considerably, partly because of the growth in size and complexity of most colleges and partly in response to changing attitudes towards authority by staff and students alike. This process was given a strong push by the DES which, much to its credit, was anxious to ensure that staff were treated as responsible, professional people and given a voice in determining the policies of their colleges. Consequently, in April 1970, it issued Circular 7/70 calling upon local authorities to submit new draft articles of government for their colleges for DES approval. The Circular recommended that members of the teaching staff be represented on the governing bodies of the colleges and, more important, that Academic Boards be set up to advise the Principal on 'the planning, co-ordination, and development of the academic work of the college as a whole'. A typical Academic Board should consist of the Principal as Chairman, the Vice-Principal, the Heads of Departments, the college Librarian, and elected and co-opted members of the teaching staff and students.

During the next few years, Academic Boards were very widely established and, as a consequence there has been some weakening of local authority control over the colleges. However, the local authorities still retain considerable influence as, for example, their powers to approve estimates which can be used as a lever for wider intervention.[15] Indeed, one critic of that system believes that as decisions are more diffuse and the outcome of bargaining and *ad hoc* situations, so the intervention of the local authority in college administration is likely to be encouraged.[16] The role of the Principal has also changed, as acting as Chairman of the Academic Board has become an essential part of his duties. Some Principals, being used to situations where on most issues they were the sole authority, have had difficulty in coming to terms with their new role; on the other hand, some Academic Boards seem content to allow the Principal to exert authority much as he has always done. In other cases, staff and student participation in the development of the colleges, through their membership of the Academic Board, has reached a very high level and, indeed, it is not unknown for the Principal to delegate almost entire responsibility for the academic work of the college to his Academic Board.[17] In general, however, as Academic Boards are in part democratically elected bodies they inevitably suffer from the problem of constantly changing membership so that if they are to function effectively they need a strong lead from the Chairman, a stance which most Principals are only too happy to adopt.

In some ways, the most difficult and demanding responsibility which devolves upon the Principal is the effective management of men and women. This is a complex matter, involving not only the teaching staff, but also the college administrative staff, technicians, and ancillary staff and, of course, the students. An essential aspect of successful management, certainly where the teaching staff are concerned, is to devise an effective programme of staff development both in the interests of the college at large and the individual teachers themselves. Indeed, many Principals are increasingly regarding this aspect of their work as one of cardinal importance.

As the work of the colleges has become more complex and the

administration more bureaucratic, so the proper financial management of the institution has become more demanding, especially since local authorities tend to delegate more authority to the Principal in this regard than to the headmaster of a school. This calls for the Principal to be possessed of a knowledge of financial management of a fairly high order and, in this respect, the Further Education Staff College at Coombe Lodge has been of great assistance in running courses on college management for Principals and the senior staff of colleges. In addition to his statutory duties in running the college, the Principal must also establish successful relationships with local industry, with government agencies such as the Manpower Services Commission, and with the community; he must make known the work of the college both locally and, in many cases, also regionally and nationally. This part of his activities has grown considerably in recent years as the work of the colleges has ramified and in many instances spread well beyond its immediate locality.

In all these concerns, the Principal has to work with and through his Board of Governors who are charged with general responsibility for the direction of the college and its educational provision, including staffing, financial control and the approval of courses. A typical governing body includes members appointed by the local authority; representatives of local industry, the professions and trade unions; the Principal; members of the Academic Board and representatives of the full-time teaching staff and students; together with a number of co-opted members. In most cases, the Chairman of the Governing Body, who is elected to his office, is the key figure who gives a lead to his colleagues and it is essential, therefore, to the smooth operation of the college that the Principal and his Chairman establish an effective working relationship.

Although we have concentrated on the role of the Principal as the single most important member of the college administrative hierarchy, we would not wish to gainsay the important part played in the life of the college by other senior staff such as Vice-Principals and Heads of Departments, especially in the larger colleges where they have considerable administrative responsibilities devolved upon them. However, space does not permit us to examine their roles and the interested reader is referred to a number of texts on the subject.[18]

Other bodies

At all three levels of administration — national, regional and local — there are many other interested bodies which, to varying degrees, influence the administration of further education. For convenience, they may be divided into four main categories. First, there are the validating and examining bodies including the Council for National Academic Awards, the City and Guilds of London Institute, TEC and BEC, the Regional Examining Bodies and the Royal Society of Arts. Second, there are the Professional Bodies such as the Institute of Chartered Accountants, the Hotel, Catering and Institutional Management Association and the Royal Institute of Chemistry. Third, there are the teachers', colleges' and administrators' organizations such as the National Association of Teachers in Further and Higher Education, the Association of Polytechnic Teachers, the Committee of Directors of Polytechnics, the Standing Conference of Principals and Directors of Colleges and Institutes of Higher Education, the Association of Principals of Colleges, the Association of Colleges for Further and Higher Education and the Association of College Registrars and Administrators. And, fourth, there are bodies representing industry and business such as the Confederation of British Industry, employers' associations, the trade unions, and government agencies such as the Manpower Services Commission.

It is clearly not possible in a book of this kind to do justice to the work of the wide range of validating and examining bodies which exist in this country and which directly determine much of the day-to-day operation of the colleges. However, mention must be made of three of the most important: the Council for National Academic Awards (CNAA), the City and Guilds of London Institute (CGLI), and the Council of Technical Examining Bodies (CTEB). The CNAA is an autonomous body established by Royal Charter in September 1964 with powers to award degrees comparable in standard to those awarded by universities to students who have successfully completed part-time, full-time or sandwich courses in establishments of further education which do not have the power to award their own degrees. The Council operates through five committees known as the Committee for Art and Design, the Committee for Arts and Social Studies, the Committee for Education, the Committee for Research Degrees, and the Committee for Science and Technology, each of which has its own Subject Boards who ensure that the content and character of courses, submitted by the colleges, and the arrangements for conducting them, are satisfactory. By the end of 1977, there were over 113,000 students studying for CNAA awards, the great majority of whom were on first degree courses.[19] The work of the CNAA has been central to the development of higher education within further education and perhaps its most important contribution has been to ensure the maintenance of high standards and thus the sound academic repute of the colleges offering its awards.

The CGLI, like the CNAA an autonomous body incorporated by Royal Charter, celebrated its centenary in 1978 and in the hundred

25

years of its existence it has awarded more than five million certificates.[20] It remains one of the largest national examining bodies in further education and in 1977, for example, there were over 250,000 candidates for its examinations. With the introduction of new technician courses by TEC and BEC, it is gradually withdrawing its courses at that level so that eventually it will concentrate on craft examinations. Within the CGLI structure there are currently 19 specialist advisory committees and panels, all of which include representatives from the further education colleges, each covering a broad sector of industrial activity such as engineering, vehicles, construction, catering and agriculture. In addition to its craft certificates, the Institute introduced its Foundation Courses in 1976: based on schemes of general education centred on the world of work, they are now offered in schools as well as colleges. The Institute has also given valuable support to the schemes of unified vocational preparation. Finally, as with the advent of TEC it is losing its technician-level courses, so it has found it necessary to rethink its pattern of courses. Accordingly, it has decided on a new policy of certificates and other awards which form a progression matched to career stages and related to other forms and levels of vocational preparation.[21]

The Council of Technical Examining Bodies (CTEB), which has existed in one form or another for more than 20 years, was set up to achieve co-operation between the CGLI and the Regional Examining Bodies. It has recently made proposals for a unified system for national standards and national certification for operative and craft vocational preparation, based on the existing structure and operating through and as part of the modified CGLI and allowing for extensive regional participation. At the time of writing, the scheme is being considered by the Regional Advisory Councils who seem to be favourably disposed towards it. If it comes about, it will be very significant as it will effectively transform a regionally based system, operated by the Regional Examining Bodies, into a national one to which the regions contribute.

Among the teachers' organizations which influence the provision of further education, perhaps the most important is the National Association of Teachers in Further and Higher Education (NATFHE). The largest of the bodies representing further education teachers, it is both a trade union and a professional body and was formed from the amalgamation in 1976 of the Association of Teachers in Technical Institutions (ATTI) and the Association of Teachers in Colleges and Departments of Education (ATCDE), as a result of the merging of the colleges of education into the further education sector. In addition to its role in promoting the interests of its members in respect of salaries and status, it also presses vigorously for improvements in the quality of further education provision. Its publications include the monthly

NATFHE Journal and the quarterly *Journal of Further and Higher Education*, two of the few periodicals devoted specifically to further education, and from time to time it issues authoritative statements of policy on important issues in further education. Its political influence is not inconsiderable and it is represented on most of the major national bodies dealing with further education such as the Oakes Committee and the ACSTT Further Education Sub-Committee.

The Association of Polytechnic Teachers (APT) is a much smaller body and describes itself as the only professional organization and trade union specifically for polytechnic teachers and senior library and administrative colleagues. It was formed in May 1973 as a breakaway union from the ATTI by some members of polytechnics who felt that existing unions did not adequately represent their interests − a view very vigorously contested by NATFHE − and, as such, is not affiliated to the Trades Union Congress. Its membership has grown somewhat during the past six years but it still represents only a minority of the staff of polytechnics, most of whom belong to NATFHE; inevitably, therefore, it lacks the political and educational influence of its much bigger rival. Its headquarters are at Portsmouth and it issues a newsletter, *APT Bulletin*, which is a useful forum for the discussion of some of the major topics of importance to further education. APT has recently attempted to obtain full negotiating rights with the local authorities on behalf of its members of certain polytechnics, rights enjoyed by NATFHE. However, the ACC and the AMA have unanimously opposed the recognition of APT locally on the grounds that it would disrupt existing negotiating arrangements. The matter went to the Advisory, Conciliation and Arbitration Service who found against APT on the grounds that recognition would fragment the present local collective bargaining machinery.

A third professional body with considerable influence due to the status of its members rather than their numbers is the Association of Principals of Colleges (APC), which has taken over the role of the former Association of Principals of Technical Institutions (APTI). It makes a significant contribution to the debate on further education by publishing occasional discussion documents, such as a recent one advocating the establishment of a new Vocational Preparation Council to co-ordinate and finance mandatory 'programmes of learning experience' for all school-leavers up to the age of 19; the Council should be chaired by a New Minister of State drawing responsibility both from the DES and the Department of Employment.[22]

The Committee of Directors of Polytechnics, the Standing Conference of Principals and Directors of Colleges and Institutes in Higher Education and the Association of Colleges for Further and Higher Education are all, as their titles imply, bodies representing specific groups of colleges and seek to act as pressure groups on their behalf and as forums for the exchange of views. Finally, the Association of College Registrars and Administrators (ACRA) is a professional organization for the administrative staff of further education establishments. It holds regular meetings and conferences, it publicly represents the views of its members — in response to the Oakes Report, for example, it expressed regret that the Committee had not taken up the question of granting corporate status to polytechnics and some other colleges — and it issues useful publications from time to time.[23]

The fourth group of bodies which plays a part in the shaping of further education provision consists of those representing employers and employees, notably the Confederation of British Industries (CBI) and the trade unions. The former through its Education and Training section and its journal *Education and Training Bulletin* has long played a part in further education. The trade unions have for some years looked to the further education colleges to provide courses for shop stewards designed to increase the efficiency of trade unions' representation on the shop floor and to encourage a broad understanding of industrial relations. In the last few years, legislation on labour issues such as the Employment Protection Act, the Health and Safety at Work Act, the Equal Opportunities Act and the Equal Pay Act and the consequent need for trade union officials to be expertly informed, has led a number of colleges to provide specialized courses on these matters. An interesting recent development, with obvious implications for the colleges, has been for individual unions to establish their own residential centres offering specialized courses: for example, the General and Municipal Workers' Union, the Transport and General Workers' Union and the National Union of Railwaymen have all opened centres in recent years, while the Trade Union Congress has its own training college at Congress House in London. Indeed, the TUC understandably devotes much energy to educational considerations and, for example, has for years consistently advocated a policy of statutory day release for all those in the 16 to 19 age group. More recently, it has recommended sweeping changes in our system of industrial training in order to overcome what it describes as the rigid segregation of apprenticeship schemes. These changes, which would emphasize the imparting of common skills, are not dissimilar from those recommended by the Manpower Services Commission; if implemented, they would have very considerable implications for much of the further education sector.

Another major force which is shaping the present character of a good deal of further education is the Manpower Services Commission itself. As we shall see, the proper provision of co-ordinated industrial training inevitably involves a measure of associated further education. Consequently, the MSC, through its Training Services and Special

Programmes Divisions has introduced developments such as its Training Opportunities Scheme and its Youth Opportunities Programme which directly involve a contribution from the further education establishments. It is, therefore, a logical development that in planning for future needs the MSC should, as it has now begun to do, invite comments from the further education sector on possible lines of action.

Finally, in addition to the four main groups described above, there are many other voluntary and political organizations with strong interests in further education. For example, such bodies as the National Association of Boys' Clubs, the National Federation of Young Farmers' Clubs, the Sports Council, the Fabian Society and the Bow Group, and others too numerous to mention all play an educational role in stimulating and influencing provision in areas of particular interest.

In conclusion, it is apparent that further education offers such a wide range of opportunity geared to meet the needs of so many people and to cater for so many interests that innumerable influences, operating at all levels, are brought to bear upon it. While this variety of provision is one of its greatest glories, it does inevitably result in a degree of overlap, wastage and conflict. Moreover, this is made more acute by the absence of a rational structure which, for example, inhibits the proper provision for the 16 to 19 age group, creates a 'binary line' between higher education provision in the public sector colleges and in the universities, and retards the proper integration of education and training. These developments, as we shall show later, are like many others in our educational system, often the product of our predilection for seeking *ad hoc* solutions to specific problems rather than seeing them in the context of the system as a whole. There seems little prospect that, under the pressure of events, things will change for the better in the foreseeable future.

3   The 16 to 19 age group in further education

One of the major concerns of further education has always been with the education and training of a substantial proportion of school-leavers, nowadays consisting of the 16 to 19 age group.* This proportion has grown steadily in the post-war period. However, in recent years, increasing attention has been paid to the needs of this important age group as a whole, whether in secondary schools or further education establishments or in neither sector and, as a result, we are at last beginning to make concerted and co-ordinated provision for it. This development has been stimulated partly because of the greater physical and psychological maturity of this age group than in the past, partly by the growing degree of overlap between the secondary school and further education sectors, and partly by the fact that this age group has suffered disproportionately from unemployment and changing employment patterns.[1]

For the purposes of this chapter, we take the term '16 to 19 Age Group' to comprise those 16 year-olds who have reached the statutory school leaving age (thereby excluding those who have reached the chronological age of 16 but who have not achieved the statutory school-leaving age), together with all 17 and 18 year-olds. The group so defined numbered approximately 1,983,000 in November 1976. As Figure 3 shows, 357,000 or 18 per cent of this group were staying on in school, 568,000 or 29 per cent entered further education in one form or another, and consequently 1,058,000 or 53 per cent were without any form of formal education, either in employment or unemployed. For the sake of convenience, we shall examine the courses presently provided for these young people by the further education colleges under two heads: full-time provision and part-time provision.

---

*These are also described as the 16-18 age group, as for example, in documents issued recently by the DES and the Department of Employment.

Full-time provision

Of those entering further education upon leaving school, just over a third, 191,000, were embarking upon full-time, including sandwich, courses, a proportion which has grown steadily during the last ten or fifteen years. The same is true of secondary schools so that the proportion of 16 to 19 year-olds staying on voluntarily in full-time education has grown from 16 per cent in the academic year 1965-6 to 28 per cent in 1976-7. At the same time, the distribution of students as between secondary schools and further education has changed in the direction of the further education college though, as Figure 3 shows, in November 1976, still nearly twice as many were in the schools as in the colleges.

The proportion of the age group which stays on in full-time education, whether in schools or colleges is, however, very low by the standards of the developed countries, being exceeded by every country in

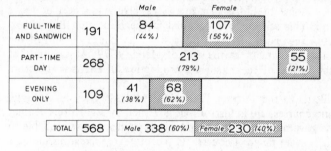

Figure 3   *The 16 to 19 age group in further education and schools*
Source: Non-advanced further education DES Report on Education No. 94, December 1978.

Western Europe with the exception of the Republic of Ireland and Portugal. In an attempt to encourage more youngsters to stay on in full-time education, the DES in May 1978 announced its intention of introducing a system of mandatory means-tested awards for 16 to 18 year-olds, known as Education Mandatory Awards (EMAs). The arrangements presently in operation are clearly unsatisfactory; in 1974-5, for example, only 2.5 per cent of pupils between 16 and 18 received educational maintenance allowances to stay on at school and these averaged only £2.50 a week for the school term. For those staying on in the further education colleges, the awards were at the discretion of the local education authorities and in 1974-5 were made to only 7 per cent of the age group. Even the dubious attractions of these grants have been undermined by the activities of the Manpower Services Commission whose Youth Opportunities Programme, at the time of writing, pays school-leavers who are unemployed for more than six months £20.55p. a week to attend a work experience or training course. Although this sort of anomaly is bound to persist, the proposal for EMAs is to be welcomed in so far as it persuades a higher proportion of the age group to stay on in full-time education. However, as the cost of the original scheme, estimated at £100 million, proved unacceptable to the Cabinet, the Secretary of State had to settle for a pilot programme of EMAs in a few areas, involving a cost of about £10 million. This scheme was included in the Education Bill and so has unfortunately been lost with the rest of the Bill as a result of the dissolution of parliament at the end of March 1979. At the time of writing, the future of the planned introduction of EMAs is therefore uncertain.

All students in the Further Education sector, be they on full-time or part-time courses, are in institutions governed by regulations distinct from those governing the schools and, as we shall see, have available to them a much wider range of courses. In recent years, increasing numbers of 16 year-olds have opted to stay on in full-time education, a tendency which is evident in other developed countries as well as in the United Kingdom. It has, if anything, been accentuated by the economic constraints of recent years and, in response, the further education establishments have attempted to cater more effectively for the needs and wishes of these young people by providing a wider range of full-time and sandwich* courses. Moreover, there has been a greater willingness on the part of local education authorities to allow transfer at

---

*Sandwich students are generally proportionally fewer on non-advanced than advanced courses. For a definition of the term 'Sandwich', see p. 94n.

16-plus from school to Further Education, in itself a recognition of the wishes of many young students. Finally, a number of important institutional developments have taken place, of which perhaps the most significant is the establishment of the Tertiary or Junior College, whose role we discuss later in the chapter.

Full-time and sandwich courses are offered principally by Colleges of Further Education, Technical Colleges, and Tertiary Colleges, together with certain specialist establishments such as Colleges of Agriculture and a diminishing number of Colleges of Art. In the three general institutions, both academic and vocational courses are available, unlike the schools which are restricted by School Regulations predominantly to the former. The academic provision consists very largely of courses leading to the General Certificate of Education (GCE), both at Ordinary and Advanced levels. Rather more than one quarter of all GCE students are in further education establishments and of these almost 60,000 were 16 to 19 year-olds studying full-time in November 1976. If we examine the courses that are provided and the ways in which they are organized we will see that there are significant differences to those provided by the schools. For one thing, the Ordinary Level courses are commonly of one year's duration, while those at Advanced Level consist of both one-year and two-year courses. For another, the groups of students in further education tend to be more heterogeneous, being drawn from a wide variety of educational institutions and spanning a considerably greater age range. Moreover, the colleges frequently offer subjects not commonly available in schools, such as Economics, Sociology, British Constitutional History and, occasionally, Science subjects which schools cannot provide because of a lack of qualified staff. Finally, provision varies much more between one further education college and the next than is the case with schools, sometimes for historical reasons and sometimes because the local education authority concerned is not prepared to allow duplication of courses that are available in their schools. All in all, however, the development of GCE courses in further education has been a major growth point in recent years and has come about in large part because of student demand. This has occurred partly because many youngsters prefer what they regard as the more adult atmosphere of the college, partly because it provides a second chance for those who have failed or not done well enough at school, and partly because, as we have seen, the further education colleges often provide courses in subjects not available in schools.[2]

An interesting, but as yet little developed, alternative to GCE A Levels is the International Baccalaureate Diploma (IB). This examination is based on a curriculum designed to achieve a balanced education by requiring students to undertake studies in six subject areas, three of which have to be offered at a higher level and three at a subsidiary level.[3] The six subjects are the mother tongue; a foreign language; the study of man, in one subject such as history, geography, or psychology; an experimental science such as biology, physics or chemistry; mathematics; and one subject chosen from Art, a third language, a second subject from the study of man and so on. It will be seen that the IB differs from GCE A Levels in that candidates are required to follow a grouped curriculum consisting of a broad range of subjects. A major problem arising from this curriculum is the requirement for mathematics which has proved so difficult for some students that an attempt is being made to develop a course in mathematics for the non-mathematical. The requirement that all students should study some science is less of a problem as most candidates on the arts side choose a biology course which has a strong element of human biology in it.[4]

In the 1977-8 academic year, three further education colleges were offering the IB programme with about 100 students in all; of these, the largest group was some 75 students, most of them from overseas, at the Hammersmith and West London College of Further Education whose curriculum had a language and social science orientation. In the session 1978-9, the IB is being offered by another four colleges and others will probably join in thereafter. The numbers are likely to grow as the demand from overseas students increases and encouragement seems to be forthcoming from the DES on the grounds that if the proposed N and F Levels are not introduced, then the IB does provide a broadly-based alternative to A Levels. Although the numbers involved are as yet quite small, it seems likely that the IB will become a significant growth point in the further education sector. It is difficult to predict the effect of its introduction on the colleges themselves but it seems inevitable that it will pose special problems for part-time and evening only students.

Other predominantly academic courses offered by further education colleges, though on a very much smaller scale than GCE, include the Certificate of Secondary Education (CSE) and the Certificate of Extended Education (CEE). CSE students in further education probably only number a few hundred and with changes in 16-plus examinations on the horizon these may not grow. The CEE is intended to be analogous to the CSE but suited to candidates of greater maturity. A Schools Council Report, published in two parts in 1972 and 1973,[5] recognized the need for sixth-form curriculum reform, not least for the so-called 'new sixth-formers', namely those for whom A Level is irrelevant and for whom O Level or CSE courses do not provide adequate motivation or a worthwhile education. It concluded that an overall strategy for reform was required, of which the introduction of the CEE would be an integral part, specifically designed for those who at present follow no course beyond O Level or CSE. The CEE, which is available to further education establishments as well as schools, was originally designed primarily for students who have obtained CSE with grades 2-4. In practice, however, the target population has varied greatly from school to school and from region to region and includes students who have achieved both higher and lower CSE grades than 2 to 4. CEE is normally a one-year course available in a range of non-vocational subjects and, like GCE and CSE, culminates in a single-subject examination. A number of pilot CEE schemes were introduced and the number of subject entries grew rapidly, rising to 6,500 in 1974, a rate of growth that was constrained by the policy of restricted entry operated by the examination boards. Not surprisingly, the attitude of further education teachers to the CEE has been ambivalent, some accepting that there is a need for it, others being unconvinced that any such development is necessary.[6] It is, of course, a normal requirement for further education courses to have a vocational purpose and not merely a vocational flavour, whereas schools in general are not well equipped to provide even a meaningful orientation towards the world of work. Consequently, reservations have been expressed about the whole purpose of CEE on the grounds that if a year of continued education at 16-plus is desirable, might not the student be better served by a course with a vocational orientation? Moreover, it is by no means clear whether the CEE will be acceptable to industry and the professional bodies or what its currency will be as an entry qualification to vocational courses. These are problems which should have been resolved at the outset and failure to do so has been one of the main reasons why a moratorium on the further developments of CEE was declared by the Secretary of State towards the end of 1976.

More recently, in April 1978, the DES announced the setting-up of a study group, under the chairmanship of Professor Kevin Keohane, head of the Roehampton Institute of Higher Education, to examine the CEE proposals in relation to other courses and examinations for those for whom CEE is intended. The 'other courses' to be looked at include the CGLI Foundation Courses which we describe later in this chapter. All being well, the study group will report to the Secretary of State in the Summer of 1979. It is to be hoped therefore, that satisfactory solutions will soon be forthcoming. Perhaps the best solution lies with the development of the tertiary college which, as we shall see later, is able to provide a range of courses which bridge the gap between school and work.

Another possible solution lies in the Certificate of Further Education (CFE), a vocationally-biased alternative to CEE and the type of course which may turn out to be well suited to the needs of many of the 16 to

35

19 year-olds who stay on in full-time education. CFE is a broad-based, one-year full-time vocational course devised by the six Regional Examining Boards. It is open to students of average ability and has three main aims: to enhance the student's prospects of employment in the specialist field of his choice; to enable him to make an informed decision on his aptitude or suitability for a particular career; and, where possible, to allow him exemption from parts of vocational further education courses. The basic CFE course pattern is of two or three core courses together with a range of options; for example, the Union of Educational Institutions is currently operating a pilot scheme of which the common core consists of courses in Numeracy and Computing and Communication and Complementary Studies, and options include a very wide range of subjects such as Carpet Technology and Manufacture, Agriculture and Horticulture, Catering, Community Services, and Electrical Installation Practice. To date, two specific inter-regional schemes have been made available: Engineering/Construction in 1977, and pre-Nursing Services in 1978.

By comparison with the CEE, CFE is more structured in that, as we have seen, it consists of a grouped rather than a single subject course. Its orientation is vocational rather than general and many of the courses cater for workshop placement or, in the case of Pre-Nursing and Caring Services, visits to hospitals. Finally, unlike CEE, it can provide a direct route to other directly vocational further education courses in the appropriate field.

Although CFE has much to be said in its favour, its future remains uncertain, not least because of the changes in the examination system for the 16 to 19 age group which are presently being mooted by the Schools Council. These take three forms: the CEE, which we have already discussed, a common examination at 16-plus combining GCE O Level and CSE, and the replacement of GCE A Level by a more broadly-based programme comprising 'Normal' and 'Further' (N and F) Levels. Clearly, these proposed changes are matters of vital concern to many further education establishments who, with good reason, are worried that these will be effected without taking fully into account the needs and interests of their students. Hitherto, as far as GCE courses are concerned, arrangements concerning syllabuses and examination procedures have been somewhat unfairly dominated by the school and university viewpoints, despite the fact that as we have seen a substantial proportion of students undertaking GCE courses do so within the further education sector.

If, and when, a common examination at 16-plus is introduced, then some major implications for further education need to be borne in mind. First, the further education colleges, receiving the school student who has successfully completed the common 16-plus examination, will need to know what vocational courses he is qualified to enter. Second, the standards of the new examination must be acceptable both to industry and also to the professional bodies. Third, and perhaps most important, the new examination, should it become widely accepted, will allow the further education sector to extend its provision and cater for a wide range of ability in non-vocational courses. For these reasons, it is a matter of concern that, so far, further education colleges have been very little involved in the feasibility trials for the new examination. To a considerable extent, this has been the fault of further education teachers themselves for not actively seeking involvement in the trials. However, the Schools Council has not been entirely blameless, for when considering such changes in the examination system it has tended to see them in terms of the academic school sixth-form and not in the broad context of overall provision, in which further education figures largely.

Finally, there are the proposals to replace the present GCE A Level examinations by N (Normal) and F (Further) Levels. Both N and F Levels are single-subject, one-year courses, the latter following on the former. A typical sixth-former might well undertake five N Level subjects in his first year and continue with three of them as F Level subjects in his second year. The new scheme would have two major advantages over the present one: it would enable sixth-formers to undertake a more broadly-based and less specialized programme and, in the case of the N Levels, it would cater for those who presently attempt A Levels but for whom they are unsuitable. Clearly, such a scheme, if it is implemented, will have considerable repercussions for the further education colleges who will be both providers of N and F Level courses and recipients of students who have taken them at college and school. While the colleges doubtless have the resources to provide the courses, they will be faced with at least two specific problems. Firstly, there will have to be much more co-operation between college departments than is presently the case in many instances and, secondly, the mature student who frequently comes to the college one evening a week and takes one A Level at a time will find it difficult to cope with the group certificate character of N and F Levels. On the other hand, as recipients of students who have completed N and F Levels, polytechnics and other colleges running courses in subjects like business studies and architecture will be happier with the broadly-based preparation which N and F Levels provide than many university departments, especially in science and technology, who have opposed the new courses on the grounds that they do not allow sufficient time to develop expertise in specific subjects such as Mathematics and Physics. Given that further education will have a strong stake in the new programmes, should they come about, it is pleasing that a number of colleges have been included in the case studies being used in the working-out of the scheme.[7] This is all the more important in that further education is only just beginning to articulate a response to the proposals and, in that respect, it is well behind both the schools and the universities. However, when a final decision is made concerning the introduction of N and F Levels, it is to be hoped that the interests of the colleges will be borne clearly in mind.

As far as non-advanced vocational courses are concerned, the further education establishments provide a very substantial number and it is, of course, this predominant feature of their work which distinguishes them from the secondary school sector. The more important of the full-time vocational courses include the various Ordinary National Diploma courses; those leading to the City and Guilds of London Institute (CGLI) Certificates and Diplomas and various professional qualifications; a wide range of courses in such specialist areas as Art, Pre-nursing, and Agriculture; and the numerous courses presently being developed under the auspices of the Technician Education Council (TEC) and the Business Education Council (BEC).

The Ordinary National Diploma (OND) is, like its part-time equivalent the Ordinary National Certificate (ONC), a two-year course. It is available in seven main subject areas: Engineering and Technology, including Building; Food Technology; Mining and Textile Technology; Agriculture, including Forestry; Science; Business Studies; and Catering and Institutional Management. In November 1975, there were over 25,700 students taking OND courses, the largest groups by far being 10,500 in Business Studies, and almost 9,000 on Engineering and Technology. Secondly, each OND course consists of a group of subjects — for example, an OND in Business Studies includes courses on Law, Economics and Accounting — which are externally assessed. It was originally intended by the Joint Committees which organize them that an OND course should include a substantial element of practical training and should, if possible, be a sandwich course. However, that principle has been gradually eroded, largely because it is difficult to include it in a course of only two years' duration. It is for this reason that a few OND courses extend for as long as three years; understandably, however, they sometimes prove less attractive to students. Another reason for the erosion of the practical element has been the difficulty which many colleges have experienced in finding placements for their students in industry or business. In general, the achievement of a satisfactory standard in OND is regarded by Universities, Polytechnics and Colleges of Higher Education as the equivalent of two GCE A Levels and is accepted by them as a qualification granting entry to a course of higher education.

It is the vocational and practical flavour of an OND course which proves attractive to many students and it is for this reason that they leave school and GCE A Levels and opt for the Technical College and OND. Girls in particular are attracted to Business Studies and Catering and Institutional Management and it is in these two areas that they outnumber the boys; boys on the other hand almost totally monopolize the Engineering and Technology courses. However, having once embarked on an OND course, some students find its vocational orientation rather narrow and its subject matter tedious, and revert to A Level studies. Although the entry qualifications are nominally four O Levels, or their equivalent, as in the case of students wishing to undertake a GCE A Level course, in practice the Colleges are able to exercise more flexible selection procedures in order to ensure viable groups. In such cases, the first year is essentially a diagnostic one and students who find OND too difficult can normally be switched to alternative courses, such as some of those offered by the CGLI. At the time of writing, the future of the OND is not completely settled; however, it seems certain that virtually all of them will in time be replaced by the new courses validated by TEC and BEC. A full discussion of these changes and their implications is to be found in chapter 4.

CGLI courses are by and large undertaken on a part-time basis; however, of a total of 235,000 students in the 16 to 19 age group in November 1976, over 39,000, or more than 16 per cent, were studying on a full-time or sandwich basis. Irrespective of the attendance pattern, the potential range of courses is virtually the same and the most important subject areas include a very wide range of Engineering courses, Building, Printing, Agriculture and Catering. Whether or not a specific course is offered on a full-time basis depends on a number of factors, including the recruitment of sufficient students, the willingness of the local authority to finance it, and the likely availability of jobs for those who successfully complete it. Full-time CGLI courses are of one or two years' duration and lead to the award of Certificates and Diplomas. Some practical experience is included in the course, although this is clearly very much less than would be obtained by a student on a part-time course. On the other hand, the study pattern is broader and deeper; however, the job prospects for full-time college-based students are less certain, there being no guarantee of a post at the end of the course. Generally speaking, however, a student who successfully completes a vocational course is probably better placed to secure a job than one who is on an academic course like GCE. CGLI courses are currently available at essentially two different levels: those for craftsmen and those with a greater theoretical content, for technicians. The latter are progressively being replaced by the new TEC and BEC courses.

An interesting recent development sponsored by the CGLI is its one year full-time Foundation Courses. Broadly-based and with a vocational element, they are designed for young people of average ability who for the most part elect to leave school for full-time further education, though they can also be provided by schools. Both colleges and schools are free to design their own courses subject to CGLI approval and the vocational element is intended to provide a base for subsequent vocational courses. These Foundation Courses which may centre on such subject areas as Construction, Engineering, Food, Science, Community Care, Agriculture, Business Studies, and Retail Distribution, are now becoming firmly established both in colleges and schools, the latter frequently on a linked basis. In 1977, for example, over 150 courses were offered and nearly 1,700 candidates examined, and the number is continuing to grow. Foundation Courses are significant for two main reasons: firstly, they are an attempt to prepare youngsters for broad occupational and industrial areas and, to this end, may be tailored to local needs and, secondly, they can be made available to young school-leavers for whom no employment is immediately available, thereby giving them a useful preparation for the world of work. Provided they are properly developed and effectively monitored, Foundation Courses would seem to have a great deal of potential and a number of important advantages: they combine vocational direction with continuing general education, they include a diagnostic element in their assessment procedures, and they can help to strengthen links between the secondary school and further education sectors.

Many students also follow courses leading to the examinations of professional bodies such as the Institute of Bankers and the Institute of Marketing. Most professional bodies require entrants to have at least completed GCE O Levels before entering on the courses, and their examinations can lead eventually to the Associateship or Fellowship of the particular institution. Until recently, the Certificate in Office Studies was also available on a full-time basis. However, like its more popular part-time equivalent, it is being replaced by courses leading to BEC General Awards. Indeed, some colleges devise their own certificate and diploma courses, often in specialist subjects related to local industry and commerce.

Finally, there is a considerable variety of other specialist full-time courses in such subject areas as office arts, pre-nursing, agriculture and art. These are very important areas of study which attract very large numbers of students, especially in office arts which principally comprises shorthand and typewriting and is, of course, taught in virtually every college of further education.

The tertiary college: the changing institutional pattern

As we have already mentioned, one of the ways in which a number of local education authorities have attempted to meet more effectively the needs of the 16 to 19 age group is by the establishment of Tertiary* or Junior Colleges. These are institutions which cater for all students in this age range in a given geographical area; they therefore replace post-16 provision in the form of school sixth forms and technical colleges by a single establishment.[8] Operating under further education regulations, Tertiary Colleges offer the whole range of non-advanced courses, both academic and vocational. The concept of the Tertiary Colleges owes much to Lord Alexander who was perhaps its earliest and staunchest advocate.[9] The first one was opened in Exeter in 1970 and by late 1978 sixteen were in operation,[10] with two more planned; with the exception of Cricklade College, Andover, Hampshire, which was purpose-built, they have all been based on existing further education colleges. As a recent NFER report points out, there are a number of reasons why local education authorities have decided to create Tertiary Colleges.[11] One is a hoped-for economy resulting from their size, especially important in the near future with the coming decline in the size of the 16 to 19 age group. More important, however, is the expectation that as they offer a much wider range of subjects than either the school sixth form or the college of further education, they will enable students to combine both academic and vocational courses, thereby providing a broader curricular diet for 16 to 19 year olds. However, it remains to be seen whether it will work out like this in practice, as the difficulties of timetabling and the preference of many youngsters for either a wholly academic or wholly vocational course may inhibit such a development. The Tertiary College, unlike the secondary school, does of course achieve another kind of 'mix' in that it provides for both full-time and part-time students.

However, whatever the advantages of the Tertiary College as compared with the sixth form college, or the traditional secondary school sixth form, it is becoming increasingly clear that the demarcation lines between the secondary school sector and the further education sector are breaking down. Clearly, no one institutional pattern will suit every part of the country, nor could it be unilaterally imposed on local education authorities. What are needed are institutional patterns that provide for a range of opportunity and maximum flexibility. In planning for the 16 to 19 age group as a whole, three major constraints

*Some confusion may arise over the use of the term 'Tertiary' in that it is also taken to mean a third stage of education beyond primary and secondary, that is post GCE A Level courses or higher education. However, it is more commonly and increasingly being used to denote the education of the 16 to 19 age group.

must be recognized: the need to provide for individual requirements; the fact the national resources are limited; and the fact that the 16 to 19 population is not static, either in numbers or characteristics.[12]

Part-time provision

Part-time courses, at one time the 'bread and butter' of non-advanced further education, are provided on two bases of study, Part-Time Day or Block Release, and Evening Only. In November 1976, of the 16 to 19 age group 377,000 young people, or about 19 per cent, were engaged on one or other of these two types of courses.

Of the two groups, *Part-Time Day and Block Release* is numerically more significant with about 268,000 students. Part-time day courses are taken by students who are released from work with pay by their employers to attend a further education college, normally for one full day a week or the equivalent in half days, together with in some cases an extra evening. These youngsters are serving apprenticeships or are under training for skilled occupations, including pre-apprentice courses in employment, and many will thus be attending CGLI craft and technician courses, which are available in over 300 different subjects. As in the case of full-time CGLI courses, the technician-level courses are being phased out and being replaced by TEC and BEC courses.

Part-time day release is not a very satisfactory basis of study, for a variety of reasons. The demands of the courses may be so great that a student during his day at college may be required to study almost continuously from nine in the morning until about 7.30 and sometimes later at night and may also be required to attend on another evening of the week; students may also have to undertake a considerable amount of work at home as a normal part of the course; and, given that many students have social and family commitments, there is the constant problem of readjustment between work and study. In the circumstances, it is hardly surprising that there is a high wastage and failure rate among day release students.

A now well-established alternative course pattern to day release is that of *block release*. Under this system employees are released with pay for periods of full-time study usually lasting about 12 weeks or less a year, according to the level of the course. Block release courses may typically consist of 12 consecutive weeks followed by an examination, or of three periods of four weeks each spread over the session with the examination at the end of the session. In the latter case, continuity of study is maintained by arranging for the students to attend the college one evening a week in the intervals between full-time study. Although there is still a great deal of research to be done to determine the relative effectiveness of day and block release, there seems to be little doubt that the latter is a superior method of instruction. However, it is often difficult for small firms to operate block release schemes as they may be deprived of the services of most, or all, of their apprentices for relatively long periods. To overcome this problem, a few firms, especially those in business, occasionally employ two junior members of staff for each post so that one of them is always at work while the other is attending college.

As will be seen from Figure 3, of the 268,000 students on day and block release courses in November 1976, almost 80 per cent of them were boys. This reflects the fact that certain major industries, for example, engineering and construction which employ principally boys, are much more generous in releasing their young employees for study at the technical college than the business offices and retail distributive trades which traditionally employ mainly girls. In any case, the overall percentage of young people obtaining release has been, and remains, low. Thus, between 1971 and 1975, the percentage of youngsters under the age of 19 years on day release courses at colleges of further education in England and Wales, as a percentage of those not in full-time education, has remained more or less stable at about 20 per cent. In absolute terms, this represents a decline in actual numbers consequent upon the decline in the population of the age group. The reasons for this unsatisfactory position are attributable partly to the growing proportion of young people remaining in full-time education after the age of 16, partly to the present difficult employment situation, and partly to the reluctance of industry to increase provision. This is in some respects an ironic state of affairs, given that the 1944 Education Act legislated for compulsory day release to county colleges for all 15 to 18 year-olds not in full-time education, a provision which has remained a dead letter ever since.

In this regard, we differ very sharply from such highly-industrialized countries as West Germany and Sweden, where structured preparation for work is the norm and where, perhaps as a result, the productivity of the work force is considerably higher. Our own further education system has to date catered essentially for our more able school-leavers and has made little provision for those who leave school at 16 to seek employment. Is there then, as some very powerful advocates have argued, an over-riding case for providing compulsory day release for the 16 to 19s?[13] Our own view is that the answer to this question is probably 'No'. For one thing, compulsory day release may not suit everybody's needs; it is one thing to grant the right to continuing education as and when the individual feels he will benefit most, but it is another to require all young people to attend college courses when they have just completed compulsory schooling. In any case, it is by no means certain that the present day release courses, normally vocational craft courses, are appropriate for the great majority of students, who have yet to commit themselves to a set vocation either because their career pattern is undecided or because jobs are unobtainable. For many, what are required are broadly-based courses with an element of work orientation and, as we shall see, the present economic climate has stimulated a number of government agencies to develop initiatives of this sort. Finally, it may well be the case that compulsory day release is by now neither a practical proposition nor educationally a live issue. Increasingly, influential educational opinion seems to be of the view that a more viable alternative will be to provide continuing education of some sort to be taken up as an entitlement by the student at the most appropriate time according to his own needs and wishes.

Evening Only students, of whom there were 109,000 in the 16 to 19 age group in November 1976, or about forty per cent of those on day release, attend college courses on one or more evenings a week. Many of them are unable to obtain day or block release and have no choice but to attend college in their own time. More than 60 per cent of these students are girls, many of them taking courses in office arts for which they are unable to secure release by their employers. Thus, they are following courses leading to the same qualifications as those studying on a full-time or part-time day basis, components of which are often taken by two or more of these groups. Evening only students are required to undertake a considerable amount of work at home; for many, therefore it is a difficult and very taxing form of study and it is hardly surprising if the wastage and failure rates are high. It is for the same reason that the numbers of students on evening only courses have declined in recent years.

Education and training

As we have indicated, the further education sector still caters very largely for our more able school-leavers, with the result that more than half of our youngsters who have achieved the statutory school-leaving age do not enter further education at all. Totalling over 900,000 young people, many of them are in jobs for which they have been provided with very little training.[14] Moreover, an increasing proportion of the age group is suffering from unemployment and changing employment patterns. Thus, the number of unemployed young people registered at Careers Offices went up from 35,000, representing 6 per cent of the total unemployed, in October 1974, to over 400,000, 30 per cent of all those unemployed, in October 1978. If one adds to these stark facts the growing awareness of the need to train a competent work force in order to compete with the other developed countries, it is not surprising that government attention is at last being given to this large group of under-privileged youngsters. As a result, a number of substantial developments have taken place in recent years, with very important repercussions for the further education service. These developments have occurred under the auspices of two separate government departments: the Department of Education and Science (DES), and in greater measure, the Department of Employment through its agency, the Manpower Services Commission (MSC).

The MSC is composed of representatives of employers, trade unions, local authorities and educational interests and was set up under the Employment and Training Act, 1973, as were its two executive bodies, the Training Services Agency (TSA) and the Employment Services Agency (ESA). In April 1978, the MSC was reorganized into three divisions, two corresponding to the old TSA and ESA, and a third under Geoffrey Holland with responsibility for MSC's special programmes for unemployed young people and adults. It is significant that in spite of persistent appeals from educational bodies such as the ATTI and its successor, NATFHE, and also the NACEIC,[15] pointing out that it was high time that a remedy was sought to the inequalities in the educational provision for the less able 16 to 19 year-olds, successive governments have hitherto been reluctant to answer these appeals. As a consequence, it has taken a major economic recession both in the United Kingdom and in the other EEC countries to initiate some form of provision. While the developments that have flowed from this initiative are generally to be welcomed, it is disturbing, from an educational point of view, that they have arisen not from a policy recommended by educational bodies but from the TSA discussion paper, 'The Vocational Preparation of Young People', published in May 1975.

The document, which was produced to stimulate discussion among employers, trade unions, educationalists and other interested parties, clearly indicated the serious deficiencies in the present system and suggested the sort of action that would be required to meet the economic and social needs of young people by providing them with adequate vocational preparation. Central to such action was the development of widely-based, off-the-job 'Gateway' courses of a recognized national standard, inculcating knowledge relevant to jobs within broad educational bands. Predictably, reaction from both industry and education was mixed. One cogent view put by the Director of the Engineering Industry Training Board was that it was not fair to ask industry to repair the ravages of an inadequate education system. Support for this view came from the Confederation of British Industry which reported that it had more comments from its members about school work than on any other part of the document. Some college principals felt, perhaps rightly, that properly-devised link courses in truly co-operative ventures between school and further education offered a better alternative solution. Furthermore, having experienced the relative lack of success of non-vocational day release, they foresaw great difficulty in persuading both students and employers of the value of gateway-type courses. Unfortunately, but typically, no reaction seems to have been forthcoming from teachers in secondary schools, apparently because the document was not circulated amongst them.

By this time, the DES was with good reason becoming concerned about the issues raised by the discussion and determined to take an initiative of its own. Consequently, it called a major conference in March 1976 on the theme, '16 to 19: Getting Ready for Work'. Addressing the conference, the then Secretary of State for Education and Science, Mr F. Mulley, outlined government proposals for making much greater provision for 'some 300,000 youngsters who each year leave school at 16 to go straight into jobs – or, in present circumstances, unemployment'. He conceded that 'part of the problem has been the development in this country of separate arrangements for education and training stemming from different traditions and different philosophies'. Nevertheless, he thought that the barriers were crumbling and, announcing a programme of ten pilot vocational preparation schemes, he said that the really unified approach to vocational preparation was a departure from established practice requiring the development of new courses and teaching methods and a 'joint effort by the further education and training partners'.

Inevitably, perhaps, these fine words were greeted with some scepticism at the conference, particularly when the Minister also indicated that as funding would only be possible through the Rate Support Grant, the DES could neither ensure that specific sums of money would be made available nor dictate how they should be spent. However, the government's intention was crystallized by the issuing shortly afterwards of DES Circular 6/76, 'A Government Statement on Unified Vocational Preparation', announcing its intention of setting up the ten pilot schemes. Each of twelve weeks' duration, these were originally designed to cater for 300 youngsters in employment, the numbers rising to 1,000 within 5 years. Subsequently, as a result of the widespread demand for the extension of the programme, the government announced in July 1976 its intention of doubling the number of pilot schemes to 20, catering eventually for 6,000 young people.

This is an extremely important development in that for the first time it represents an attempt to co-ordinate education and training through two separate agencies: the DES working through the local education authorities, and the Department of Employment working through the Training Services Division of the MSC. Clearly, the success or failure of this venture will depend in large part upon the degree of effective co-operation between the DES and the Department of Employment. If this co-operation is not forthcoming, it will further prolong a division of responsibility which, it has been argued, is 'one of the greatest impediments to the coherent development of continuing education and training in Britain'.[16] In recognition of this danger, the arrangements for the schemes of unified vocational preparation (UVP) are being overseen by the Training and Further Education Consultative Group, which was established in December 1976 to implement recommendations originally proposed by a planning group on links between the TSA and the education service set up jointly by the TSA and the DES in 1974. Under the chairmanship of R.L. Helmore, Principal of the Cambridgeshire College of Arts and Technology and the Education Member of the MSC, the Group's remit is to look into ways of providing a national consultative forum to bring together the training and education services to discuss matters of common interest. The group aims to provide a means of full consultation between the education service and the MSC on major developments in the field of education and training and proposes to issue occasional bulletins to the press and interested national bodies recording such developments. The first major recommendation of the Consultative Group was, indeed, that a national forum be established to ensure the proper integration of education and training.[17] However, it is too early yet to predict whether it will be established, still less how effective it will be. Clearly, one of the major tasks of the Group must be to help overcome suspicions within the further education colleges of the work of the Training Services Division of the MSC. Undoubtedly, some staff in the colleges view with alarm some of the latter's more radical views as expressed in recent discussion documents and research reports and understandably resent the substantial financial resources made available to it at a time when financial cutbacks are being imposed on the further education sector. However, if we are to bring about a more successful integration of the work of the education service and the training agencies, then a more open-minded and receptive attitude is called for on both sides.

The 20 schemes of unified vocational preparation were originally scheduled to start early in 1977, the majority of them being based on colleges of further education, and the rest in Department of Employment Skill Centres and in industry itself. Unfortunately, but not surprisingly, by April 1977, not only had the first schemes failed to attract even half the numbers originally planned, but they also had to draw widely on unemployed youngsters for whom they were not intended. In practice, only 14 schemes were set up overall and, instead of a planned intake of about 300 youngsters, quickly doubling to 600, the total number recruited to the programme was only 110. There were two reasons for the relative failure of the first phase of the programme. Firstly, there was the difficulty of persuading employers of the value of the schemes; some firms preferred to provide their own vocational preparation while smaller firms, beset by economic difficulties, thought the financial compensations offered by the government too small to justify the release of employees. Secondly, there were basic difficulties inherent in the nature of the programme itself which was both new and challenging and also intended to meet the needs of a wide range of occupations. The chief stumbling block was the great lack of expertise available for devising and teaching such programmes.

However, most of the colleges which have participated in the schemes report that the effort of launching a successful course has its rewards in showing how a hitherto neglected group of young people can be helped in early working life.[18] Moreover, the programme is beginning to grow and in 1978 there were 47 schemes catering for over 400 young people running in Great Britain, which means that some had very small numbers. In addition, the government has been determined to carry on with the second phase of the programme and has called on the CGLI to help with the devising and running of new schemes. The CGLI has responded by developing two complementary schemes of vocational preparation which are largely project-based and which adopt a problem-solving approach; these CGLI schemes have been incorporated into the general programme of unified vocation preparation. Although it is too early to pass judgment on what is an important and worthwhile venture, arrangements for monitoring it are well under way. In October 1977, the National Foundation for Educational Research (NFER) announced the setting up of a research project, under the direction of Dr Bruce Choppin, to evaluate the pilot schemes. At the end of this project, which will take some three years, a comprehensive report will be produced. Furthermore, the Further Education Curriculum Development and Review Unit (FEU), working with further education staff and other interested parties, has recently published principles and guidelines on curricula and teaching approaches for colleges wishing to offer the UVP schemes.[19] As suggested by the DES in Circular 10/77, 'Unemployed Young People — the Contribution of the Education Service', consideration is also being given to the extension of the principles of UVP to the design of college-based courses for unemployed school-leavers. To this end, a number of joint schemes for the unemployed are currently being developed in co-operation with the MSC. More recently, in April 1978, the DES announced that the UVP programme will be extended until 1981, by which time it will have been in existence for four years.

The implications for the further education service of such developments are very important. For one thing, they represent what is really the first concerted attempt to cater for some at least of that group of underprivileged youngsters who have previously had virtually no access to further education. While one may reflect ruefully that it has taken massive unemployment to bring it about, it is nevertheless a very welcome development. For another, these developments have brought education and training closer together and in the process have locked two major government departments in a close if not always affectionate embrace.

Another important training programme is the Training Opportunities Scheme (TOPS) which has been extended to include a proportion of 16 to 19 year-olds. First introduced in August 1972 to replace and extend the previous Government Vocational Training Scheme, TOPS is run by the Training Services Division of the MSC, and consists of courses which were originally only available to those aged 19 or over who had been at least three years away from full-time education. Training is available in a wide variety of occupations, the main concentrations being in the traditional craft skills, construction and automotive engineering, and clerical and commercial occupations. Courses, which must normally be full-time and last not more than a year, are provided in colleges of further education, Government Skill Centres, and in employers' establishments. Since its introduction in 1972, TOPS has expanded rapidly and, during the year ending March 1978, about 99,000 people, including 22,000 youngsters under 19, completed courses, of whom more than 56,000 were trained in colleges of further education. In the six years from 1972 to 1978, the proportion of women on TOPS courses rose from 8 to 44 per cent. However, although TOPS reached its numerical targets, it has been criticized because of the decline in the number of trainees who obtained employment and because it has not met the demand for skilled manpower in certain categories of employment. Accordingly, the MSC instituted a review which culminated in a report issued at the end of 1978. This contains proposals for retaining the agreed targets for 1980 of 90,000 for adult training and 25,000 for young people. However, it recommends that higher-level technician training should be expanded, as well as that for design draughtsmen and computer staff. Other areas of occupational training in which TOPS would extend provision are the clerical and commercial field, and catering. In general, the review emphasizes that TOPS should be seen as an independent but complementary part of the training system which needs to strengthen its relationship with other training sectors such as the industrial training boards and with the further education service.

Of considerably greater scope and significance than the UVP and TOPS schemes is the Manpower Services Commission's Youth Opportunities Programme (YOP) which began operations in April

1978 under the aegis of the Special Programmes Division. Outlined in the Holland Report, 'Young People and Work', published in May 1977, the programme is the world's first comprehensive national scheme for jobless school leavers and is scheduled to last for five years. The target date for full-scale operations was 1 September 1978 and, thereafter, in the first full year some 230,000 young people should have a constructive alternative to unemployment.[20] The magnitude of the problem is demonstrated by the fact that in the third quarter of 1978 there were more than one in three of our school-leavers unemployed, that is between 230,000 and 250,000 and, in addition, 200,000 other young people aged between 16 and 18 may be without jobs. Under YOP, it is intended that no school-leaver in 1978 will remain unemployed without the opportunity of a place on the programme by Easter 1979.

The Youth Opportunities Programme will consist of two main forms of provision. Firstly, there will be work preparation courses which will include short modules of employment induction run on employers' premises and in further education colleges. These are planned to improve a young person's prospects of employment by helping him, or her, to form a clear view of what job would be suitable, by informing him of the requirements and satisfactions of working life, and by giving him the vocational knowledge and skills and the social confidence which should enable him to find and keep a job. Secondly, there will be work experience schemes which can take place on employers' premises, on community service schemes, in training workshops, or on projects. The schemes will contain four key elements: a systematic induction into working life in general and into a particular vocation; an opportunity to try different tasks, to develop views of suitable jobs, and to acquire basic skills; an opportunity to undertake an element of further education; and the provision of counselling and careers advice.

The programme, which will cost an estimated £200 million, will be reviewed every 12 to 18 months. Designed to lead to permanent employment or to full-time further education, it has required a whole new structure of planning and administration. Accordingly, the MSC has set up 28 area boards of part-time members representing local authorities, the education service, industry, voluntary organizations and the Commission itself, whose job it is to approve budgets and plans for the provision of places on the various schemes and courses covering the first year of operation. These include a wide range of schemes previously in operation, such as courses already being run by the Training Services Division of the MSC and job projects set up by voluntary bodies under the former job creation programmes. This organizational structure has occasioned a great deal of criticism on the part of organizations already involved in existing work experience schemes and training courses on the grounds that they are inadequately represented on the area boards. A greater cause of concern and one on which the success or failure of the programme will largely depend is the shortage of trained staff on the area boards, most of whom have been recruited from existing services and lack the experience and skill needed in dealing with youngsters and community bodies.[21]

Moreover, there is as yet a lack of clarity about how the programme will work which, together with the short time left before the full programme is operative, poses particular difficulties for the further education colleges. For one thing, the time scale in education is somewhat different from that in industry and as a consequence many local education authorities will find it very difficult to make their full contribution in the coming academic year.[22] Another problem facing the colleges is that of adequately financing the new courses. In its Circular 10/77, 'Unemployed Young People – The Contribution of the Education Service', issued in September 1977, the DES announced that money for the educational contribution to the Youth Opportunities Programme would be made available through the Rate Support Grant to the local education authorities, thereby enabling them to provide an additional 10,000 places in their colleges by 1980-1. However, as this is not an earmarked grant, it is often very difficult for local authorities to find specific sums of money. In any case, it represents a relatively small contribution to the programme; the main thrust and most of the money will come from the MSC.

Another problem facing teachers in the colleges is uncertainty about their role, as the challenge thrust upon them by the Youth Opportunities Programme is unlike anything they have met before. The young people most affected by the programme are, inevitably, those with fewest or no qualifications; they tend to be the sons and daughters of manual workers, parents who themselves left school at the statutory minimum age; and a startlingly high proportion, some two out of five according to a recent MSC survey, stayed away from school for shorter or longer periods in their last years before leaving.[23] Consequently, although some of the youngsters on the programmes will correspond to those who in times of normal employment would be on day release courses, the majority of them would prefer to obtain a job as soon as possible and have no desire to embark upon courses of further education. Accordingly, the teachers in the colleges will have to develop courses based on activities and the acquisition of skills, rather than on subject matter, a task that will prove none too easy. However, a start has already been made and there are some encouraging signs of progress, such as the programme devised by Derek Weitzel of Coventry Technical College at the Old Fire Station, Coventry, to train unemployed youngsters in specific basic transferable skills.

As everyone realizes, the Youth Opportunities Programme will not

emerge fully fledged and in full working order overnight. The difficulties it faces derive in large part from the fact that it seeks to help
precisely those young people hitherto not reached by the education
and other services, that substantial proportion of the age group whom
we have neglected for too long. In recognition of the fact that most of
the young people the programme will be dealing with have rejected
traditional education and for whom novel approaches must be found if
it is to be successful, the MSC has set up a task group to look at the
kind of skills they should be taught. The task group consists largely of
representatives from education and industry who have had successful
and direct experience of working with and mounting projects for young
people. While such a development is wholly desirable, its contribution
is bound to take some time to become effective. More immediately, the
colleges of further education are faced with a major challenge and
opportunity which will make great demands on their staff.

In the longer term, the advent of the Youth Opportunities
Programme will have far-reaching consequences. In the words of its
chief architect, it 'is bound to give the whole education and training
system new insights into helping the least able and most disadvantaged
and also into the identification and teaching of core organic skills. It is
bound to provide a means for education and training to come together
and provide learning which is work rather than institution-based.'[24]
Thus, the programme marks a major opportunity not just for unemployed
young people, but also for all our education and training services.

One final aspect of education and training worthy of mention is the
development of linked courses. These are courses in which pupils still
at school attend a further education college for one, or sometimes two,
days a week. Although they cater very largely for 15-year-olds in their
final year of compulsory schooling, they are also attended by a proportion of school students who are over 16. The majority of such courses
are vocational, being offered in such areas as commerce, engineering,
catering, applied science, and building and some lead to a CSE type of
qualification which can be used as the route into CGLI craft courses.
They give youngsters an insight into specific vocational areas and are
therefore sometimes called 'tester' or 'sampling' courses. Clearly, when
properly organized, they provide a valuable mix of education and
training. In addition, at best, they lead to effective co-operation between the secondary school sector and further education and help to
make the youngster aware of what the technical college has to offer
and also to ease the transition between school and work. Although
linked courses grew very rapidly in the period from 1969 to 1975,
expanding tenfold to 140,000, they have now virtually ceased to grow.
This is due largely to the fact that what spare capacity the further
colleges have had has been taken up by the MSC-inspired developments

we have described. This is in many ways a pity, as properly constructed linked courses have much to offer. All in all, they seem not to have received their fair share of credit; for example, the government Green Paper, *Education in Schools*, which one would have expected to look upon linked courses with favour, makes no mention of them.

Having thus reviewed the provision of courses for 16 to 19 year-olds within the further education sector, it is necessary to consider what in educational terms is the best institutional framework to cater for the needs of this age group, bearing in mind that their numbers will contract sharply within a relatively few years. One possible solution is to institutionalize transfer at 16-plus from secondary school either to a sixth form college or a further education college, as already happens in a number of areas. However, no one solution is ideal for different regions of the country and for urban and rural areas alike. To date, where transfer at 16-plus does occur, students are technically free to choose between a sixth form college and the local further education establishment. In a growing number of authorities, however, the tertiary college is seen as the best solution and thus it is important to examine the arguments for and against it.

It can be said in its favour that it caters for the whole range of students, comprising those who want an academic course, those who prefer a vocational course, and those who wish to combine the two.[25] In this respect, it provides a greater degree of flexibility than a sixth form college operating in parallel with a further education college, both in providing a mixture of academic and vocational courses and also in facilitating transfer from one to the other. Second, in the eyes of some students it provides a more adult and therefore more attractive environment than the secondary school. However, many schools have changed in this regard, as the establishment of sixth form colleges and sixth form units or centres within secondary schools testifies. Third, there is the economic argument in favour of the tertiary college, namely that its size makes it a viable proposition, an argument of increasing cogency at a time when secondary school rolls are declining. It has been suggested in some quarters that before long it will not be a practical proposition in some parts of the country to run viable sixth forms in schools and that, in those circumstances, one obvious solution is to transfer all GCE A Level work to the further education sector. However, the tertiary colleges are still few in number and no quantitative evidence is yet available to confirm the supposition that they are more economic to run.

Against the tertiary college, it can be argued that their very size, like that of some of the 'all-through' comprehensive schools, militates against effective organization and against the creation of a sense of belonging which many feel is so crucial to effective learning. Secondly, there is as yet no evidence to suggest that where tertiary colleges exist they promote on a significant scale the flexibility of course offerings and the transfer between courses of which they boast. However, it is still too early to arrive at a considered judgment of the merits and demerits of the tertiary college. In the meantime, it is obviously necessary to monitor its development and, perhaps, we can also learn much from examining closely such European alternatives as the diversified Swedish Upper Secondary schools.

But whether the 16 to 19 age group is educated in a sixth form college or an 'all through' comprehensive school or in the further education college, there seems little logic in having the institutions operating under different DES regulations, such that the provision of vocational courses is restricted to the technical college or that teachers in schools must have successfully completed a course of professional teacher training, while those in the further education sector need not have done so, even if in many cases they are teaching the same courses to the same age range. There is something to be said for the NATFHE proposal that we should establish by statute a system of Further Education with its own regulations, to begin at the school-leaving age of 16 and to incorporate what are now school sixth forms, those sixth form colleges currently operated under school regulations, and the whole of Further and Higher Education as we now understand it, including Adult Education.[26] This proposal merits detailed consideration, not least because the substantial demographic changes that the next decade will usher in strengthen the case for breaking down the lines of demarcation between secondary schools and further education and for allowing the maximum of flexibility.

Such a measure will help to ensure that the further education sector is adequately represented in the decision-making machinery for the examinations for the general education of the 16 to 19 age group. As previously indicated, this has not always been the case largely because the dominating role in devising a new 16-plus examination system has been taken by the Schools Council, upon which the further education colleges have in general been inadequately represented. Although the Schools Council itself sometimes recognizes further education's vital interest in examination matters, for example it sees the CEE as exercising a unifying role, 'both between schools and colleges and among the various FE examining bodies, provided that adequate FE involvement is ensured',[27] in practice this has not always been the case. It is pleasing therefore that in setting up a Study Group, under the chairmanship of Professor Kevin Keohane, to advise her on the future of the CEE, the Secretary of State should include among its members principals of both a further education college and also a tertiary college. However, it remains to be seen whether the reconstructed Schools Council under the chairmanship of John Tomlinson, the Director of Education for Cheshire, and the Steering Committee on the 16-plus examination to replace the GCE and CSE, set up by the DES under the chairmanship of Sir James Waddell, will enable the voice of further education properly to be heard in the future.

Another major artificial division militating against the development of a coherent policy for the 16 to 19s is, as we have seen, that between education and training. Unlike much of Western Europe, we vest responsibility for these in two separate government departments, with the DES promoting education and the Department of Employment, through the MSC, promoting training. Reference has already been made to the growing realization of the need formally to co-ordinate these two complementary activities, resulting in the establishment of the Training and Further Education Consultative Group in December 1976 and the issuing of the DES Administrative Memorandum 12/77, 'Links between the Training and Further Education Services', in August 1977. However, there are many, in further education in particular, who feel that consultation does not go nearly far enough and who would prefer a much more radical change, such as the establishment of a Department of Education, Science and Training.[28] However, not surprisingly, this proposal, put forward recently by NATFHE, has not met with much support, partly because of opposition from those who fear that it might result in less effective training, and partly because it might lead to a complex bureaucratic structure which would inhibit rather than promote the effective co-ordination of education and training.

Given that school-leavers need a broadly based preparation for work, combining both education and training, the problems we face are how to devise suitable programmes and how best to provide them. We believe that all young people should have the right of access to further education and training beyond the statutory school-leaving age but that such provision should not be compulsory. Nor need the right to access be taken up immediately young people leave school. In many cases, they might benefit from deferring their entry into further education for a few years after leaving school, in line with current thinking on what has been called 'Recurrent' and 'Continuing' Education.[29] We need properly constructed courses of education and training which are attractive to young people and which go well beyond the 12-weeks unified vocational preparation schemes. For their success, close co-operation between school, further education, industry and the MSC is essential. Significantly, a number of developments are already taking place in this area. For example, the Further Education Curriculum Review and Development Unit (FEU) set up in January 1977 to act as a focal point for further education curricular matters, has commissioned a major study into 'alternative FE curricula for those groups who will be most vulnerable to the long-term structural unemployment which the transition to a "high technology" economy brings about'. A useful document on the problems of linking education and training is the recently published Third Report on the subject by a Working Party of the Rubber and Plastics Industrial Training Board.[30] Some of the central issues have been enunciated in a number of recent books, including *Education After School* by Tyrell Burgess, and *Post Compulsory Education: The Way Ahead* by E.J. King and others.[31]

All in all, however, these represent isolated initiatives and much more needs to be done at governmental level. It was encouraging, therefore, that early in 1979 the government was belatedly considering establishing a committee of inquiry to look into the provision of education and training for 16 to 19 year-olds.[32] For once, it would seem that all the major interested parties including the MSC, the DES, industry and the TUC were in agreement on the need speedily to set up such an inquiry. The first development was the publication by the two government departments concerned of a discussion document highlighting the issues.[33] However, at the time of writing, this particular matter, like many others, has had to take a back seat and await the outcome of the forthcoming general election. It is greatly to be hoped that this much needed opportunity to examine the problems of the 16 to 19 age group as a whole will not be lost.

In his budget speech on 12 June 1979, the Conservative Chancellor of the Exchequer announced that the proposals for a pilot scheme for Education Mandatory Awards, which were contained in the previous government's Education Bill for implementation in September 1979, would not now be introduced. However, local authorities remain free to assist pupils and students over the age of 16 with discretionary grants.

Cuts in the budget will also effect the work of the Manpower Services Commission; the Youth Opportunities Programme will be cut by over £25 million, a reduction that the MSC claims will not seriously impair its commitments to offer places on its programmes to all unemployed school leavers; the Training Opportunities Scheme will lose over £22 million, leading to reductions in commercial and clerical retraining.

In June 1979, an under-secretary of the DES reviewed the progress that had been made in schemes of Unified Vocational Preparation and concluded that, on balance, they had been unsuccessful. This unfortunate development illustrated clearly what was already evident, namely that a major cause of stagnation was the disbelief of employers in the value of education and training for the 16-19 age group.

In the same month the new Secretary for State for Education, Mark Carlisle, announced that proposals to introduce N and F Levels would not be implemented and, for the present, GCE A Levels would remain.

4 Technician and business education

There is no doubt that in a complex technological society such as our own the technician is a key figure, with a vital part to play both in industry and in business. For example, it is estimated that for every engineer and scientist industry employs, it requires five or more technicians to put theories into practice. The manner of their education is therefore of overriding importance to the prosperity of the country. During the 1960s there was growing concern for technician education, concern which focused on two main aspects: the confusing and overlapping structure of technician courses arising from the separate provision by the CGLI and the Joint Committees for OND/ONC and HND/HNC; and the need to ensure that courses properly reflected the changing role of the technician in industry and business. It was this concern that led the Secretary of State in 1967 to invite the National Advisory Council for Industry and Commerce (NACEIC) to review the national pattern and organization of technician courses and examinations.

The NACEIC established a committee under the chairmanship of Dr H.L. Haslegrave, former Vice-Chancellor of Loughborough University of Technology, with the brief 'to review the provision for courses suitable for technicians at all levels (including corresponding grades in non-technical occupations) and to consider what changes are desirable in the present structure of courses and examinations'. When the Haslegrave Committee reported in 1969, it concluded that, 'The present pattern of technician courses and examinations is unsuitable in a number of important respects as an instrument for meeting not only existing needs, but also the new and changing needs likely to arise in the coming years. In particular, the present administrative machinery will not be adequate to deal effectively and economically with likely future demands.'[1] Accordingly, the Haslegrave Report recommended that new national administrative and co-ordinating machinery be set up 'to plan, administer, and keep under review the development of a unified national pattern of courses of technical education for technicians in industry and in the field of business and office studies, and in

57

pursuance of this to devise or approve suitable courses, establish and assess standards of performance, and award certificates and diplomas as appropriate'. This national machinery should take the form of two independent bodies, a Technician Education Council (TEC) and a Business Education Council (BEC), drawing upon the CGLI for their administrative personnel.

While the Report's recommendations were immediately accepted by the government, there was a substantial delay before the Councils were established. TEC eventually came into existence in March 1973, followed by BEC in May 1974, and corresponding Scottish Councils, SCOTEC and SCOTBEC, were also set up. As a consequence of the activities of the Councils since their establishment, major changes in technician and business education are being effected with very far-reaching consequences for the further education colleges. We shall now examine the nature of these changes by looking closely at the work of TEC and BEC respectively and by comparing their modes of operation.

The Technician Education Council (TEC)

The role of TEC, which came into existence in March 1973, is to set standards, validate courses, award qualifications and generally promote the advance of technician education and enhance its status. The first Council consisted of 24 members under the Chairmanship of Mr A.L. Burton and was appointed for three years. When its term of office expired on 31 March 1976, it was replaced by a council of the same size, chaired by Mr Neale Raine, a Coventry industrialist and a Governor of Lanchester Polytechnic. The Vice-Chairman throughout this period has been Mr R.L. Helmore, Principal of the Cambridgeshire College of Art and Technology, and its Chief Officer is Mr Francis Hanrott, formerly Registrar of the CNAA. The 24 members of the Council are drawn from further and higher education, industry, professional and qualifying bodies, local authorities, industrial training boards and a trade union.

The officially stated aim of the Council is to create a more flexible and simplified range of technician courses eliminating unnecessary duplication without reducing the opportunities available to students or ignoring industry's needs. Although it is much concerned with arrangements for assessing students, TEC sees itself as a validating rather than an examining body, concerned with setting standards, and awarding qualifications. It identified its functions in its first policy statement in June 1974 as, 'essentially to rationalise existing provision, thus saving valuable resources, to keep the system which it introduces under review, and to innovate — or to provide for innovation, for the Council hopes that many new developments and initiatives will originate from colleges and other establishments in the field'. As we shall see later, TEC's view of its role is, in this regard, significantly different from that of BEC. In seeing itself primarily as a validating agency, TEC closely resembles the CNAA which is not perhaps surprising given that its Chief Officer was formerly Registrar of the CNAA.

In order to carry out its functions, TEC has established a number of committees. Thus, there are two standing committees, for Education, and Resources and Organisation, together with three Sector Committees, 22 Programme Committees and a number of specialist panels and working parties which are responsible for developing and validating programmes of study. These committees, panels and working parties cover a very wide range of technician activity and consist of more than 400 members from colleges, industry, professional and qualifying bodies, technician organizations and industrial training boards. The three sector committees cover, respectively, the three main disciplines with which technician education is broadly involved — engineering, construction, and science. Under them, the 22 programme committees cover individual subjects such as computer engineering, fuel technology, maritime studies and the life sciences.

To explain its outline policy to the colleges and interested members of the public, TEC issued a Policy Statement in June 1974 which was subsequently expanded and modified by a large number of Circulars and Guidance Notes. It also publishes a news-sheet, *TECNEWS*, which is issued about three times a year. There is thus a mass of official documentation available on TEC and all its works. However, we are here primarily concerned with a critical analysis of the influence of TEC on the development of technician education and for this purpose we shall restrict ourselves to a brief summary of the way in which it operates.[2]

Whilst the Council is a registered limited company, financed initially by a 100 per cent deficiency grant from the DES, the expectation is that it will be self-supporting by 1980 with revenue entirely raised from student registration fees. By the beginning of 1978, its annual budget was over £500,000, of which only just over 20 per cent was derived from student registration fees. However, as the number of students increases, each new student paying a registration charge which is currently £15 a year collected by the colleges, so the DES grant will be phased out. Thus, by 1980, when an estimated 200,000 students will be studying for TEC qualifications, all its income will be derived from fees, and by 1982 when there should be 300,000 students taking its courses, the Council's revenues from this source should rise to an estimated £1,500,000.

From its establishment, the Council's secretariat has been provided by the CGLI, a service which it has also made available to BEC. This arrangement, recommended by the Haslegrave Report, is an eminently sensible one in that it both ensures continuing close liaison between the new Councils and the CGLI and also utilizes the services of experienced personnel who might otherwise have been made redundant as the CGLI involvement in technician examinations disappeared.

The approach adopted by TEC is based on a unitary or modular system culminating in one of the four qualifications recommended by the Haslegrave Report: the Certificate, Diploma, Higher Certificate or Higher Diploma. This range of awards provides both for different levels of performance and also for different educational experiences but is *not* associated with particular modes of attendance. Thus, it should ultimately be possible to obtain TEC awards through full-time, part-time, day release or block release, sandwich or evening study, or by a combination of more than one of these methods. Special provision has also been made for external students, such as the handicapped, who cannot attend college regularly. The Council is also exploring the possibility of combining studies undertaken by correspondence or other forms of directed private study which do not involve regular attendance at a college, with a system of occasional personal contact between the student and college. At the time of writing, the great majority of students on TEC programmes are following Certificate courses. The minimum entry for a Certificate programme is completion of a five-year secondary school course, reaching a standard recommended by the appropriate programme committee and the standard of the award is midway between Parts I and II of the CGLI Technicians' Certificate or broadly comparable with that of ONC. Whilst the time taken to complete the course obviously varies according to the pattern of study, a typical day release course, ignoring any exemptions or credits, is of three years' duration covering in all some 900 hours of study.

Both the minimum entry requirements for a TEC Diploma programme and its technical content are much the same as for the Certificate. However, the Diploma includes a broader range of studies and consists of between 1,800 and 2,200 hours of study for the average student, or approximately twice as many as for the Certificate. The programmes are so structured that a student who has successfully completed the Certificate course can then add the necessary units to obtain a Diploma, or alternatively qualify in selected additional endorsement procedures, an arrangement reminiscent of the ONC/HNC system.

Minimum entry requirements for both the Higher Certificate and the Higher Diploma are based on either the TEC Certificate or Diploma or GCE A Levels and O Levels. A Higher Certificate involves some 600 hours' study for the average student, the more broadly based Higher Diploma course taking between 1,200 and 1,500 hours. Thus, the Higher Certificate may be taken by a two-year day release course and the Higher Diploma by a two-year full-time or sandwich course.

As indicated previously, TEC awards are based on schemes of study known as programmes which, in keeping with the present trend towards modular courses, are divided up into units. For example, the Certificate and Diploma programmes contain, typically, 15 and 25 units respectively, each unit consisting of approximately 60 hours of study for the average student. There are basically two main kinds of units: 'standard units' which are devised by the TEC programme committees and made available to all colleges, and 'college devised units' which as the title indicates are devised by one or more colleges. In a given programme, some units may be compulsory, some may be optional and some may be 'supplementary units' which could yield credit towards another programme. To assist the colleges in writing their units, TEC has issued validation guidelines. These require that every programme proposal has to be prefaced by a clear statement of its objectives, including the knowledge and skills which it aims to impart to students and the career to which it is related and each scheme must include a syllabus and a proposed method of assessment. Moreover, an element of general and communication studies, equivalent to at least fifteen per cent of the total and which can be assessed, must be included in college programmes. The Council also envisages that practical units will be required in full-time programmes leading to the Certificate or Diploma, while at the higher level project work is likely to be appropriate. All TEC programmes also have to contain health and safety material, to complement the training which employers are obliged to give under the 1974 Health and Safety at Work Act.

To facilitate students' progress through the programmes, TEC introduced, in 1975, the concept of 'level' into the Certificate and Diploma and in the following year it extended it to programmes leading to higher awards. Briefly, a level is ascribed to a particular unit so that it can be compared with other units and used as an entry qualification for subsequent stages in a programme. For example, a level I unit in mathematics might be an entry requirement for a level II unit in mathematics or physical sciences. Generally, the prerequisites for a level I unit in CSE study, for level II appropriate GCE O Levels and for Level III the appropriate Level II unit. To ensure a uniform academic standard for each Certificate and Diploma programme, a minimum number of Level III units must be included. In addition to the TEC requirement of satisfactory performance in a minimum of three level III units to obtain a Certificate, some of the professional bodies are also specifying the nature of the units which must be taken at different levels by students proposing to proceed along the road to professional membership. Consequently, students gaining a particular TEC award will represent a continuum ranging from those who have followed a pre-dominantly academic programme to others with a more practical orientation.

As far as assessment is concerned, procedures may vary consider-ably, TEC being willing to give the colleges a good deal of latitude in devising what they consider most appropriate to a particular programme or unit, provided the basic requirements are met. Thus, agreed pro-cedures may in theory range from complete external assessment by TEC to a mixture of internal college assessment and external modera-tion. In practice, however, it now appears to be the case that, because of lack of resources, TEC is unable to offer an external examination system to the colleges wanting it. Instead, it has been forced to adopt a complicated system of controlling the colleges' internal assessment procedures, with consequent pressures on the staff involved. Finally, the Council has to be satisfied that the college has both the staff and the resources needed to run the programme. It takes national and local needs into account and urges colleges to consult local industry, their own local education authority and other interested bodies. TEC will normally approve a programme for a period of five years. Once it is in operation, standards are maintained by monitoring. The Council appoints an external moderator for each programme who reports on its progress and endorses students' grades on appropriate units.

It is interesting to note that the Scottish Technical Education Council, SCOTEC, which was established in March 1973, was given a similar remit for Scotland, in line with the recommendations of the Hudson Committee on Technician Courses and Examinations in Scotland. SCOTEC has a similar committee structure to TEC and has adopted the same award titles, but without the unit programme con-cept. The two councils have announced their intention of working together as far as possible to ensure that there is a national system of education appropriate to technicians.

In the relatively few years since its inception, TEC has made rapid, some would say too rapid, progress in approving courses. The first programme of study for a TEC award was approved by the Council in early 1976. By September of that year, the Council had received 330 submissions of courses, of which it had approved 290 for starting in the academic year 1976-7. This comparatively modest start was fol-lowed, a year later, by the first major phase of the introduction and adoption of the new courses. Thus, in September 1977, some 350 colleges introduced about 1,200 new programmes involving between 35,000 and 40,000 students. Though the range of courses was, in the words of TECNEWS, 'impressively catholic', the majority were in engineering, with over 200 for Mechanical and Production Engineering and about the same number for Electronics and Telecommunications.

Other programmes on offer included Building and Civil Engineering, Electrical Engineering, Fabrication and Welding, Gas Services, Estate Management, Printing, Shipbuilding, Textiles, Avionics and Science. By the beginning of the academic session 1978-9, there were over 100,000 students on TEC courses, almost all of them at the Certificate or Diploma level. The provision of courses for the Higher Certificate and the Higher Diploma is inevitably much less well advanced. The appointment of moderators has gone ahead rapidly and, by the beginning of 1978, two full time and approximately 230 part-time moderators had been appointed, each part-timer to visit three or four colleges three or four times a year. In addition, TEC is currently considering appointing more full-time moderators.

Given that the original intention of the new TEC courses was to replace CGLI and national certificate and diploma courses, it is interesting to note the progress to date in this regard. The CGLI has announced its intention of gradually withdrawing all its technician level examinations during the next few years and it is anticipated that the last normal examinations will be phased out by 1983, with the majority having disappeared by 1980. The picture for the National Certificates and Diplomas is, however, much less clear. For example, agreement was reached to phase out OND in Building for a September 1977 start and the same was the case for both ONC and HNC in Surveying, Cartography, Planning and Estate Management and Valuation. Also, the Joint Committee in Sciences has decided to phase out ONC by the end of 1979-80, but appears to have made no decision about OND. On the other hand, many colleges are expressing concern on a number of grounds at the projected disappearance of OND Technology (Engineering). They argue that, unlike TEC courses, its prime purpose is to provide a route into higher education; that its structure is different to TEC, being an integrated scheme not based on the unit model; and that establishments offering the course have only fairly recently undertaken a considerable amount of curriculum development in order to devise it. It is for these reasons that some colleges have petitioned the Joint Committee concerned to continue to administer the scheme. Finally, there are at the time of writing no plans to phase out the bulk of the HND courses in engineering, as the Joint Committees running them have expressed a lack of confidence in the proposed TEC courses and have stated their intention of continuing with the existing HND courses while suitable revisions are being considered. Although these difficulties may turn out to be temporary, they represent a major setback in the Council's attempts at complete rationalization. Whilst it seems inevitable that the phasing out of OND and HND courses will take much longer than for CGLI courses, it is the intention of the DES that it should be accomplished as soon as possible.

Finally, in February 1977, TEC accepted responsibility for another important area by agreeing to provide national validation for technician courses in Art and Design. It has accordingly set up a new Committee for Art and Design (DATEC) under the chairmanship of Mr David Carter, a well-known design consultant. In the Council's view, two main advantages will flow from these new arrangements, which are likely to affect at least 15,000 students: they will help to integrate the design factor into British productive industry and improve product design; and they will make it possible for new types of vocational courses to be developed, in which design is more closely related to technology or business. This important development is discussed at length in chapter 6.

In attempting to analyse the success or otherwise of the developments initiated to date by TEC, it is convenient to examine them under three separate but overlapping headings: the organizational aspects of the Council's work; the financial aspects; and, perhaps most important, the curricular aspects. As we have seen, TEC's governing body is the Council, which is supported by Standing Committees, Sector Committees and Programme Committees. As far as the Council is concerned, one major criticism which has been levelled at it is that the education service is under-represented. The Haslegrave Report recommended a Council of between 15 and 20 members of whom two-thirds should represent educational interests. In practice, the Council numbers 24, of whom a considerably smaller proportion than one might expect derive from further education. Another criticism levelled at the original Council was that very few members were actively involved in teaching students at the required level. Where the Programme Committees are concerned, the total membership of about 400 is divided roughly equally between education and industry. However, given that the committees are concerned with devising and approving new courses, it may not be entirely desirable that the original selection of members seems to have been based more on the political necessity of balancing the numerous interests jostling for representation than on proven curriculum expertise.[3] On the other hand, such a balancing act was probably inevitable and undoubtedly, with experience, the industrial and other non-educational members have become more knowledgeable about curriculum development. Moreover, some criticism must be levelled at the further education colleges themselves as they took some time to get to grips with the problems facing the Council and perhaps did not make their voice heard soon enough.

In retrospect, one cannot help but feel that there was also a partial failure on the part of such bodies as the DES, the NACEIC, the RACs, the teachers' unions, and the Professional Bodies to see clearly the shortcomings inherent in the Council's strategies and to voice their criticisms publicly at a much earlier stage than they did. For example, the first major written criticism of TEC policies emanating from NATFHE did not appear until October 1976, some three years after TEC's Policy Statement was published.[4] Another very vocal criticism of TEC's organizational procedures that is to be heard from many colleges concerns its complex submission structure. What has been justly called 'the wealth of burdensome paper-work'[5] that has to be sent to TEC in a college submission inevitably causes irritation and resentment and has led some critics to accuse TEC of being more concerned with the mechanics of its system than with ensuring it has adopted the right curriculum specifications.[6] Inevitably, the development of TEC courses by the colleges involves a great deal of work which puts strain on staff and facilities, particularly at a time when in many colleges no money is available to provide additional resources. While a complex submission procedure is probably unavoidable, given the range of aims and objectives that are required and the alternative forms of assessment available to the colleges, their lives have not been made any simpler by what one critic has apostrophized as the 'unspeakable jargon' in which some of the TEC paperwork is couched.[7] Undoubtedly, TEC has placed upon the colleges a considerable amount of extra administrative work at a time when no extra help is forthcoming. That the former is probably inevitable and the latter accidental is of little comfort to the staff of the colleges.

Another organizational problem to which we have already referred is that of phasing out of existing courses, in particular HND and HNC. The Council is understandably pressing the colleges to enter their students for its qualifications but as yet have only just begun to make arrangements for the Higher Diploma and Certificate. As a consequence, some students will have completed their lower level courses before the higher awards are available and there is as yet no guarantee of entry from, for example, a TEC Certificate course to HNC.[8] Indeed, the arrangements for transfer from lower to higher award programmes have yet to be worked out fully. Although the Higher Certificate and Diploma programmes have to be designed to follow on from appropriate lower award programmes, this implies a degree of co-operation between Polytechnics, for example, and feeder colleges which has not always been as healthy as it might have been.[9] As far as TEC is concerned there is no firm demarcation between lower awards and higher awards because certain level III units are likely to feature in both types of programme. However, as some students will enter higher award programmes directly from school with GCE A Levels some programmes may have to contain what the Council has termed 'balancing units' to cater for their needs.[10]

As we have seen, negotiations between TEC and the National Joint

Committees are making variable rates of progress. While some of the latter have already merged their activities into the TEC system, others are clearly unhappy about the prospect of losing the identity of a well established award, as in the case of HNDs in engineering, and in these cases, to use TEC's own terminology, 'negotiations are continuing'. However, the Council has not ruled out the possibility that certain HNDs might survive in some form within the TEC system. TEC is also engaged in negotiations with professional bodies and technician societies to secure the acceptance of, and confidence in, TEC awards. Major problems to be resolved include the maintenance of appropriate standards and the achieving of a delicate balance between academic and practical components within a given programme. In the meantime, it is significant that both the Joint Matriculation Board and the CNAA have agreed in principle that a TEC Certificate or Diploma with at least three units at level III, with merit in appropriate units, shall be an acceptable entry qualification for their degree courses. There is no reason why, in principle at least, a similar level of achievement should not be acceptable to the universities as an entry qualification for their degree courses. However, a common problem that faces both the universities and the CNAA is that, given the variation in programmes from one technical college to another, how to evaluate the qualification. It is in order to resolve this problem that consultations are proceeding between TEC, the Standing Conference on University Entrance, the Open University and the CNAA. It is for the same reason that both TEC and BEC have been involved in discussions with the CNAA and the Open University concerning a proposal for setting up a national agency to deal with credit transfer arrangements in further and higher education. The possible structure and financing of such an agency are now the subject of a feasibility study and TEC and BEC are both represented on the committee carrying out this exercise.

The financial aspects of TEC arrangements have also come in for very close scrutiny as, rightly or wrongly, one of the Council's main aims from the outset has been 'to produce a much better system of technician education ... at little or no extra cost'.[11] Clearly, a massive new structure is being erected which will be expensive to run and early indications were that the Council had underestimated the amount of money it would need to carry out its tasks. On the other hand, in the long term some savings may result from the replacing of the CGLI and Joint Committees structure by a single Council. However, it is very difficult accurately to quantify the cost of running TEC and any savings that accrue will be long-term ones that are not likely to be felt uniformly or at all levels. In the meantime, for the colleges and indirectly for the local authorities, the TEC arrangements have involved very considerable hidden costs and, as we have observed, the expenditure in staff time and in use of college facilities has been great.[12] Inevitably, too, there has been a degree of duplication as different groups of staff have undertaken the same work at the same time in different colleges.

From an educational point of view, undoubtedly the most important aspect of the new TEC courses is their curricular function. In short, when all the dust has settled shall we have produced a series of programmes which will produce better educated technicians, more suited to the country's needs than those turned out by the old system? While it is too early to answer that question, a number of criticisms can be levelled at the way in which TEC has gone about devising its new courses. Perhaps the most cogent of these is that it has underestimated the central importance of curriculum development which has tended to take second place to the establishment of an efficient organizational structure.[13] As a result, it is argued that TEC committees have spent much of their time in producing schemes into which to fit the curriculum instead of first identifying curriculum objectives as a means of defining the curriculum content. In short, the impression given by TEC to date has been that the structure is much more important than the curriculum.[14]

Much criticism has also been levelled at TEC on the grounds that it has committed itself to a form of curriculum design based wholly on behavioural objectives. Or, as one critic has put it, 'TEC guide-lines appear to suggest that stating objectives is the major and only step in curriculum design, with the assumption that lists can represent the structure of knowledge'.[15] While it is understandable that TEC should have adopted this approach in that the objectives model has for its exponents much to commend it, not least that as an aid to assessment it facilitates the Council's validating role which it sees as its main one, nonetheless in practice it has major shortcomings. In the first place, what really matters is what goes on in the lecture room and the prime aim of curriculum innovation should be to improve practice; thus, while a statement of objectives is an important prerequisite of good teaching, it does not by itself help to bring it about. Indeed, an undue emphasis on behavioural objectives may well have the harmful effect of putting the emphasis on 'a pre-fabricated and encyclopaedic notion of knowledge',[16] with the result that procedures may become shallow and geared to aims which are the quickest and easiest to put into effect and for that reason often trivial. In short, say the critics, the system is cumbersome and arid and leaves no room for flair.

Whatever the rights and wrongs of this argument, there is little doubt that a major exercise in curriculum development of the sort initiated by TEC requires considerable resources in terms of skill and time on the part of further education teachers if it is to be successful. This is particularly true of the behavioural objectives model which hitherto has been virtually unknown to many staff in the colleges, a situation aggravated by the high proportion of lecturers without professional training. It would have been better, therefore, many educationists think, if TEC had proceeded more slowly and carefully by undertaking a series of pilot schemes along the line of the Schools Council or the Nuffield Science projects which would be carefully evaluated before introducing far-reaching curriculum changes. In a typical schools curriculum project, for instance, confidential trial materials are tested in selected schools and only when they have proved their worth are they published in book form. In the case of TEC, however, there was an initial shortage of textbooks, followed in the last few years by a spate of books, many of them written understandably by personnel closely involved in TEC developments. While this is inevitable and in many ways desirable, it does create its own problems, in that once sets of textbooks become used in the colleges upon which the teaching is largely based, it becomes more difficult to modify the content of courses should that prove to be desirable. Indeed, it must inevitably make the moderator's task a difficult one.

It would seem fairly obvious that TEC should have initiated an ongoing programme of research and development looking into such aspects as its procedures, particularly that of evaluation, and how to identify the needs of industry. In practice, however, this has occurred only belatedly with the setting up in the latter half of 1977 of a subcommittee to study research and development projects relating to TEC. In this regard, as we shall see, BEC has got off the mark rather more quickly. Another even more important development that has been required from the start is a co-ordinated programme of staff development to acquaint further education teachers with the mechanics and principles of curriculum design. While it may be the case that this responsibility should lie more with the colleges themselves and the teacher training institutions than with TEC, it is nevertheless patent that the Council overestimated the degree of professional expertise available in the colleges. Moreover, although the Further Education Staff College and the technical teacher training establishments have made some attempt at offering suitable courses, the national provision has been quite inadequate to meet the needs.

Another concern about the Council's behavioural approach to curriculum planning is that it is likely to be even less appropriate for the higher level courses, where the knowledge content is necessarily greater. Concern has also been expressed about the capacity of the TEC system to accommodate the wide ability range of students who take technician courses on the grounds that a simplified structure consisting of only four awards may not be sufficient to meet the needs and aspirations that exist within the existing and potential range of technician courses.[17]

Finally, it is clear that the model adopted by TEC is very dependent for its successful operation on effective monitoring, and that the key figures will be the moderators. As large numbers of them will be needed, it remains to be seen whether sufficient well-qualified staff are available. Moreover, they cannot do their jobs properly without the help of suitable criteria and an appropriate mechanism for monitoring the relationship between curriculum content and the changing requirements of modern industry.[18] It is doubtful whether these sophisticated tools have yet been placed in their hands and it may yet turn out that the effective monitoring of standards is too vast and demanding a job given the limited resources available.

When all is said and done, however, it must be conceded that although many of the criticisms levelled at TEC are valid, they could equally be directed at any system of curriculum reform, given our uncertain state of educational knowledge and our limited resources. While it may be true that TEC is trying to do too much too quickly, there is no doubt that it has made considerable progress in what is an immense task. To design a system of courses to replace provision for more than 250,000 students in more than 500 colleges, thereby replacing nearly 300 different courses and about 90 CGLI committees and Joint Committees, in so short a time, is no mean feat. Moreover, matters were not helped by the delay of four years between the Haslegrave Report and the establishment of TEC, responsibility for which must be laid at the door of the DES. As a consequence, the Council has been under considerable pressure, particularly from the DES, to introduce its schemes rapidly. While a more leisurely approach would doubtless have been more effective in educational terms, it would have been more expensive and have involved further delay.

Perhaps of greatest significance is the fact that with all its faults TEC has at least one considerable achievement to its credit, namely the stimulation of curriculum development in a sector of education where little existed before. Moreover, in this regard, the Council has been forced by events to change its approach. Originally, for example, it was hoped that colleges or groups of institutions would write units and devise suitable programmes to be validated by TEC. When this proved to be impracticable, the Council gave greater emphasis to programmes based on standard units rather than college-devised units, particularly at the lower levels. Although this change was made for operational reasons, it can be argued that it also confers educational advantages in that by providing comparability across courses it furnishes a 'common core' which in turn establishes a common foundation on which the more varied higher level courses can be erected. TEC has also been responsive to the criticism that its submission procedures have been unnecessarily complicated and in mid-1976 simplified them by reducing the amount of documentation required.

In conclusion, it would perhaps be no exaggeration to describe the activities of TEC, in the words of a Polytechnic Director, as constituting the greatest single change which further education has had to assimilate in recent years, not excepting the establishment of the polytechnics and the evolution of the CNAA.[19] Dr Law of Preston Polytechnic, while acknowledging that TEC has generated some hostility and suspicion, believes that this is in part a reflection of the perennial clash between immediate career needs, as advocated by industry, and the desirability of preparing students for a higher stage in the educational process. In such circumstances, conflicting interests are inevitable and should be harnessed constructively. In short, all sides should concentrate on optimizing the opportunities afforded by the creation of the new body.

The Business Education Council (BEC)

As we have seen, the establishment of BEC, like that of TEC, fulfilled a recommendation of the Haslegrave Committee on Technician Courses and Examinations in its 1969 Report. However, partly because business education was less well developed than technician education and partly because of some reluctance on the part of the professional bodies concerned to endorse the proposed changes, BEC took even longer than TEC to come into existence and was not set up until May 1974. The original Council was constituted for three years and, accordingly, was reconstituted in May 1977. Its part-time chairman is Mr J.M. Bruce Lockhart, its chief officer Mr John Sellars and it has 24 members, about half of whom represent educational interests and half business interests. Like TEC, it is a registered company limited by guarantee and for the first two years of its existence received a deficiency grant from the DES. However, it is now self-supporting, deriving all its revenue from fees. Its potential income is much smaller than that of TEC and in the financial year ending September 1977 its fee revenue was about £530,000. Like TEC, it issues a range of publications including major policy documents, detailed course syllabuses, and BECNEWS.

Its terms of reference are very similar to those of TEC in that its role is to plan, administer and keep under review the establishment of a unified national system of non-degree courses for people whose occupations fall within the broad area of business and public administration. It interprets the word 'business' to extend to all those who need education, other than for scientific and technical qualifications, to equip them for their work in any part of the private or public sector, whether in industry, commerce, central or local government. However, as we shall see, although BEC's origins and purpose are similar to those of TEC, its awards, methods and style are in many ways quite different.

As we have observed, the Scottish equivalent of BEC is the Scottish Business Education Council, SCOTBEC. It was established somewhat earlier than BEC, in July 1973, in line with the recommendations of the Hudson Committee Report on Technician Courses and Examinations in Scotland. SCOTBEC replaced the Scottish Council for Commercial, Administrative, and Professional Education (SCAPE) by what amounted to virtually a change in name only. As SCAPE had devised and introduced a comprehensive series of recognized courses in the 1960s, it was felt that these were well able to meet known requirements and that there did not appear to be any significant gaps in the material available. However, it was thought that a change of title would be desirable to bring about a uniformity of description, particularly for those bodies, like the industrial training boards, whose activities cross national borders.

Many of the differences between BEC and TEC are identified in BEC's Consultative Document published in June 1975. A particular difficulty was that, with the exception of those courses which were the responsibility of the Joint Committee for National Awards in Business Studies and Public Administration, the Joint Committee for National Certificates in Distribution, and the National Committee in Office Studies, there was no national structure in business education at sub-degree level.[20] Moreover, the need for business education was not so widely acknowledged by employers as the need for craft or technical training, and in any case employers' needs varied widely. It identified some 40,000 candidates who were enrolled annually at that time on ONC/OND courses in Business Studies, and approximately 25,000 candidates on other further education courses in the business field; in addition, the annual intake of candidates for qualifications through professional body examinations in the broad field of business studies was in excess of 150,000. All this made it difficult to estimate the potential size of BEC's market.

It was for these reasons that BEC, in its First Policy Statement, issued in March 1976, stated that the requirements for BEC courses were in some significant ways different from those of TEC. Thus, the Council decided to adopt different terminology in those instances where it was felt that to use the same words to describe something different could be confusing. In contrast to TEC, BEC became involved with the administration of existing courses from an early stage in its development and, from 1 September 1975, it took over administrative and policy responsibility for the awards offered by the three committees listed above. As we shall see, BEC is replacing these awards by its own which are available at three levels: General Awards, National Awards and Higher National Awards. The introduction date for General Awards was September 1978 and 327 colleges have been approved for these courses. Provision for national and regional examinations for pre-BEC courses at this level such as the Certificate in Office Studies and the General Certificate in Distribution has been withdrawn except for those students who, at the time of writing, are in the second year of existing programmes. As far as its National and Higher National Awards are concerned, BEC policy is to phase them in over the two academic years 1978-9 and 1979-80. Thus, there will be no further first year enrolments to existing ONC/OND or HNC/HND courses after the academic year 1978-9. A number of colleges were in a position to embark upon National and Higher National Awards in September 1978 and BEC approved 83 of the former and 17 of the latter. The remainder will be approved for a start in September 1979.

The Council also differs from TEC in that its committee structure is based on three main committees, Education, Research and Monitoring, and Finance and General Purposes. Moreover, by comparison with TEC, BEC has realized the importance of establishing a Research and Monitoring Committee from the beginning. As indicated in its First Policy Statement, the Council is concerned at the inadequacy of the available data about the effectiveness of the existing provisions for business education and considers that an essential feature of its work programme is to ascertain both the market for business education and also the costs of meeting these requirements, using a range of alternative methods and routes of study. The information, when assembled, will be published as a basis for discussion.

Undoubtedly, however, as far as BEC awards are concerned, the key committee is the Education Committee, which is the body with the responsibility for developing and maintaining a structured set of awards. Under the Education Committee are four boards, set up in 1976, with responsibility for devising and validating individual courses, syllabuses and curricula. The first board, the Business Studies Board, oversees courses of a non-specialized nature for students planning careers in a wide range of commercial, manufacturing or service organizations. The second, the Financial Sector Studies Board, is responsible for courses aimed at employees in occupations such as accountancy, banking and insurance. The third, the Distribution Studies Board, has to provide courses for those who are or wish to be employed in wholesale and retail trading, or on the sales staff of customer service industries, both privately and publicly owned. Finally, the fourth board, the Public Administration and Public Sector Studies Board, is responsible for those in the non-industrial public sector, including central and local government, hospital administration and the police. Each board is made up of equal numbers of educationalists and employers, together with advisers brought in from outside to help with the development of courses. In addition, specialist committees have been set up to advise on courses which cut across the responsibility of more than one board, including the Secretarial Studies Committee, which has a status equal to that of the four boards, the Directed Private Study and Correspondence Course Committee, and a Modern Languages Panel. The establishment of the Secretarial Studies Committee represents a major change in BEC policy from that originally advocated. It represents a realistic acceptance of the fact that whilst training for secretarial skills is the province of well-recognized and long-established bodies with international reputations, there is also a need for young people trained as typists or secretaries to have the opportunity to study for suitable BEC awards. Moreover, it is necessary to provide appropriate optional secretarial modules within BEC programmes so that students, immediately on completion of their courses, can find jobs requiring office skills. For this reason, the Secretarial Studies Committee is responsible for devising and validating option modules and for formulating recommendations regarding exemptions from secretarial studies. To sum up, BEC has assumed responsibility for the administration of courses of business education at all levels between school and higher education, unlike TEC which is concerned only with technician education, leaving craft level courses to the CGLI and the Regional Examining Boards.

Details of BEC awards were announced by the Council in its First Policy Statement in March 1976; these are aimed principally at students in the 16 to 21 years age band, but with the clear understanding that many older employees would wish to qualify at the same levels. As we have seen, there are three levels of award and at each level courses will lead to either a Certificate or Diploma. As in the case of TEC, these terms no longer identify a method of study; the standard of attainment is the same in each case, but a Diploma will indicate a greater breadth of performance. The first level awards are called BEC General Certificate and Diploma, the second BEC National Certificate and Diploma, and the third BEC Higher National Certificate and Diploma.

There will be no formal entry requirement for courses leading to the BEC General Certificate and Diploma which are designed in large part to provide a 'second chance' for those students, whether full-time or part-time, who have little or no record of academic success. The courses are aimed at providing a broad educational foundation with a stress on literacy and numeracy and students have to be 16, indicate their suitability for the courses and be able to benefit from them. Pass levels in the courses will be at least equivalent to the present Certificate of Office Studies. In order to obtain a BEC General Certificate, a student will have to attend at least one year part-time and to get a Diploma at least one year full-time or two years part-time. Students taking a

General award can gain either a pass or a credit.

BEC National Certificate and Diploma courses take students to at least the level of the present ONC and OND in Business Studies. They will recruit from 16-year-olds and older age groups holding a BEC General Certificate or Diploma at credit level, or at least 4 GCE O Levels or their equivalent. The National Certificate will require a minimum of two years part-time study and the National Diploma will take two years full-time or three years part-time.

At the Higher National level, students will usually be over 18, hold a BEC National Certificate or Diploma or a combination of GCE A Level and O Level passes. The terminal level will be not less than the present HNC and HND awards and the minimum time will be two years part-time study for the Higher Certificate and two years full-time or three years part-time for the Higher Diploma. Arrangements are also being made for well-motivated students without the minimum academic entry requirements to gain direct entry into appropriate courses at the discretion of the Council. At both National and Higher National levels, it is intended that the awards should be recognized for entry to and, where appropriate, exemption from, part of degree courses and/or the examinations of professional and qualifying bodies.[21] Indeed, by the end of 1978, both the Standing Conference on University Entrance (SCUE) and the CNAA had recognized BEC awards for the purposes of entrance to degree courses: SCUE agreed that the BEC General Certificate or Diploma shall be acceptable as an alternative to the 'O' level component of the general requirement and that the National Certificate or Diploma shall be acceptable as an alternative to the 'A' level component, and the CNAA has agreed that the National Certificate or Diploma shall be acceptable as meeting the minimum general entrance requirements for courses leading to their first degrees and Dip. HE.

BEC awards can be gained through a variety of study patterns. Thus, in addition to the normal full-time, sandwich, and part-time routes, it is hoped that directed private study, linking oral and postal tuition, and correspondence courses will be available, initially on an experimental basis. It is intended that a pilot scheme will shortly be in operation at some six centres.

In its First Policy Statement, the Council announced its underlying philosophy. Firstly, its courses should be based on a modular system consisting of 'core' modules and 'option' modules. Second, four central themes, considered basic to BEC's concept of business education, should be an integral part of all courses, whatever the level of award. These themes are: an understanding of the role of money in business; an understanding of how to work with people; an ability to speak and write clear English and communicate effectively; and an ability to understand and propose solutions for business and administrative problems which arise in an advanced technological society. Third, initially at least, the designing of courses at the general and national levels would be undertaken entirely by BEC, another significant difference from the procedure adopted by TEC.

Subsequently, in its Initial Guidelines on the Implementation of Policy issued in May 1977, the Council announced that its General and National awards would be based on standard modules provided centrally and that all General awards would be examined centrally for a period of at least three years, when the policy would be reviewed in the light of experience. In the case of National awards, the Council requires all colleges to use standard courses for the first three intakes of students, in order to build up experience in the new approach but, thereafter, colleges will be given the opportunity of devising their own courses and submitting them to BEC for validation. However, where standard units do not meet specific needs, colleges can exceptionally submit for validation options devised by themselves. When the three years are over, the colleges will have the right, if they choose to exercise it, to design their own alternative courses and to submit them to BEC for validation. However, judging by past experience, very few colleges will avail themselves of the opportunity.

In its May 1977 policy document, the Council intimated that it would in due course publish standard courses for Higher National awards for colleges wishing to adopt them and, indeed, by the end of 1978 it had already begun to do so. As far as the polytechnics and some of the major colleges offering degree courses are concerned, they have already had experience of devising and examining their own courses; thus, the Council's approach to them is that they should have freedom to innovate within certain parameters. These include a well-defined course structure, based on core modules and options, and a requirement that the four central themes be so introduced that the students' understanding of them is developed within the core of any course. All courses will normally be approved initially for five years and where assessment is carried out by college staff, BEC, like TEC, will appoint moderators to monitor standards, as it does for all its courses. Indeed, a small number of BEC Higher National courses have started during the academic year 1978-9 and moderators have been appointed. However, many of the colleges presently running HNC and professional body examination courses are much more used to working to externally determined syllabuses and have little or no experience of devising their own. The Council is anxious that the latter colleges should gradually be brought to the standard of the better colleges of the former group. For some years to come, therefore, they are likely to rely on Higher National courses provided by the Council.

All BEC programmes are designed on a modular basis and for each level of award the Council defines a core of compulsory modules, designed to cover what it describes as 'fundamental knowledge and skills'. In some instances, the core modules are common to all Boards but, in others, there are variations which reflect the particular interests of particular Boards. In general, there is a greater degree of flexibility in courses leading to National awards than in those that lead to General awards. For Certificates at all levels, the core modules will account for three-quarters of the course, for General Diplomas they will account for three-eighths and for National and Higher Diplomas one half of the course. In addition, the Council encourages the devising of courses which incorporate an appropriate period of concurrent work experience. The assessment procedures prescribed by the Council are based on three criteria: they must reflect the need to measure the extent to which the student can interrelate and apply the knowledge and skill gained from the study of a number of modules; they must include an adequate recognition of the student's work during the course; and they must include a significant emphasis on written examinations.

In assessing the changes in business education being wrought by BEC, it is instructive to compare the differences in awards, methods and style between it and TEC. At the time of writing, BEC seems to have come in for rather less public criticism than TEC. This may be partly due to the fact that BEC has adopted a more centralized approach by providing more courses rather than by giving colleges freedom initially to put forward their own course proposals, thereby causing less work and upheaval for the colleges. This may be seen as a more conventional approach than that of TEC; however, BEC would argue that, in terms of the way in which it has asked the staff of the colleges to think about the implications of how they need to teach and the relationship between the different parts of the courses, its approach has been more radical in its requirement for change.[22] Nevertheless, like TEC, it has not wholly escaped criticism that it has insufficiently involved and consulted those college staff who will be teaching its courses.

As we have seen, the Council will be making awards at three levels, including level I, which is the equivalent of a craft course; by contrast TEC will be making only two awards, leaving craft level courses to the CGLI. Doubts have been expressed about the appropriateness of, and necessity for, BEC's level I awards, on two grounds: that existing qualifications such as GCE and CSE might be further developed to meet this need, and that the future of the part-time route to a Diploma may be in doubt, given that the two-year Certificate in Office Studies courses have been markedly less successful than the one-year full-time courses. However, while the latter criticism is not without merit, it is surely desirable that the further education colleges should offer truly vocational courses, in place of GCE and CSE, for those young people who require them?

BEC have explicitly stated that their new awards are designed to offer a broad integrated educational experience relevant to industry and to this end devised their four central themes as a major integrative factor in course design. In addition, the Council has indicated that these themes should not become separate subjects developed by particular academic specialists. If such courses are to be successful, then lecturers will have to work more closely together than has always been the case hitherto. Moreover, given that their own education and teaching methods have hitherto been largely subject-based, they will not find it easy to devise the broadly based lectures and examinations that are necessary to achieve integration.[23] Clearly, the higher the level of the award, the more difficult it will be to achieve. Moreover, the introduction of an inter-disciplinary approach may well cut across the academic structure of many colleges, which is essentially subject-based, and may therefore lead to serious administrative problems. It may also cause difficulty in securing recognition for BEC courses from some of the professional bodies and from some quarters in industry. While BEC has never stated that there shall be no subject-based modules, nonetheless it sticks to its guns on the admirable grounds that the weakness of many business education courses at present is precisely the over-concentration on separate subjects, which results in the practical, vocational application of knowledge not being mastered by the student. What is indisputable, however, is that the radical changes in the structure and content of the Council's courses will require changes in teaching methods and attitudes. Clearly, if these are to be successfully implemented, then a major programme of staff development will be required. While BEC acknowledges the need for this, it remains to be seen how far it will be able to stimulate and support appropriate in-service training for further education teachers.

Another matter of considerable concern to many staff in the colleges is the position of general or liberal studies in the BEC programmes. Unlike TEC, which as we have seen includes a compulsory, assessed component of at least 15 per cent in all its Certificate and Diploma courses, BEC makes no such specific requirement. It certainly regards some of the aims of general studies as basic to all its courses and, as we have seen, includes in its four general themes such requirements as an ability to speak and write clear English and to understand and propose solutions for business and administrative problems which arise in an advanced technological society. However, this is not the same as requiring that general studies shall be an integral part of the curriculum; indeed, BEC's Chief Officer has intimated that general studies do not need to be imposed and are at the discretion of the colleges. This, it is argued, could lead to their omission or to their being given an unnecessary or irrelevant bias.[24] Hitherto, general studies has constituted an officially recognized, non-vocational, non-examined subject which has been taught in the colleges for more than twenty years. Traditionally, it has been concerned with such issues as the environment, political awareness, ethical problems such as euthanasia and abortion, social issues such as law and order and racial discrimination, and economic issues. It has involved a great deal of experiential education whereby students are encouraged to engage in discussion, to watch and make films, to solve problems, to conduct surveys, and so on.[25] In the last few years, however, increasing emphasis has been laid on Communication Studies which can be interpreted narrowly as remedial language competence or more broadly as the ability to communicate fluently in a variety of complex ways. As a result of the emphasis given to Communication Studies by both TEC and BEC schemes, together with the taking-up by some colleges of the CGLI Certificate in Communication Skills, there is growing concern among teachers of general studies that, as presently conceived, the subject may disappear altogether from further education. Communication Studies are both easier to assess and also have a more easily demonstrable utility,[26] and these are powerful attractions. However, young people need both to be able to communicate effectively and also to develop the attributes of a liberal mind. Given the submission of suitable curricula by the colleges, with support from TEC and BEC, these two objectives are by no means irreconcilable.

As far as assessment is concerned, there are substantial differences between TEC and BEC. While TEC accepts that it can be either internal, with or without external moderation, or external, BEC normally requires that awards be based both on an external examinations element and also an in-course assessment element. For TEC, the purpose of assessment is to ensure that a student on an approved programme merits the grades given for individual units; BEC, on the other hand, requires both an overall classification of the award as well as one for each module.[27] This requirement is reflected in the procedure whereby, in its Level 2 and 3 awards, BEC uses the term 'Distinction', and not 'Credit', to denote what it describes as the 'implied higher standard of assessment'.

Although some criticism has been levelled at BEC on the grounds that its assessment procedures, being based partly on external examinations, will reduce the involvement of teachers, it is not clear that these criticisms can be substantiated, at least as far as the General awards are concerned, for in these courses BEC is requiring teachers to accept responsibility for the in-course assessment of all modules, a procedure for which there has been no equivalent in the CGLI and Regional Examining Board courses which they are replacing. Moreover, in-course assessment is the only form of assessment for the option modules of General awards. On the other hand, in so far as BEC General awards are based on performance at external examinations, their procedures resemble those of the CGLI and the REBs; TEC, in contrast, is not directly involved with programmes at this level. It is hardly surprising, therefore, if the development of a national system of awards at this level by BEC is seen by the REBs, in particular, as a financial threat to them.

As in the case of TEC, BEC has rightly required that courses be devised on the basis of aims and general objectives and in its literature has talked of learning objectives, some of which have necessarily been of limited prescription. This has led to criticism that such an approach does not seem to be in line with the Council's insistence on a broad integrated curriculum, that it may tend to emphasize the learning of routine, unimportant material, that it constrains coursework, and that it inhibits valuable but unexpected developments in the learning process.[28] However, the Council does realistically draw attention, in its course specifications for National awards, to the central role which the professional teacher must play and the dangers of being unduly prescriptive.[29] A more fundamental criticism concerns the terms of reference of the two councils. As we have seen, they were required to devise new courses for technician and business education respectively. One of the major reasons for this requirement was to take account of the fact that the concept of a technician has changed considerably. However, while the concept of a technician may be reasonably clear in manufacturing industry, it is much more problematic for the commercial and administrative sectors of the economy.[30] Indeed, in any given commercial enterprise it may be very difficult to state precisely who are the 'technicians' who are operating between the managerial level on the one hand and the clerical and typing grades on the other. Given this difficulty, the argument that curricular change is necessary because of the changing concept of the technician becomes less convincing. However, BEC points out that its terms of reference are different to those of TEC, that the word 'technician' has no formal part in its remit, and that it was asked from the beginning to accept responsibility for courses for a range of students who were in no way limited by the normal interpretation of the word 'technician'.

Another reason put forward by BEC for curricular change in business education is to meet the changing needs of employers. However, as BEC itself concedes, very little is known about what employers want, or even that they are dissatisfied with present provision. As we have seen, BEC in its First Policy Statement has indicated its intention of finding out the requirements for business education and the costs of meeting them. That being so, it may not seem entirely logical first to institute substantial curricular and organizational changes and only subsequently set up a research programme to determine the necessity, direction and costs of these changes.[31] On the other hand, BEC did undertake a very considerable amount of consultation before introducing its awards and has continued to do so since. Moreover, the Council points out that of those young people entering employment in the business field each year, only about fifteen per cent enrolled on the pre-BEC courses. This would appear to provide strong *prima facie* evidence that these courses were not meeting the needs of the vast majority of young people seeking employment in business.[32]

At the time of writing, it remains uncertain whether the professional bodies will fully accept the changes being implemented by BEC. Certainly, the Council has already assumed responsibility for a range of examinations previously controlled by a variety of Joint Committees, a development which will simplify procedures. Moreover, by the end of 1978, a substantial number of professional bodies had given formal recognition to BEC awards including, for example, the Association of Certified Accountants, the Building Societies Institute, the Institute of Bankers, the Institute of Marketing, the Institute of Work Managers, and the Civil Service Commission. However, within the Distributive Industry, for example, there is much concern that the BEC General Level award is considered to be of a higher standard than the General Certificate in Distribution which it is replacing. The industry is apprehensive lest the supposedly higher standard will result in too few qualified students coming forward to make viable classes at National Level, still less at Higher National Level.[33] This concern also brings into sharp focus the problems which BEC faces both in rationalizing an extremely diversified system and also in ensuring comparability of standards. Not surprisingly, BEC, like TEC, has experienced some difficulty in keeping to its stated timetable; however, thanks largely to its centralized policies, it has succeeded reasonably well in making available to the colleges the documentation essential to facilitating their entry into the new system. However, it remains to be seen if the college staff will be prepared fully to translate BEC policy into acceptable practice, especially as NATFHE's general policy on BEC courses has been to insist that extra resources are made available to lecturers for preparation in the form of additional funds or remission time. If this is not forthcoming from local authorities, it may well cause delays in starting BEC courses in certain colleges.

In any case, it is by no means certain that the new courses will bring about major changes in the actual practice of business education. Although the new BEC curricula are attempting to achieve desirable educational and vocational aims, these will remain statements of high intent until they are translated into students' learning and teachers' teaching. This in turn requires that teachers and students be supported with appropriate and carefully devised material such as books, worksheets, and visual aids; in addition, teachers need help and advice on suitable teaching and learning methods. To date, BEC has only begun to scratch the surface of this problem. As a result, while BEC will bring about substantial organizational changes, it will only effect a change in curricular practice when its statements of intent are translated into operational terms and accompanied by the necessary support in the form of staff development and teaching materials.[34]

There is a significant difference in the attitude taken by TEC and BEC towards the correspondence course and Directed Private Study (DPS) routes to their awards. While TEC is prepared to accept submissions based on these methods of study, it insists that they be supplemented by attendance at college and face-to-face contact between student and tutor. BEC adopts a similar approach as far as DPS is concerned and is arranging for its awards to be available to students undertaking courses based on this method of study in which a primarily correspondence course is supported by periods of compulsory full-time face-to-face tuition. However, it is also making available a correspondence-only route by which a limited number of centres will be permitted to offer this form of tuition for BEC courses and the results will be monitored and compared with those of students studying by traditional college routes.[35] The main reason for this difference in emphasis is essentially a practical one: it is easier to accommodate a typewriter in the home than a lathe and an exercise in typing, for example, can more easily be posted to an external tutor than a component manufactured by turning.[36] Both TEC and BEC, however, appreciate that circumstances such as geographical remoteness, or family pressures, or shift working, may prevent students from attending college, even on a part-time basis, so that studying at home in their own time is their only practicable route to a qualification. They have therefore set out to develop these routes to their awards: of the two, TEC has made the greater progress and by the end of 1978 had enrolled some 500 students on Directed Private Study courses; although, as we have seen, BEC has set up a Directed Private Study and Correspondence Course Committee, which is presently considering applications from many colleges to become approved BEC DPS centres, it has yet to enrol any students and does not contemplate doing so until 1980.

One other difference in outlook between the two councils should be mentioned, that is in their attitude towards the European Economic Community. While TEC makes only a passing reference to liaison with the EEC, BEC is quite specific on this point. It recognizes the importance of mutual recognition of awards between the United Kingdom and her EEC partners and declares its intention of working towards

81

European recognition for all its awards. It also recognizes the need for a growing proportion of business employees to have a reasonably competent grasp of foreign languages and declares that its Boards will be considering the requirements for modern language options as part of BEC courses.

In conclusion, a comparison of the differences between BEC and TEC should not be allowed to obscure the fact that they have much in common, nor that there is a degree of overlap between their areas of responsibility. The Councils themselves acknowledge these facts and accept they can learn from one another. They also appreciate that there are certain subject areas which they have in common and for this reason they have set up a Joint Consultative Working Party to explore ways of achieving effective co-operation. More specifically, they have set up two joint committees: one for Computer Studies, administered by BEC, with the responsibility for producing courses in computer studies and for devising and validating units and modules which can form part of either a TEC or BEC course; and one for Mathematics and Statistics, administered by TEC.

As we have seen, the Haslegrave Report laid down the terms of reference for TEC and BEC, namely that they should plan, administer and keep under review the establishment of a unified national system of non-degree courses of technical education for technicians in industry and in the field of business and office studies. To achieve this aim, which is designed to bring about an improved standard of technician and business education, the two councils have followed somewhat different routes. How far they will succeed in achieving their very worthy aims still remains to be seen. What can be said, however, is that there is no going back to the pre-Haslegrave position. Whatever their defects, TEC and BEC are here to stay and cannot be allowed to flounder. The colleges themselves are well aware of this just as they appreciate that, despite the upheaval and greatly increased workloads created by the councils' demands, their stimulation of curriculum development can be extremely beneficial. There are perhaps three important criteria by which the councils' success, or failure, can be judged over the next few years: their willingness to adapt their courses and procedures to changing circumstances; the broadening of their horizons to embrace a European dimension; and, perhaps most important of all, the extent to which their awards are accepted by industry, business, the professions and higher education.

The achievement of their aims will clearly be enhanced by the closest co-operation between the two councils. Indeed, it would seem sensible that despite their different approaches, TEC and BEC might before long consider coming together as one body. Further education has suffered for too long from a multiplicity of courses and validating and examining bodies and the amalgamation of TEC and BEC would, if practicable, be a heartening move in the right direction. The secretariat for the two councils is, after all, provided by the CGLI under the same roof and together all three bodies have a crucial role to play in the development of further education. It was the Haslegrave Report itself which concluded that although a single council might not be wholly acceptable to all the interests concerned, 'it might well be to benefit of students, their employers, professional bodies and the education service that such a single council should ultimately emerge, and we have been careful to frame our recommendations in a way that will not make this more difficult to achieve'.[37]

5   Higher education in further education

One of the major features of the growth of our education system over the last 30 years has been the enormous increase in provision of higher education. By 'higher education' we mean all courses of a standard beyond GCE A Level or its equivalent (see p.219). Although the 1944 Education Act placed upon all local education authorities the statutory duty to provide adequate facilities for further education, defining further education as full-time or part-time education and leisure-time occupation for persons over compulsory school-leaving age, it made no reference to higher education as such. This was understandable as at that time higher education was very largely concentrated in the autonomous university sector and the then teacher training colleges. Few further education colleges provided courses of higher education, the main ones being those leading to external degress of the University of London and HND and HNC.

However, in the period up to the Robbins Report of 1963, there was a considerable growth in the provision of advanced courses in the further education sector, mainly in science and technology. By the end of this period, Regional Colleges of Technology were offering full-time and sandwich courses of university first degree and post-graduate standard and were attracting students from the country as a whole and from overseas. Ten Colleges of Advanced Technology (CATs) had come into existence and, from 1958, the Diploma of Technology (Dip. Tech.) had been available, validated by the National Council for Technological Awards (NCTA), the predecessor of the Council for National Academic Awards (CNAA).

Then, in 1963, the Robbins Report appeared.[1] Perhaps the most important document on higher education in the post-war period, it provided a detailed blueprint for the development of higher education into the early 1980s. Taking as its basic premise the principle that courses of higher education should be made available to all those able and willing to benefit from them, it affirmed its belief that the pool of ability, especially among girls who at that time were grossly under-represented in higher education, was sufficiently deep to warrant an

84

expansion in the numbers of students in higher education in England, Scotland and Wales from 216,000 in 1962-3 to 390,000 in 1973-4 and 560,000 in 1980-1. At that time, in 1962-3, 55 per cent of students in higher education, or 116,000, were in universities, the other 100,000 being shared between the teacher training sector and further education. Significantly, the Robbins Report recommended that the universities' share should rise to 60 per cent, or 336,000, in 1981, thereby leaving 224,000 for the public sector. However, as we shall see, although the gross target recommended by Robbins has been exceeded, the proportions between the university and the public sectors have in practice worked out rather differently. In addition, the Report made a number of other detailed recommendations which were designed to encourage an increase in technological studies. Thus, it advocated that the Colleges of Advanced Technology should become technological universities awarding their own degrees, the National Council for Technological Awards should be replaced by the Council for National Academic Awards, the Regional Colleges of Technology should develop a wide range of advanced full-time courses, and that some of them might eventually form the nucleus of other universities or become universities in their own right. Other recommendations concerned the expansion of the teacher training colleges. They were to be renamed Colleges of Education; a new degree, to be called Bachelor of Education and validated by the universities, would be introduced for their more able students; they should be removed from the public sector and closely linked with the universities; and some of them should become universities in their own right.

In short, Robbins saw the university model as playing the major role in the expansion of higher education and its recommendations were essentially an attempt to convert an unco-ordinated provision of higher education into a system based on the university. In retrospect, it is hardly surprising that although the government of the day duly accepted its general strategy for expansion, it rejected the university model as the main basis of that expansion. Thus, within months of the publication of the Report, the government had taken action to implement some of its main recommendations. Its planning figures up to 1980-1 were endorsed, the CATs were authorized to appoint Academic Advisory Committees to advise on how best to obtain university status and to assist in the planning of their future development, the CNAA was established in 1964, and the teacher training colleges were renamed Colleges of Education and were encouraged to work with the universities to introduce the new B.Ed. degree. However, the recommendation that some regional colleges and colleges of education should become universities was not implemented, nor was the proposal that the colleges of education should move out of the public sector to become closely associated with the universities.

Instead the government opted for a 'binary' system, whereby the provision of higher education was to be shared by the universities, the colleges of education, and new institutions to be called Polytechnics. Not that the binary system was a creation of the government for, as the then Secretary of State for Education, Anthony Crosland, observed in a speech in 1967, 'I did not invent the plural or binary system which we inherited . . . Alongside the universities we had the training colleges under local authority or denominational control; and we had a strong and growing sector of higher education within further education. Indeed, 40 per cent of students in full-time higher education were outside universities. Were we then to convert it into a unitary system entirely under university control?' Clearly, the answer was 'No', and one suspects it would have been the same answer whatever the political flavour of the government in office at the time. In any case, the decision to create the Polytechnics emanated from a policy devised by a small group of senior officials at the DES who, among other things, were concerned to create a top tier of institutions within the public sector to replace the CATs which were in the process of becoming universities.[2]

The government's position on the structure of higher education was articulated publicly for the first time by Crosland in his famous speech at Woolwich Polytechnic in 1965, in which he declared the government's acceptance of the need for a 'system based on the twin traditions which have created our present higher institutions'. He gave four reasons for deciding in favour of a binary system: the demand for vocational, professional and industrial based courses required a separate sector with a separate tradition and outlook; a ladder system with the universities at the head would inevitably depress and degrade morale and standards in the non-university sector; there was a need for a substantial part of the higher education system to be under social control and directly responsible to social needs; and, lastly, no other country in the western world down-graded its non-university professional and technical sector. Whatever the merits of these reasons, and not all of them carry complete conviction, it must surely be true that no government, given that the enormous and growing cost of higher education was coming very largely out of public funds, would have been prepared for provision to have been largely concentrated in the 'autonomous' university sector? Furthermore, the Robbins proposal that some colleges of education and colleges of technology be taken out of local authority control and made into universities would never have been acceptable to the local authorities and was politically a non-starter.

Accordingly, in 1966, the Government issued its White Paper, 'A Plan for Polytechnics and Other Colleges: Higher Education in the

Further Education System', outlining its programme of developing higher education within the public sector. The main instrument for this purpose was to be the Polytechnics and the White Paper provisionally recommended that 28 be established, to which two more were added in the following year, making 30 in all. They were to be based on existing regional and other colleges already substantially engaged in higher education. As a result, in the course of the next six years all 30 polytechnics were officially designated and the binary system of education was consolidated.[3]

At this time, the colleges of education occupied a halfway house between the universities and the further education sector. On the one hand, they were part of the public sector, in that they were administered under DES teacher-training regulations — but not under further education regulations — and two-thirds of them were under local authority control, the rest being denominational colleges. On the other hand, they were members of university Area Training Organisations (ATOs) and their courses were exclusively validated by the universities. However, as we shall see, this position was later to change. The numbers of students at the colleges of education grew rapidly in the late 1960s, reaching a total of 114,000 by 1972. Even as late as 1970, the official position as set out by the DES was that they would continue to grow slowly to about 130,000 by 1981, marginally below the Robbins projection of 131,400 for that year.[4] However, it was beginning to be apparent that the decline in the birth rate would radically affect these calculations.

The next landmark in the development of higher education in this country occurred in January 1972 with the publication of the James Report on 'Teacher Education and Training'. Although it proposed no major institutional changes, apart from greater co-operation between colleges of education, universities and polytechnics, it did recommend that the colleges should broaden their base by offering other courses alongside teacher-training, notably the two-year Diploma of Higher Education (Dip. HE), a development which is discussed in detail later in this chapter. Although the Report made virtually no references to the need for a cutback in teacher-training, it seems certain that the James Committee discussed the possibility, or even the probability of such a development. For various reasons, however, the Report was silent on the subject.[5]

The subject was, however, broached in another landmark document on the future development of higher education, the Government White Paper, published in December 1972, 'Education: A Framework for Expansion', in retrospect an ironically-titled document. It envisaged expansion of higher education considerably beyond that recommended by Robbins, whereby student places would be increased to 750,000 by

1981. These places would be shared equally between the universities and the public sector colleges so that each would eventually have 375,000 students, a marked change from the Robbins proportional allocations. Of the 375,000 in the public sector, which included Scottish institutions as well as those in England and Wales, the polytechnics would be expected to expand to accommodate 180,000 students by 1981. The White Paper also recognized publicly for the first time a stark fact that was becoming increasingly obvious: that with the steep decline in the birth rate the number of teachers in training would have to be sharply reduced to avoid a gross overproduction of teachers. Accordingly, it announced the government's intention of reducing the numbers on teacher-training courses in the public sector colleges from the maximum of 114,000 in 1972 to between 75,000 and 85,000 initial and inservice places by 1981.

Unlike the James Report which had envisaged the colleges of education remaining as a coherent sector, effectively separate from the universities and the polytechnics, the White Paper proposed that, for the most part, they be merged with the polytechnics and other further education colleges. Although it did envisage some mergers with universities, the emphasis throughout was very much on strengthening the public sector of higher education. Finally, the White Paper endorsed the James Report recommendation concerning the introduction of the Dip.HE. Thus, the stage was set for the disappearance of the colleges of education as a separate sector of higher education.[6] In this context, it should be noted that the rapid demolition of the colleges of education which followed was made possible by a unique regulator placed in the hands of the Secretary of State; unlike the universities which are protected by a degree of autonomy and the polytechnics which are subject to a variety of controls and influences, overall teacher-training numbers and their distribution between individual institutions are directly controlled by the DES.[7] Accordingly, in March 1973, the DES issued Circular 7/73, 'The Development of Higher Education in the Non-University Sector' which required local authorities and voluntary bodies to put forward detailed plans for every one of the 155 colleges of education within the guidelines of the White Paper. A strict time-table was to be adhered to whereby reorganization was to be completed by the end of 1974. Unfortunately, this schedule was overtaken by events, as a major economic crisis and a continually falling birth rate reduced still further the need for more qualified teachers. As a result, the reorganization only reached its final stages in the summer of 1977.

Even at the time that the White Paper was being issued in 1972, it was becoming clear that the rapidly declining birth rate would have very serious repercussions for the colleges of education; however, it was not until the decline began to steepen in the mid-1970s that the full implications were publicly announced by the DES. The extent of the decline may be measured by the figures for live births: 832,000 in 1967, 784,000 in 1970, and levelling-off at just over 600,000 in 1975. As the full impact of these figures was borne in on the DES, it reacted by successively cutting back teacher-training places in the colleges of education. This happened no fewer than four times between 1974 and 1977 until, finally, at the end of 1977, the Secretary of State announced that instead of the 75,000 to 85,000 places indicated in the 1972 White Paper, the target would be 45,000. The whole burden of these cuts fell on the colleges of education partly because, as we have seen, their numbers could be swiftly regulated and partly because they were still for the most part institutions predominantly concerned with teacher education.

Clearly, the difference between the original proposals put forward in the White Paper and the final solution in 1977 is enormous. As David Hencke points out, it is possible to take two views of this.[8] One is the magnanimous view that the DES was caught out by economic circum-stances and a declining birth rate and that circumstances combined to overthrow its carefully planned reorganization. Another, less charitable, view suggests that because of lack of ministerial direction – occasioned in part because there have been no fewer than four different Secretaries of State between 1972 and 1978 – and lack of consultative machinery between the DES and those most closely affected in the colleges, little attempt was made to anticipate events which should have been foreseen much earlier. Consequently, the DES failed to devise a coherent strategy for teacher-training and to work out its role in relation to higher and further education and its priority within the whole education pro-gramme. Instead, it chose the easy way out of its dilemma by demolish-ing the colleges of education. Whatever view one takes of this matter, the facts are indisputable. Of the 155 colleges of education that existed in 1972, not one has remained untouched by the dramatic upheaval of the last few years. By 1981, the number of institutions in the public sector concerned with teacher-training will have been substantially reduced, at least 14 colleges will have closed altogether, over 60 will have merged with polytechnics and other further education institutions, a few will have joined universities, and even those that remain 'free standing', that is untouched by institutional reorganization, are finding themselves offering a diversified range of courses including teacher-training, thereby fundamentally altering their academic role. Some measure of the enormous change which is taking place can be gauged by the fact that in 1981 not one of the former colleges of education will be offering the same courses it provided in 1972. As a result of these developments, a group of new institutions has evolved, known generally as Colleges or Institutes of Higher Education. Later in this chapter we examine in detail their major characteristics and the nature of the courses which they offer.

In the meantime, as part of the administrative reorganization aimed at bringing public sector teacher-training into the further education system, as envisaged in the 1972 White Paper, the university-based Area Training Organisations have been abolished. However, it has yet to be decided what to put in their place and this particular problem has thrown into sharp focus the acute difficulties surrounding the management and financing of Advanced Further Education as a whole, not least the role of the local education authorities in the government of polytechnics and other colleges. In the guarded prose of the DES, 'It is widely acknowledged that more effective and coherent management arrangements are required'.[9] As a result, a working group was set up in 1977 under the chairmanship of Mr Gordon Oakes, Minister of State at the DES, to consider the management and financing of advanced further education. The main aims of the Report, which was issued in March 1978, are to increase the accountability and co-ordination of a service which is currently costing about £394 millions a year and to permit more forward planning by the polytechnics and colleges of higher education. The Report's recommendations and its implications for the further education sector are discussed in detail later.

Despite the gradual run down in the number of students on teacher training courses, overall numbers in higher education in the public sector, as in the universities, have grown steadily throughout the 1970s. Thus, in England and Wales, and Scotland, in 1969 there were 374,000 full-time students in higher education, 190,000 in the public sector and 184,000 in the universities; by 1974 these had risen to 421,000, 210,000 in the public sector and 211,000 in the universities; and by 1977 to an estimated 520,000, approximately 240,000 in the public sector and 280,000 in the universities. In an announcement at the end of 1977, Mrs Williams stated in parliament that the government was planning for an increase of student numbers in higher education to 560,000 by 1981, to be divided between the public sector and the universities in the ratio of 45:55, that is approximately 250,000 and 310,000 respectively. Predictably, this announcement aroused considerable objections from the polytechnics and other public sector colleges on the grounds that the government was going back on its intention stated in the 1972 White Paper, namely that by 1981 the students in higher education would be shared equally between the public sector institutions and the universities. To a considerable extent these objections lacked conviction because although on the face of it there would· appear to be only a very small expansion of student numbers permitted to the public sector colleges over the next few years, in practice the run-down in students on teacher training courses will release some 30-40,000 places for developments in other areas, representing a growth somewhat larger than that which took place in the public sector institutions between 1974 and 1977. In any case, the DES has made it clear that its decision was dictated by present circumstances and did not represent a permanent departure from the policy enunciated in the 1972 White Paper. It remains to be seen how far this will be borne out by events.

Having thus briefly outlined the background against which the enormous postwar growth in public sector higher education has taken place, we shall now proceed to examine in detail the institutions which make up the public sector of higher education. These may be divided into two major groups: the Polytechnics, and what the DES terms 'Other Institutions', including of course the newly-established Colleges and Institutes of Higher Education.

Polytechnics

As we have seen, the policy for the polytechnics was outlined by the government in the White Paper, 'A Plan for Polytechnics and Other Colleges', issued in May 1966. The official purpose in setting up these institutions was to meet the rapidly growing demand for higher education within further education without prejudicing opportunities for students following non-advanced courses and to make more rational and effective use of the resources available. In the next six years, 30 polytechnics were officially designated and by the academic session 1975-6 they had become the major institutions of higher education within further education, catering for over half the full-time, including sandwich, students in advanced further education, approximately 108,000 (including students at colleges of education expected to merge with polytechnics by 1981), together with 54,000 part-time students.[10]

A considerable literature on the nature and purpose of the Polytechnics is already in existence and it is not our intention to add to it.[11] Indeed, we have attempted in our previous book on further education succinctly to summarize their chief characteristics and we intend therefore to restrict ourselves to a discussion of the ways in which the polytechnics have changed and developed in the twelve years or so since their creation. As originally conceived in the White Paper, the main characteristics of the polytechnics were that they were to be large, comprehensive, have an applied philosophy, be primarily teaching institutions with a brief to develop courses in new areas, and their courses were to be validated by the CNAA.

As far as their size is concerned, the 1966 White Paper envisaged that they would average about 2,000 full-time students each, together with a substantial number of part-time and occasional students. By the optimistic view of the 1972 White Paper, they were to increase to an average of 6,000 full-time students each by 1981, making 180,000 students in all. It would appear that the somewhat magical figure of 6,000 full-time students in each institution was initially used by the DES in a document which went out to all the polytechnics requesting them to submit development plans for expansion to these numbers. Subsequently, despite the fact that it became increasingly obvious that growth of this order was impossible, the figure of 6,000 assumed a totemic significance and remained as a notional target. However, despite the harder times upon which higher education has fallen since then, the polytechnics have nonetheless become quite large institutions for, as we have seen, in 1975-6 they catered for about 108,000 full-time students or an average of over 3,500 each. If the government's latest plans for development up to 1981 is adhered to they will increase very little in size over the next few years. As indicated earlier, much of the increase in student numbers in polytechnics in the last few years has been brought about by the absorption of the former colleges of education so that the polytechnics now play a major role in teacher training in the country. Indeed, a small number of them have trained teachers since 1967, when seven education departments were established specifically to train primary school teachers, and a few others came into existence in the next few years, often with particular orientations such as the provision of in-service courses for practising teachers. However, when the reorganization of the colleges of education is completed, some 34 colleges will have merged into about 20 polytechnics bringing with them approximately 14,000 teacher-training places. The scale of this development, which is taking the form academically of a growth in Education Studies at degree and sub-degree levels, is such that it adds a major new dimension to the academic interests of the polytechnics.

By describing the polytechnics as 'comprehensive', the 1966 White Paper meant that they should provide both degree and sub-degree courses; post-graduate and post-experience courses; full-time and part-time courses; and a wide range of short courses. They have since then also covered a wide academic spectrum — including science and technology, the social sciences, the humanities, and art and design — so that in a sense the term 'Poly-technic' is something of a misnomer. In so far as the polytechnics today do in fact offer a wide range of advanced courses on different bases of study, they can also be said to live up to the description of being 'comprehensive' in that respect. However, during the past 12 years the balance between full-time and part-time students has shifted markedly in favour of the former. In 1969, for example, the polytechnics contained 163,000 students, of whom

67,000 were full-time and 96,000 part-time. By 1975, as we have seen, at 162,000 the overall number of students had hardly changed, except for the very substantial difference that the total was made up of 108,000 full-time and only 54,000 part-time and evening students. There are those critics of the polytechnics who regard this as a most unfortunate development and would go so far as to castigate them for betraying their primary purpose, which they see as providing for the communities in which they are located, something which of necessity can only be done primarily through part-time provision.[12] The reply of the polytechnics to this charge is that while they are fully prepared to maintain part-time provision at a high level, students are simply not coming forward in sufficient numbers to make it possible. This argument, while it is in many ways irrefutable, does in part assume that the present trend away from part-time studies as a route towards membership of professional bodies such as the Council of Engineering Institutions and the Royal Institute of Chemistry is unlikely to be reversed.

A similar picture emerges if one compares the proportion of sub-degree to degree courses. According to Burgess,[13] at the time of the designation of the polytechnics the proportion of sub-degree level work to degree work was of the order of 70 per cent; by 1974, this had fallen to about 50 per cent and is doubtless lower still today. Burgess and Pratt attribute this development, like that of the growth in full-time as opposed to part-time students, to what they apostrophize as 'academic drift'.[14] This is the tendency for the polytechnics to emulate the universities by concentrating primarily on advanced course provision, especially degree courses, thereby rejecting students they would previously have accepted and transferring elsewhere many of the courses they previously offered. As a consequence, their student body becomes increasingly homogeneous and tends to contain only the 'normal', that is university, proportion of the sons and daughters of manual workers, a process that Pratt and Burgess regard as running counter to one of the original intentions behind the setting-up of the polytechnics. While it is indisputable that the proportions of both sub-degree and part-time courses in the polytechnics have declined, it remains to be proved that this is the result of policy on the part of the Directors and their staffs; it would seem much more likely to be a case of students 'voting with their feet' by opting for full-time degree courses. Nor does it necessarily follow that if polytechnics were somehow to promote part-time and sub-degree courses, that they would be taken up by large numbers of children of manual workers.

The third characteristic envisaged for the polytechnics, namely that they should have an 'applied philosophy', means that their courses should have a vocational orientation and be designed with specific

93

career outlets in mind, thus distinguishing them from many university courses which are sometimes described as 'pure'. Another aspect of the applied philosophy of the polytechnics is that they should maintain close contacts with industry and business. In these respects, it can certainly be claimed that the polytechnics have by and large measured up to their original specification. The great majority of their courses, whether in the sciences and technologies or in the social sciences, prepare students for specific career outlets; thus modern language courses for the most part give attention to the practical application of the language with a view to the student's ultimate employment, for example as an interpreter, while courses in social science often include options in such areas as community work, social planning, industrial relations, and public administration. In addition, a proportion of the courses offered are sandwich courses, either of the 'thick' or 'thin' variety,* though there has been some decline in the relative proportion of sandwich courses available over recent years. For example, the CNAA Annual Reports show that of its first degree courses, the proportion of sandwich courses declined from 33.7 in 1974-5 to 29.3 in 1977-8. In any case, the merging of colleges of education with polytechnics and the development of the Dip. HE has led to a range of courses predominantly of general education, and to that extent the vocational orientation of the work of the polytechnics has been somewhat diluted.

Fourth, the 1966 White Paper made it plain that at that time it was the government's intention that the polytechnics should remain primarily teaching institutions; as the DES notes of guidance subsequently indicated, research would be justified only in so far as it was of educational value to the teaching staff and of benefit to industry and business. Understandably, this has been a bone of contention with many of the staff of the polytechnics ever since, who maintain that for teaching at degree level to be lively and effective it needs to be supported within the institution by an active research programme. As a result of their continued advocacy, research for its own sake has been developed on an appreciable scale. For example, a typical Research Report issued by Sunderland Polytechnic in 1976 lists some 230 active research projects being carried out by staff members, and most polytechnics now advertise regularly for senior research staff and assistants. However, the volume of research varies considerably from one polytechnic to another

*In respect of their degree courses, the CNAA describe 'thick' sandwich courses as those 'in which there are two years (October-July) of academic study followed by a calendar year of practical training with a final year of academic study' and 'thin' sandwich courses as those 'in which there is a maximum amount of interleaving of academic study and training, usually on the basis of alternative periods of approximately six months'. (*CNAA Directory of First Degree Courses, 1977-78*, 7.)

and, in general, it has a very long way to go before it begins to approach that generated within universities. Nonetheless, it is clear that as indicated by a Science Research Council Report of a Working Party on Research in Polytechnics in 1977, research in the polytechnics will continue to grow, if only for reasons of prestige, and the same trend is discernible in some of the Colleges of Higher Education. What is less clear, however, is how funds derived from such government-financed bodies as the Research Councils should be divided up between the universities and the public sector institutions of higher education.

As far as the introduction of new courses is concerned, the polytechnics, through the aegis of the CNAA, have certainly succeeded in developing undergraduate courses in areas of study in which they were not previously much, if at all, concerned. Consequently, they now offer a very wide range of first degree courses, not only in Science and Technology, Business Management and Art and Design, but also in the Social Sciences and the Arts, including such subjects as Librarianship, Politics and Government, Humanities and Communication Studies. However, a number of the polytechnics have for some years nourished the hope that they will eventually be permitted to award their own degrees. In response to pressure from the colleges, the CNAA has set up a working party to look into the question of validation and it seems likely that, as a result of its deliberations, the polytechnics and colleges will be allowed a bigger part in validating their own courses. Such a move might also result in financial savings, as a recent estimate puts the total cost of CNAA validation of polytechnics, including staff time and resources, at £6 million a year. Indeed, the Committee of Directors of Polytechnics is arguing for a system whereby 'mature' institutions have considerable independence such that the CNAA would delegate its charter responsibilities to licensed institutions.[15] At the time of writing, the report of the working party is still awaited but it seems both desirable and likely that, in the relatively near future, a more flexible system of CNAA validation will come into being.

At present, the CNAA approves courses for a period of five years, at the end of which time it institutes a quinquennial review. It was just such a review of Teesside Polytechnic, in 1978, which blew up an unprecedented storm, highlighting the strained relationships which, inevitably, occur from time to time between the Council and the colleges. The Teesside Polytechnic review was followed by the most critical report on an institution ever issued by the CNAA: among other things, it criticized the Director for a failure in internal management and the local authority for its inadequate support for the Polytechnic. In conclusion, the Council announced its intention to cease recognition of the Polytechnic's courses after the 1979-80 academic year unless substantial improvements occurred, a development described as 'one of the most disturbing episodes in the recent history of higher education'.[16] Although it seems almost certain that Teesside Polytechnic will meet the CNAA's standards and thus avoid closure, the matter does raise fundamental questions about the validation role of the CNAA. It is undoubtedly of considerable concern to the polytechnic directors that an independent chartered body should have the power, through an adverse report, to induce the collapse of an institution.[17] This has led them to suggest to the CNAA that it sets up an independent inquiry to investigate its system of quinquennial inspections.

On the other hand, the CNAA's task is a very difficult one: while respecting the *amour-propre* of the colleges and welcoming innovations in course structure, it has the prime responsibility of maintaining academic standards and must have the power to do so. Notwithstanding the Teesside Polytechnic affair, it has on the whole been very successful in maintaining a balance between innovation and tradition. However, the balance is a delicate one and the polytechnics are for most part sufficiently experienced and mature to be given the greater degree of flexibility in validation that they are striving for. In any case, if the Oakes national bodies come into being it will undoubtedly affect the relationship between the colleges and the CNAA, if only because, as the Oakes Report itself acknowledges, academic standards are intimately linked to management and financial decisions. The Report concludes that, where necessary, the national body should be prepared to enter into discussion with validating bodies about standards.[18]

Although the 1966 White Paper laid down guidelines for the development of the polytechnics as academic institutions, it did not explicitly adumbrate the philosophy to be adopted, with the result that this is something for which they have been searching ever since. As we have seen, in his 1965 Woolwich speech Crosland declared that the polytechnics were to form the basis of a sector of higher education separate from the universities, with a separate tradition and outlook. But wherein precisely lies that difference? There are those like Robinson, and Burgess and Pratt who have consistently argued that the polytechnics should eschew emulating the universities by remaining faithful to their traditions, which they interpret as serving the community, and especially the working class, by offering a wide range of courses both degree and sub-degree, and especially part-time courses. Attempts to secure independence from the local authorities and the establishment of a professoriate, as has happened in a number of polytechnics, are thus deprecated as foolish emulation of the universities.

That a degree of 'academic drift' has occurred is indisputable; for example, as Donaldson has shown, the student body in at least some of the polytechnics is as high in social class composition as in that of the universities and probably the general trend throughout the polytechnics is in this direction.[19] As a result, the polytechnics will not promote social mobility to any greater extent than do the universities at present. While this may or may not be a bad thing, according to one's point of view, it seems to a considerable extent to be inevitable. In any case, it is probably a mistake to think of the polytechnics as a homogeneous group, for in practice they have developed in different directions. Anthony Crosland, when commenting on their progress in 1972,[20] identified three separate groups of polytechnics: those which were set on emulating the universities by, for example, creating a professoriate; those which were concentrating on serving regional needs, as in their Regional College days; and those which were striving to express the vision of the mid-1960s when the polytechnics were seen as a major instrument of social change. In a crude sort of way, this is probably a useful categorization, though it is doubtless the case that most polytechnics see themselves as falling into more than one of Crosland's three groups. In any case, there seems to be no obvious reason why the polytechnics, any more than the universities, should conform to one particular model.

Understandably, what they have been trying to achieve, against the background of financial and other constraints, is a corporate identity which among other things can serve as a pressure group on their behalf. To this end, the Committee of Directors of Polytechnics (CDP) was formed in 1970. Analogous to the universities' Committee of Vice-Chancellors and Principals, it describes its remit as being 'to discuss matters of common interest to Directors, and to contribute to the evolution of policy for the development of polytechnics within the total provision for higher education'. As part of its task, the Committee from time to time issues statements and publications describing polytechnic policy and philosophy.[21] Another, more recently formed, group is the Association of Polytechnic Teachers (APT), which as the name indicates is open to the teaching staff of the polytechnics. In practice, only a small minority belong to this organization, the great majority being members of the National Association of Teachers in Further and Higher Education (NATFHE), which represents all teachers within the further education sector, not just those in polytechnics. This division of allegiance reflects the dilemma in which the polytechnics find themselves: on the one hand, they are within the further education sector of which higher education is but part, and on the other they may seek to be regarded as the equivalent of the universities which are exclusively institutions of higher education. It is for this reason that the APT has recommended that the term 'polytechnic education' should be used in a way similar to 'university education' as being more specific than the comparatives 'further' and 'higher' education. It has also expressed concern lest the new colleges and institutes of higher education bring about a devaluation of the term 'higher education', on the grounds that in some of them only a minority of their work is at advanced level and consequently it is misleading to include the word 'higher' in their titles.

One matter on which the great majority of the Directors and staffs of the polytechnics seem to agree is their desire to achieve a greater degree of autonomy *vis-à-vis* their local authorities. Certainly, the DES has been anxious to secure for them a reasonable amount of self-government. For example, when approving polytechnic Articles of Government before designation it stressed that the Governing Bodies should, within the estimates as approved, be free to incur expenditure without reference to the local authority. In practice, it has not always worked like that, as is well illustrated by the decision of the Inner London Education Authority to use the Greater London Council's own accountants to undertake a detailed audit of the accounts of the five London polytechnics early in 1978, following their unwillingness to abide by its request that they reduce their proportion of overseas students to 10 per cent by 1982. Any polytechnic which refused to do so was warned that its grant from the ILEA would be cut and at one time it appeared that two of the five, the Polytechnic of Central London and Thames Polytechnic, risked losing £50,000 as a direct consequence of their stand against the local authority. The final outcome of this dispute is unclear at present as it is part of a much larger problem facing higher education in both the public and the university sectors. In April 1978, for example, the government indicated that it was debating a new plan to exclude from the controversial quota system for overseas students those who were able to pay the full cost of fees at universities and polytechnics and it remains to be seen whether this proposal will be implemented.

In the meantime, difficulties and disagreements have arisen between the polytechnics and their local authorities on important issues such as this as well as on small but irritating bureaucratic procedures which some authorities have imposed on their institutions. Such a matter of major disagreement occurred between the Coventry authority and Lanchester Polytechnic when the former insisted that Coventry College of Education be merged with the polytechnic instead of the University of Warwick, against the wishes of the great majority of the staff concerned. It was somewhat fortuitous that the local authority changed its mind and that the college and the university were eventually given authority to merge. It was for reasons such as these that one polytechnic Director put forward the suggestion that a national forum of polytechnic Governing Bodies be formed to act as a counter to the power of the local authorities, a proposal which did not however meet with much favour.

While these may be isolated examples of major disagreements between polytechnics and their local authorities, they do arise because of fundamental problems in the complex relationship between them. In this respect, it was probably unrealistic of the DES to assume as it did in its original notes of guidance to polytechnics that their Governing Bodies would be granted by the local authority more than a very limited degree of freedom in the disposition of public funds. Whilst, for historical reasons, each polytechnic is accountable to a single local authority education committee (with two or three exceptions), it is at the same time both a regional and national institution drawing its students from, and therefore serving, the whole country as well as the immediate locality. Moreover, the local authority responsible for the polytechnic meets only part of its costs, which is just as well, as the cost of running a very large establishment of higher education is such that few individual local authorities could contemplate it if they had to rely solely on their normal sources of income, that is the rates and the Rate Support Grant.[22] If this were the case, then clearly a large polytechnic's annual budget could prejudice other provision; in Sheffield, for example, the Polytechnic's share of the Education Committee's budget allocation for 1977-8 was 18 per cent compared with 26 per cent for primary education and 26 per cent for secondary education.[23] It is for this reason that a 'pooling' system operates, by which the cost of local authority higher education is shared at present among all the local authorities. Each authority is assessed for a contribution towards the 'pool' on the basis of its school population and non-domestic rateable value and is entitled to charge to the pool its expenditure on higher education courses. In practice, this means that a polytechnic or college of higher education can obtain a 100 per cent grant for that proportion of the establishment's work which falls within the definition of 'poolable advanced further education' as agreed by local authorities. This system creates a number of anomalies and problems. In the first place, it means that while financial responsibility for the polytechnic falls on its local education authority, it is effectively financed by all the authorities collectively, a fact which perhaps strengthens the institution's claim for more autonomy. Second, it could be argued that this system removes any incentive for sound financial control at local level and, indeed, a matter of concern to the DES has been that an authority can promote advanced courses secure in the knowledge that, once in operation, the major proportion of the cost will be chargeable against the pool. Finally, a number of local authorities without polytechnics or much in the way of advanced further education provision consider it unfair that they should nevertheless have to pay sizeable sums of money into the pool.

All this being said, however, there are what many, particularly those among the local authorities, would consider to be compelling reasons for retaining strong local and regional links between the polytechnics and their hinterlands and for making them at least partly accountable to the communities in which they are placed. Many authorities have invested a great deal of time and money into building up polytechnics of which they are justly proud and with which they have a close emotional involvement and they still provide directly a part, albeit a small part, of the polytechnics' revenues. Moreover, if one of the major functions of the institution is to serve the needs of the community, then that community must be involved in its government. On the other hand, there are those who argue that because the polytechnics now exhibit more national than regional characteristics, in such matters for example as course provision and student recruitment, they should be much freer of local authority control, despite the fact that historically they have always been subject to it. Indeed, it is argued that the existence of a national pooling system has provided a stimulus to the development of advanced courses in further education.[24] However, when all is said and done, it is almost certainly not practical politics at the present time to construct a radically different general structure of government into which advanced further education might fit, however desirable this might be.[25]

Nonetheless, there is general agreement that the arrangements under which public sector higher education are presently managed and financed are both complex and unsatisfactory. In addition to the central issue of the relationship between the local authorities and the polytechnics and other colleges offering advanced courses, two other major problems require resolution. Firstly, as we have seen, the existing pooling arrangements by which advanced courses are financed need revision, mainly because they constitute a divorce between management responsibility and financial accountability of the kind severely criticized by the Layfield Report on local government finance published in 1976.[26] Secondly, the abolition of the University Area Training Organisations has left a gap which has yet to be filled. The Advisory Committee on the Supply and Training of Teachers (ACSTT) proposed that regional bodies for teacher education be established, distinct from the Regional Advisory Councils, on which both the universities and the public sector institutions would be represented. The Council of Local Education Authorities (CLEA), on the other hand, advocated that regional bodies only be set up, thereby making no provision for the national co-ordination of teacher education in the public sector institutions. It was to resolve these major administrative and financial problems that a Working Group was established in March 1977, under the chairmanship of Gordon Oakes, Minister of State at the DES. The Oakes Committee, as it has come to be called, issued its report exactly one year later.[27]

Its terms of reference were 'to consider measures to improve the system of management and control of higher education in the maintained sector of England and Wales and its better co-ordination with higher education in the universities'. The Oakes Report made a number of recommendations of which perhaps the most important was that an independent national body be set up with specific terms of reference that include the 'general oversight of the development of maintained higher education' and the responsibility to 'collect, analyse and present where appropriate in conjunction with the Department of Education and Science and the University Grants Committee information affecting the demand for and supply of higher education in the maintained sector'. The Report envisaged that these arrangements might also apply to Wales, at least until such time as a decision on devolution were forthcoming. In practice, as we have seen, the government subsequently decided to recommend the establishment of two national bodies, to be known as Advanced Further Education Councils (AFECs) one for England and one for Wales. If these Councils eventually come into being, their terms of reference should ensure that they evolve into authoritative and influential bodies, analogous in some ways to the UGC. By collecting information on the demand for and supply of higher education in the public sector they should gain a considerable insight into its detailed workings thereby enabling them to make more informed and coherent decisions than have been made previously.[28]

Each AFEC will also be required 'to consider and issue guidance on the programmes and estimates submitted to it by authorities ... to allocate funds for recurrent expenditure.' In other words, it will have to decide how much money should be spent by local authorities on advanced further education and how it should be divided between individual polytechnics and colleges. One of the important changes proposed by the Report is that the total amount of money for public sector higher education be earmarked at the beginning of each financial year. The pooling system will continue but there will be two significant differences in the way in which it operates. First, instead of, as at present, the size of the pool being determined solely by the demands made upon it by the local authorities, the global sum to be spent on advanced further education will be determined by the AFEC in con-sultation with the DES after it has received estimates of expenditure from the local authorities in respect of the provision of higher educa-tion within their boundaries, on the grounds that the local authority will behave more responsibly if it pays a proportion of the cost rather than reclaiming all of it from the pool. Consequently, the local authori-ties will make a 5 per cent contribution rising in yearly increments to an absolute maximum of 15 per cent, the residual cost of 85 per cent being reclaimed from the pool. However, where an authority considers that a particular course is essential to the national or regional interest but regards the cost as excessive, it can propose to the AFEC that it covers the whole cost of that course.

For institutions offering a substantial programme of advanced work, it will be possible to submit estimates of expenditure through the local authorities for a programme of work three to five years ahead. The AFEC will consider the programme in the light of such factors as potential student demand and competing provision and allocate a block of money through the authority to the institution with the specific purpose of running that programme. It is then the responsibility of the institution itself to decide upon the detailed allocation of resources within the programme. In this way, the institution is given more flexibility and at the same time has to live with any mistakes it may make. This system is closely modelled upon that which operates successfully between the UGC and the universities. These sensible recommendations are also designed to harmonize relationships between institutions and their local authorities, in that the granting to institutions of considerably more discretion in the control and allocation of resources should help to avoid the kind of disputes that have erupted between them and the local authorities in the past.

Finally, the Oakes Report recommends that nine new Regional Advisory Councils (RACs) for England be established to improve the co-ordination and provision of courses and to ensure co-operation with the universities. Their remit will now include courses of initial teacher-training in public sector institutions, and universities involved in teacher-training will be invited to join in the regional planning. Initially, the boundaries of each RAC region should be as at present, with modifications where necessary to be the subject of negotiations between the RACs as soon as they are established.

Clearly, the recommendations of the Oakes Report are a compromise and, to that extent, will wholly satisfy none of the parties concerned, be they polytechnics, teachers or local authorities. Moreover, the Report leaves a number of important questions unanswered; for example, it will be necessary to work out the precise relationship of the voluntary colleges to the AFECs, a matter which was beyond the terms of reference of the Committee, and to finalize the details of financial allocation to institutions, matters which will have to be resolved if and when the AFECs come into being. The Report has also attracted considerable criticism: for example, it has been argued that it will result in a weakening of public control; it will impose a layer of bureaucracy that will inhibit development and innovation; it has ignored the unfortunate division between advanced and non-advanced further education and, to that extent, strengthened it; and it gives universities a place on RACs without making the Councils responsible for them.[29]

Whatever the rights and wrongs of these arguments, the Secretary of State announced in Parliament in March 1978 her broad agreement with the Report's proposals and invited comments on them from interested parties. These comments were received by the end of June 1978, enabling legislative proposals to be included in the parliamentary session which began in November 1978. As we have indicated, an Education Bill including provision for the establishment of the two AFECs had reached the Committee stage in the House of Commons when it was halted in its tracks by the dissolution of parliament at the end of March 1979. Thus, the future of the Oakes proposals is presently a matter for conjecture.

If, however, the AFECs eventually come into being, it is hoped that at least three major benefits will result. First, the polytechnics and other colleges offering advanced courses should obtain a greater degree of autonomy from their local authorities than at present. Second, long-term planning by the polytechnics and their authorities should be facilitated and the former should be freed, in large part at least, from the need to submit courses for approval to the Regional Advisory Councils, which are themselves to be reorganized. Third, greater financial accountability on the part of both the institutions and their local authorities should result in more economic and efficient management. However, these benefits will not accrue if, as some fear, the AFECs turn into an 'arthritic bureaucracy'.[30] Given their wide range of responsibilities, they would have to approve the programmes of over 400 institutions, for example, this is clearly a distinct possibility.

We have dealt at some length with the financial control and management of advanced further education because of their complexity and of the way in which they affect provision in the public sector. As we have indicated, the recommendations of the Oakes Report, if implemented, will be brought to bear both on the polytechnics and the other further education colleges offering courses of higher education. It is to a detailed examination of the latter that we now turn.

Other institutions offering advanced further education

As we have seen, the wholesale merging of the college of education sector mainly with polytechnics and other further education establishments has placed the provision of advanced further education into the hands of a wide variety of institutions, many of them quite new. For the sake of convenience, the DES has divided those institutions which provide education other than polytechnics into three main categories: those with over ninety per cent of their students on advanced courses; those with between thirty and ninety per cent of advanced work; and those with less than thirty per cent of advanced work. The numbers of institutions and their full-time and sandwich students are as follows:

Table 1
Advanced courses in further education: expected pattern of institutions, 1981

Groups of Colleges	Numbers of Colleges		Student Numbers 1975-6 (Full-time and Sandwich) '000s
1 With over 90% Advanced work			
Former colleges of education, free-standing or amalgamated with other colleges	57		54
Other colleges	10	67	4
2 With between 30% and 90% Advanced work			
Former colleges of education amalgamated with other colleges	18		20
Other colleges	39	57	11
3 With less than 30% Advanced work			
Former colleges of education amalgamated with other colleges	2		1
Other colleges	262	264	8
Totals		388	98

(Based on Table 2, 'The Management of Non-University Higher Education', *DES Report on Education*, No. 90, May 1977.)

As can be seen from the above table, the great majority of students on advanced courses are located in colleges which come into the first two categories, that is at least thirty per cent of their work is advanced. The majority of these colleges are, in turn, either institutions which have amalgamated with colleges of education or are free-standing colleges. Collectively, they are known generally as *Colleges and Institutes of Higher Education* and, as we have seen, their principals have come together to form an association called the Standing Conference of Directors and Principals of Colleges and Institutes in Higher Education, whose 67 members are shown in Figure 4. They make up a group of institutions which has been described as the 'third force' in higher education, alongside the universities and polytechnics, and are known variously as Colleges of Higher Education, Institutes of Higher Education, Colleges of Education or just plain Colleges. This somewhat confusing diversity can best be illustrated by examining what has happened in a particular region, the East Midlands (Figure 5). Here, before the recent upheavals, there were ten colleges of education: seven of them were members of the University of Nottingham Area Training Organisation; one, Loughborough College of Education, was attached to Loughborough University of Technology; and two to the University of Leicester. With the abolition of the ATOs and the drastic cutback in teacher-training, they have suffered a variety of fates. Two of them, Nottingham and the City of Leicester Colleges of Education have been merged with Trent and Leicester Polytechnics respectively; one, Loughborough College of Education, has merged with Loughborough University of Technology; two, Bishop Lonsdale College of Education, Derby, and Northampton College of Education, have merged with other further education colleges in their towns to form new institutions known respectively as Derby Lonsdale College of Higher Education and Nene College; two colleges, Bishop Grosseteste, Lincoln, and Matlock College of Education, have remained free-standing; four, Kesteven College of Education, Grantham; Mary Ward College, Keyworth; Eaton Hall, Retford; and St Paul's Rugby, have closed down or are in the process of doing so. As part of these changes, the number of public sector teacher-training places in the region is being drastically reduced, from over 8,000 in 1974 to about 3,400 in 1981. Those colleges which have merged with polytechnics and other further education colleges are *ipso facto* part of a diversified institution, though in the case of Derby Lonsdale and Nene Colleges a substantial proportion of their students are on non-advanced courses. Of the two free-standing colleges, Bishop Grosseteste is endeavouring to diversify by offering courses of general education not directly related to teacher training, while Matlock is remaining essentially a monotechnic institution, offering initial and in-service teacher-training courses. As far as validation of the courses is concerned, this is being undertaken either by the CNAA or by the Universities of Nottingham and Leicester. The picture is further complicated as the former pattern of teacher-training consisting of Certificate of Education and 'old-style' B.Ed. courses – is phased out and being replaced by new B.Ed. courses. This complex pattern is being repeated, *mutatis mutandis*, all over the country.

As we have seen, the three groups of colleges listed in Table 1, are characterized by varying proportions of advanced work. However, they also vary according to the types of courses which they offer, a criterion which results in a somewhat different grouping. First, there are those institutions like Derby Lonsdale College of Higher Education formed

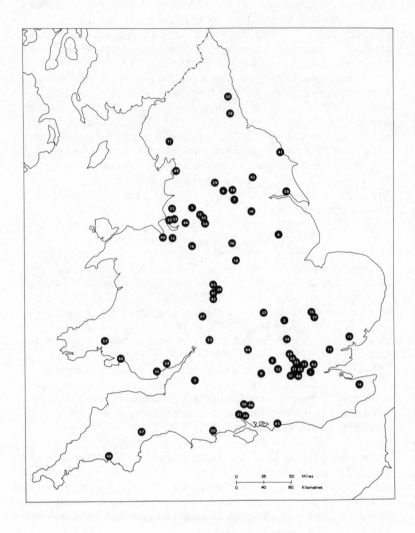

Figure 4   *Colleges and institutes of higher education (based on information supplied by the Standing Conference of Principals and Directors of Colleges and Institutes of Higher Education).*

Key to Figure 4

1 Avery Hill College, London
2 Bath College of Higher Education
3 Bedford College of Higher Education
4 Bishop Grosseteste College, Lincoln
5 Bolton Institute of Technology
6 Bradford College
7 Bretton Hall College, Nr. Wakefield, Yorks
8 Buckinghamshire College of Higher Education, High Wycombe
9 Bulmershe College of Higher Education, Reading
10 Cambridgeshire College of Arts and Technology, Cambridge
11 Charlotte Mason College, Ambleside
12 Chelmer Institute of Higher Education, Chelmsford
13 Chester College
14 Christ Church College, Canterbury
15 Colchester Institute of Higher Education
16 Crewe and Alsager College
17 De la Salle College of Higher Education, Manchester
18 Derby Lonsdale College of Higher Education
19 Doncaster Metropolitan Institute of Higher Education
20 Dorset Institute of Higher Education, Poole
21 Ealing College of Higher Education
22 Edge Hill College of Higher Education, Ormskirk
23 Gloucestershire Institute of Higher Education, Cheltenham
24 Gwent College of Higher Education, Newport
25 Harrow College of Higher Education
26 Hertfordshire College of Higher Education, Watford
27 Homerton College, Cambridge
28 Hull College of Higher Education
29 Ilkley College
30 King Alfred's College, Winchester
31 La Sainte Union College of Higher Education, Southampton
32 Liverpool Institute of Higher Education

33 City of Liverpool College of Higher Education
34 Luton College of Higher Education
35 City of Manchester College of Higher Education
36 Matlock College of Education
37 Nene College, Northampton
38 New College, Durham
39 Newman College, Birmingham
40 North East Wales Institute of Higher Education, Connah's Quay
41 North Riding College of Education, Scarborough
42 North Worcestershire College, Bromsgrove
43 Oak Hill College, London
44 Padgate College of Higher Education, Warrington
45 College of Ripon and York St. John
46 Roehampton Institute of Higher Education, London
47 Rolle College, Exeter
48 College of St. Mark and St. John, Plymouth
49 St. Martin's College, Lancaster
50 St. Mary's College, Newcastle-upon-Tyne
51 St. Mary's College, Twickenham
52 Shoreditch College of Education, Egham
53 Slough College of Higher Education
54 Southampton College of Higher Education
55 South Glamorgan Institute of Higher Education, Cardiff
56 Stockport College of Technology
57 Trinity College, Carmarthen
58 Trinity and All Saints College, Leeds
59 Watford College of Technology
60 West Glamorgan Institute of Higher Education, Swansea
61 Westhill College, Birmingham
62 West London Institute of Higher Education
63 West Midlands College of Higher Education, Walsall
64 Westminster College, Oxford
65 West Sussex Institute of Higher Education, Bognor Regis
66 Winchester School of Art
67 Worcester College of Higher Education

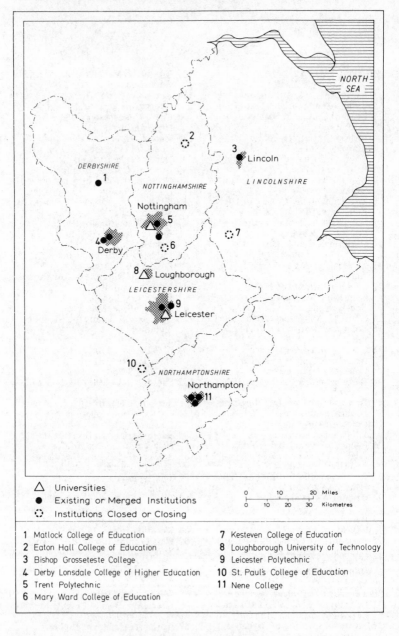

Figure 5   *Higher education in the East Midlands*

from the linking of one or more Colleges of Education, which by definition offered only advanced courses in teacher-training, with a College of Technology which offered a considerable number of advanced vocational courses. Another example is the West London Institute of Higher Education formed out of two former Colleges of Education, Borough Road and Maria Grey, and Chiswick Polytechnic, which to make confusion more confounded was not a polytechnic as we would understand it but, in effect, a College of Technology. The results of such changes are institutions which concentrate largely on advanced vocational and general courses and come into one of the first two groups. Second, there is a category of institutions formed by a single former college of education or by the amalgamation of two or more of them, such as Bishop Grosseteste College, Lincoln, and Crewe and Alsager College, Cheshire. These institutions offer almost exclusively advanced courses and come into the first category. As the result of a planned diversification, they now provide a blend of teacher-training and general education courses with, as yet, a small number of vocationally-oriented courses in such areas as business management. Third, there is a large group of institutions where only a minority of students are on advanced courses. These consist very largely of Colleges of Technology and Technical Colleges which offer only a few advanced courses and where most of their students are in the 16 to 19 age group and taking non-advanced courses. Also in this category, however, is a group of establishments formed from the amalgamation of a college of education with one or more further education colleges, for example the North East Wales Institute of Higher Education consisting of the former Cartrefle College of Education, Wrexham; Wrexham College of Technology; and Kelsterton College of Technology, Connah's Quay, Flintshire. This institution now provides a mixture of non-advanced and advanced vocational courses as well as general courses and would therefore be more accurately described as a College of Further and Higher Education. For reasons of status, however, the attribution 'further education' is generally omitted.

When the colleges of education existed as a separate sector of higher education, all their courses were validated by the universities to which they were attached. Since re-organization, however, many of the new colleges of higher education have turned to the CNAA for validation, a process that has not been without its stresses and strains. For the Council, the creation of the new institutions has greatly added to its work, while for the colleges the rigours of course submission and CNAA validation procedures have, in some cases, been traumatic. Indeed, some of the colleges have felt that the Council is dominated by the polytechnics and, as a result, neither wholly understands the rather different outlook of the colleges and institutes nor entirely sympathizes with

109

their aspirations.[31] The problem received a thorough airing in the middle of 1978 when the CNAA approved new regulations occasioned by changes such as the introduction of the Dip.HE, and the developments in art and design education following the merger with the National Council for Diplomas in Art and Design. These regulations, which will take effect in September 1979, were criticized on the grounds that they were far too detailed, that they sought to settle by regulation questions which are properly matters of judgment, and that they would extend the Council's authority over the colleges and, indeed, the polytechnics.[32] The Council, on the other hand, pointed out that formal regulations have always existed and that the new ones reflected the philosophy of liberality which it had always traditionally shown. Whatever the rights and wrongs of this issue, there is no doubt that some of the new colleges and institutes have found the process of CNAA validation a long and difficult one involving years of hard work and intensive planning. On the other hand, having been forced to question the validity of their courses, they have undoubtedly benefited from the self-examination required.

As a result of the disappearance of the college of education sector, we are witnessing therefore the emergence of what has been called a 'third force' in higher education, alongside the universities and polytechnics, namely the colleges and institutes of higher education. Many of them are not unlike the American liberal arts colleges, offering for the most part courses of general education. Some educationists, in the polytechnics and elsewhere, have criticized this process as a looking backwards to the 1960s, when there was a fast-growing demand for higher education, rather than a looking forward into the 1980s when the demand may well decline. It is argued that the creation of a large number of relatively small institutions of general education offering degree courses, many of them increasingly unlikely to obtain sufficient students to make them viable, cannot be justified at a time when there will be spare places in polytechnics. Another unfortunate by-product of the reorganization of teacher training, some believe, is the closing of the route into higher education for students with GCE O Levels which the Certificate of Education provided. While this may well be a retrograde step, blame for it cannot be fairly laid at the door of the new colleges of higher education as the movement towards an all-graduate teaching profession has proceeded independently of their creation.

What then does the future hold for them? Certainly, for those colleges which very largely provide courses of general education at degree level it looks particularly bleak. However, there are at least two important roles which they should be able to carve out for themselves. The first and psychologically the most difficult for the majority of them is to turn their back on academic drift, the emulation of the universities and polytechnics, and instead accept their role as providing a mixture of courses, both vocational and academic, at advanced and non-advanced levels. In other words, they should proudly accept the designation of College of Further and Higher Education. In this way, they would form a valuable institutional framework in which non-advanced and sub-degree courses of general and technical education could co-exist creatively. The second and complementary role which they might progressively adopt is to provide recurrent or continuing education for mature adults who wish to alternate work with education. The increasing provision of in-service teacher training is but one form it might take and with spare capacity likely to be released by declining numbers of 18-year-olds on initial courses of higher education, it is for the first time becoming a realistic proposition. For the colleges of higher education to adopt a strategy of this sort would make for two very considerable advantages: it would promote the imaginative recon-struction of the present system of tertiary and higher education, thereby allowing the universities and polytechnics to get on with their jobs; and it would encourage the growth of more local and less pretentious centres of higher and tertiary education which would be accessible to a much wider range of the population.

The Diploma of Higher Education

In many ways the most remarkable thing about the Diploma of Higher Education (Dip.HE) is the suddenness with which it appeared upon the educational scene. Even as recently as the late 1960s, the idea of introducing a two-year course into polytechnics and colleges of educa-tion was regarded by many as unacceptable and hardly worth consider-ing. By contrast, it is today an accepted, if not yet widespread, feature of the educational landscape. The Dip.HE was first formally recom-mended in the James Report, 'The Education and Training of Teachers', in January 1972. The report's main recommendation was that the education and training of teachers should be divided into three consecu-tive stages or 'cycles': a two-year full-time Dip.HE, followed by profes-sional teacher training, followed by in-service training for practising teachers. The first cycle, the Dip.HE, was to be a course in general education, equivalent in standard to the first two years of a first degree course, designed not only or directly for teachers. In this way, the Dip.HE could be regarded as a terminal qualification in its own right, or could lead on to a 'post-Dip.HE' course of teacher training or of academic study. In its recommendations concerning the content of Dip.HE courses, the report said they should 'combine the advantages of study in depth with those of a more broadly-based education' and 'should be so organised that each student could select a suitably com-posed course from a range of options'. In addition, one-third of the two-year course should be devoted to 'general studies'.

Although these recommendations were couched in general terms and might be thought by some to be mutually exclusive, they did provide the basis for discussions which culminated in recommendations in the government White Paper, 'Education: A Framework for Expansion', which was issued at the end of 1972. The White Paper in welcoming the Dip.HE said that it should adhere to three general principles: it should be an acceptable terminal qualification in its own right; it should be of a standard equivalent to the first two years of a degree programme; and it should be convertible to a degree wherever possible without loss of time. In keeping with the last principle, courses might be developed on a 'unit basis', thereby 'offering students the opportunity of a programme which could be modified as their interests and career plans unfolded'. Finally, courses should be validated by existing degree-awarding bodies, that is the universities and the CNAA. The White Paper also expressed the belief that universities would wish to offer the Dip.HE themselves, a belief not borne out by subsequent events.

The next stage in the development of the Dip.HE was the appoint-ment of the so-called Transbinary Study Group, representing the Committee of Vice-Chancellors and Principals, the CNAA and the Open University, to draft guidelines for the construction of Dip.HE courses. In its report, issued in May 1973, the Study Group promulgated a set of criteria for the new courses. These may be summarized as follows: entry qualifications should be the same as existing first degree pro-grammes, that is at least two passes at GCE A Level, though institutions 'should use their discretion in waiving normal entry requirements in the case of mature students who have appropriate experience or alternative qualifications'; the course should be two years full-time or the equiva-lent in part-time or sandwich study; the Dip.HE should only be classi-fied on a Pass/Fail basis, but a transcript should be provided showing the courses successfully taken with their grades; the course should be so designed as to facilitate transfer to a degree programme with two years' credit, though this would depend upon the interlock between the particular Dip.HE and the course of further study; and, lastly, as far as content is concerned, it would be up to the validating body to be satisfied that the course possessed the necessary degree of coherence.

This report was accepted by institutions on both sides of the binary line and with the recommendation of the DES to local authorities early in 1974 that the Dip.HE should carry a mandatory grant, the way was now set clear for the introduction of the first courses. These came in the following September when North East London Polytechnic and Bulmershe College of Higher Education, Reading, each introduced a

Dip.HE course, with about 100 students altogether. Since then there has been a gradual growth in the number of courses, which have taken two main forms. The first, commonly known as a 'freestanding' Dip.HE, is designed *ab initio* as a self-contained programme of studies, not being a part of an existing degree course for further study; and the second is a course which though internally-coherent is designed as part of a larger degree course. In both cases, the student can if he wishes terminate his studies with the Dip.HE award.

Gradually, the numbers of Dip.HE courses have built up and in the academic year 1977-8 it is estimated that there were about 50 of them, with 31 validated by CNAA and the remainder by universities. Of the CNAA-validated courses, 14 were freestanding and 17 degree-linked, while as far as university-validated courses are concerned, the likelihood is that they are virtually all degree-linked. In 1977, there were 3,350 students undertaking CNAA courses, so that assuming a proportionally-similar take-up on university-validated courses there were about 5,000 students on all Dip.HE courses. It is already clear that some colleges are having great difficulty in recruiting viable numbers of students, especially from those coming in at 18-plus. This is because, given that for school-leavers entry qualifications for the Dip.HE are the same as for degree courses, students understandably prefer to opt for the latter. It is for this reason that most colleges are running their Dip.HE programmes as part of linked degree courses, though understandably this is much easier to arrange in the larger colleges. It is interesting too to look at the destinations of students who have successfully completed Dip.HE programmes. Incomplete figures issued by ACID (the Association of Colleges Implementing Dip.HE Programmes) reveal that 586 Dip.HE awards were made in 1977. Of these no fewer than 500 transferred to post-Dip.HE courses in the same institution, of which 405 went into teacher-training courses and 95 to other degree courses. Of the remaining 86, 40 transferred to post-Dip.HE courses in other institutions and 46 were 'turned loose on the world' with the Dip.HE qualification.

These last figures highlight three of the main problems which the Dip.HE faces: can it be both a preparatory and a terminal course, will it become a generally accepted route into a wide range of courses, and will there develop a national system of transfer from one institution to another? As we have seen, the great majority of students on Dip.HE courses at present are intending to move on to a subsequent course of one sort or another and for the most part are taking degree-linked courses. Many of the students on free-standing courses are mature students and as they represent in many areas a fairly shallow pool the number of such courses is likely to decline. In the words of a percipient commentator on the Dip.HE, 'the tendency will be to design curricula for maximum transferability to degree programmes . . . even to the point of making them almost identical with the first two years of a three-year degree'.[33]

As far as the range of Dip.HE courses is concerned, this is unlikely to continue to expand to any considerable extent. The needs of industry and commerce are served by the well-established vocational courses such as HND and HNC, which are being replaced by TEC and BEC courses, and which require only one GCE A Level as entry qualifications. Where transfer to another institution for a post-Dip.HE course is involved, the numbers of students doing so is as yet relatively small and much of the success of the Dip.HE will depend on making transferability much more widespread. To this end, in June 1977 the DES set up a working party to examine all aspects of a national credit transfer agency. The working party, whose membership is 'transbinary' and includes representatives of the universities as well as of the public sector institutions, has established a project to examine the feasibility of setting up a national information centre for credit transfer in higher and further education. If a national credit-transfer agency does come into being, it will do much to increase the viability of the Dip.HE, though of course its implications go well beyond it, potentially to embrace the whole field of recurrent education.

Despite the relatively rapid growth in the numbers of students taking the Dip.HE, it is difficult to be optimistic about its future. For one thing, some Dip.HE courses are effectively no more than the first two years of a degree course, with the added minor advantage that a student can if he wishes leave after two years with an award. Moreover, a serious disadvantage is that a student enrolling for a Dip.HE course is not guaranteed, in every case, that on successful completion of the course he will secure a place on a subsequent degree course. But, more important, what casts a large shadow over its future are the likely changes in the size of the 18-year-old population over the next fifteen years or so. Government estimates of student demand for higher education predict that, given that the pattern of higher education remains much as it is now, the system will face an increase of some 80,000 students over the next six years rising to a total population of about 600,000 in 1984-5. Thereafter, the numbers will level out at that figure until 1990 when they will fall back sharply to about 530,000 in 1994 and possibly further contraction will occur after that.[34] If these developments occur and inevitably the calculations on which they are based are speculative, then clearly they will have considerable implications for the whole of higher education, implications which we discuss in our final chapter. However, if it turns out that by the 1990s there is spare capacity in the polytechnics and other colleges offering advanced courses and that the entry qualifications for degree courses are the same as for Dip.HE courses, then it seems probable that students will opt for the former. If that turns out to be the case, then in fifteen years' time we may look back on the Dip.HE as a brave educational experiment that failed.

Following the General Election of 3 May 1979, which resulted in the election of a Conservative government, the Chancellor of the Exchequer, in his budget speech of 12 June 1979, announced a number of specific reductions in public expenditure within the government's direct control, including education. Among them was the abandonment of provision in 1979-80 for Advanced Further Education Councils; thus, it remains to be seen if, and when, the proposal to create AFECs is resubmitted to parliament.

Although the Conservative government has at present (June 1979) not fully articulated its policy towards higher education, some hint of what may come was given quite recently by Dr Rhodes Boyson, a Junior Minister at the DES. He advised the polytechnics to look carefully at their terms of reference such that they should strive to become what he called 'centres of vocational excellence'. He also indicated that the polytechnics and the Open University would be expected to take the initiative in developing recurrent and continuing education on the basis of part-time courses.

In June 1979 the Council for National Academic Awards announced a modification of its validation procedures for polytechnics and other public sector institutions offering its degree courses. Instead of approving what it calls 'well established' courses for five years, it will now grant approval to most of them for an indefinite period. This means that courses, once approved, can continue without a full revalidation; instead, the CNAA will oversee courses by a system of progress review visits which will encourage future development. For this purpose, the Council will create a new body to be known as the Committee for Institutions. It is hoped that this new system will enable many institutions to develop a greater degree of autonomy whereby they can put forward their own ideas on initial validation or subsequent modifications.

6 Education for art and design, agriculture and management

Education for Art and Design

Education in Art and Design is carried on in many different institutions ranging from polytechnics and colleges of higher education through specialist colleges of art to colleges of further education and technical colleges. Courses are available at all levels and exhibit a considerable diversity, from foundation courses which provide a basic general education in art and design to CNAA post-graduate courses leading to Master's degrees in such specialist areas as Fashion and Textiles, Fine Art, and Graphic Design. The provision of art and design education has grown relatively slowly in the post-war period so that in November 1975, for example, there were only 30,000 students taking courses leading to recognized qualifications in art and design of whom 18,000 were on non-advanced courses, and 12,000 on advanced courses; these represented approximately 1½ per cent of all students in further education studying for recognized qualifications. In addition, there is a much larger number of students taking recreational courses in art and design.

The field of art and design education represents a very broad spectrum of study and as far as it is possible to distinguish between 'Art' and 'Design' the former is generally used to denote painting and sculpture and the latter is concerned with the production of graphic material, three-dimensional or textile/fashion artefacts by hand or machine processing. Moreover, design for industrial production consists much more in supplying the needs of commerce, professional and public bodies, often quite small in size, than those of large-scale manufacturing organizations.[1] In general terms, the present structure of courses in art and design may be subdivided into five main categories: (1) foundation courses, (2) non-degree vocational courses, (3) degree courses, (4) courses of teacher education, and (5) recreational courses.[2] We will now briefly examine each category, outlining the developments which have taken place since the beginning of the decade.

1 Foundation courses

As the title implies, foundation courses are primarily designed to offer a preparatory training for students wishing to enter more advanced courses or to pursue an activity in art and design. In this regard they are a vital element in the system and serve two very important functions: they provide a basic general education in art and design and thus constitute a valuable educational experience in their own right; and they are diagnostic in that they enable students to determine their abilities and select further courses of specialist study. In so far as they have grown up in an *ad hoc* fashion, designed by the art colleges on an individual basis, it is difficult to generalize about them.[3] However, they are usually one-year, full-time courses, though some extend over two years, and entry is normally at 17 or 18. In some cases, however, the exigencies of timetabling for examinations and the demands made on students by applications for courses of further study can reduce the effective time available to the one-year foundation courses to as little as 20 or 24 weeks. Entry qualifications are generally the same, that is five Ordinary-level GCE passes or their equivalent, as those required to continue on to degree and other higher level courses, which is indeed what the great majority of students do when they have successfully completed their foundation courses. Another form of entry is available in the form of pre-foundation courses which are offered by some colleges. These are one-year full-time courses which are normally designed for 16-year-olds.

It is also the case that the great majority of students entering advanced courses in art and design have come from foundation courses, a few having come from school with GCE Advanced level passes in Art. To some extent, therefore, A Level Art/Design classes offered by the schools are in competition with foundation courses offered by art colleges; however, the two are not strictly comparable in that the former are considered by many to be less suitable as pre-entry training for higher level courses in that their diagnostic value is much less than that of foundation courses. The latter therefore, constitute a vital sector of art and design education about whose future there is a good deal of debate. The basic problem is that, unlike other courses in this field, they have never been given into the care and custody of a national body so that there is no established basis for recognition, either as equivalent to qualifications at a similar level in other fields or as a stage leading to higher level courses.[4] Both the recently-formed Inter-Regional Standing Committee for Art and Design Education (IRSCADE) and NATFHE have pressed for some form of national validation of foundation courses and the former organization, having collected views from the colleges offering the courses, has listed five future possibilities.[5]

These are: that they remain as at present, organized and administered on an ad hoc basis; that responsibility for them be given to the CNAA; that they become the responsibility of TEC; that they become the responsibility of a joint CNAA/TEC body to be set up; and that a new and independent validating body be established specifically for foundation courses. IRSCADE, itself, has recommended that TEC and the CNAA get together to explore ways of establishing a joint validation procedure.[6] While it remains to be seen which, if any, of these options is adopted, it is not very encouraging that in recent years a number of offers of adoption have apparently been made by national bodies, only to be discouraged by the DES.[7]

2 Non-degree vocational courses

Both in the number of students involved and the colleges and departments offering the courses, these form the largest part of art and design education. The great majority of vocational courses are concerned with design and related subjects so that the fields of employment for students taking them include graphic design; typographic design; technical illustration; display; fashion; interior design; silversmithing and the making of jewellery; engineering model-making; stage, film and television design; and industrial design. They include a wide range of full-time and part-time courses which vary considerably in length, level and objectives.

The courses may be broadly subdivided into 'advanced', and 'non-advanced'. As far as the former are concerned, the term 'advanced' is applied to vocational courses in the sense that the level of work achieved is similar to that of other high-level courses, although the entry standards may sometimes be lower, and the majority of students taking them have already successfully completed Foundation Courses. Among the better-known of the high-level vocational courses are those leading to awards of a professional body, such as Diploma and assessment for Diploma membership of the Society of Industrial Artists and Designers (SIAD), one of the more influential bodies in this area. Such courses which may relate to graphic design, fashion/textile design, interior design, and product design are usually of similar duration to those leading to CNAA degrees, that is three-years full-time, and the numbers taking them have grown gradually over the years. In 1977, for example, over 1,200 candidates from more than 200 courses were assessed for the SIAD Diploma membership, of which over 80 per cent were accepted.

Non-advanced courses in some instances presently lead to CGLI examinations and are taken on both a full-time and part-time basis. In addition, there are a number of well-established and successful regionally-validated schemes, such as those run by the East Anglian, Northern and Southern RACs, leading to the award of Certificates and Diplomas. However, in contrast to the position in further education generally, vocational courses in art and design show a preponderance of students on full-time rather than part-time courses. Full-time provision includes courses of one to three and four years' duration, some of which may be studied as separate 'end-on' courses and many of which provide opportunities for transfer of suitable students to degree courses. Many of the full-time courses include opportunity for short-term release for industrial experience and some are organized on a more clearly defined 'sandwich' basis. Part-time courses which are available for similar periods of study as for full-time courses usually involve an average of eight hours' attendance at college each week, predominantly on a 'day release' basis. There are also short intensive courses available on a part-time basis, designed to develop a particular craft skill or to bring practical or technical studies up to date.

For some years now, there has not surprisingly been a strong feeling among colleges and faculties and departments of art and design that a rational and nationally-recognized structure for vocational courses is long overdue. As long ago as 1970, the Coldstream-Summerson Report[8] reflected the growing concern about vocational courses and suggested they be recognized so that they became design 'technician' courses along the lines of the definition laid down in the 1969 Haslegrave Report. This initiative led in turn to the setting-up of a working party, under the chairmanship of Mr A.S. Gann of the DES, to survey the provision of vocational non-advanced courses in art and design, to consider the extent to which that provision met employment needs and to propose a pattern for the future. The Gann Report[9] appeared in April 1974 and made a series of recommendations designed to fit non-advanced vocational courses in art and design into the general pattern of further education. Its survey of the field showed that there were some 13,000 students taking these courses, mostly on a full-time basis, in 176 institutions including art colleges, polytechnics and other further education establishments. Having concluded that it was not possible accurately to assess industry's wishes, the Report then proceeded to make a number of far-reaching recommendations. First, however, it disposed of the concept of 'design technician' put forward by the Coldstream-Summerson Report, a concept which had evoked a hostile reception from the are colleges in 1970, on the grounds that the expression seemed to be in use only in the ceramics industry.[10] The Report stressed the need for a nationally recognized form of certification and recommended the establishment of an autonomous body for vocational courses in art and design whose validating functions should resemble those of TEC and BEC, thereby enabling it where necessary to devise suitable courses as well as receiving submissions from colleges. It then suggested a pattern of full-time study consisting of two courses, which were dubbed C1 and C2. C1 was to be a two-year course for 16-plus school-leavers with suitable qualifications, leading to a certificate or diploma comparable in status to an OND, while C2 would normally be of two years' duration and would be for students not so highly qualified or well-motivated as those taking C1 courses. Students who obtained a C1 Certificate and who did not wish to enter employment immediately should be able to undertake further studies; in some instances, this might be a Diploma in Art and Design course, but in most cases it would lead to a Higher Certificate of the validating body. While C2 Certificate holders would normally proceed directly into employment, there should, however, be opportunities for some students to acquire credits allowing them eventually to obtain a C1 Certificate. In summary, the Gann pattern of courses represents a rationalization of existing national and regional schemes, under the aegis of the proposed national body.

The Gann Report received qualified approval from the colleges, though in many quarters regret was expressed that it had not taken the opportunity to recommend a single validating body for all courses in art and design, and not just non-advanced ones, and that its proposal for two different types of courses was 'elitist' and a vain attempt to separate the sheep from the goats.[11] It was widely felt in the colleges that the Gann C1 and C2 groupings were an over-simplification of the existing situation, as the potential C1 students who possessed suitable qualifications and had clear objectives were in a minority. Most students start with vague objectives or change direction quite fundamentally during their first year so that a wider range of courses is required including some broadly-based and some of a more specialized nature.[12] It is likely that this view is still held by a majority of the art colleges. In any case, nothing happened for more than two years, a fate common it would seem to reports on aspects of further education, until July 1976 when, in response to a parliamentary question, the then Minister of State for Education and Science, Mr Gerald Fowler, announced that the DES would reject the Gann proposal for an autonomous validating body, in favour of handing over control of non-advanced vocational art and design courses to TEC and BEC. In the upshot, responsibility was formally passed over to TEC in February 1977, and, as we have seen, the Council established its committee for art and design education (DATEC) late that year under the chairmanship of Mr David Carter.

The establishment of DATEC was by no means universally welcomed in the art world, many artists and designers being strongly opposed to links with TEC; the Association of Art Institutions, for example, urged the DES to recognize it as the appropriate organization to represent all aspects of art and design education.[13] On the other hand, the National Society for Art Education regarded the forthcoming introduction of TEC courses as an important development which would emphasize the needs of the design area to be better served by more appropriate courses and examinations.[14]

DATEC issued its first major proposals in June 1978 which stated that students would be studying for awards conforming to the existing TEC pattern of certificate, higher certificate, diploma and higher diploma via any mode of study. The major validation procedures are to be carried out by the new area committees covering graphic and visual communications, fashion, surface patterns and textiles; three-dimensional design which includes interior design; and general art and design which takes in areas such as fine art study. In November 1978, DATEC issued further proposals[15] in which it affirmed its philosophy that colleges should have the maximum opportunity to develop courses which they consider to be most appropriate to educational, commercial and professional needs as they are able to identify and define them. The structure of courses should be such that the majority will require a form of integrated study such as that described in the Grouped Course Scheme within existing TEC policy. Alternatively, courses may be designed as unit-based programmes to reflect the character of particular subject areas and requirements for a flexible credit award system. In both cases, assessment will be conducted internally and moderated externally in accordance with general TEC policy. The minimum length of courses will be as for existing TEC courses at the equivalent level. The intention is that the majority of courses will start from the autumn of 1980 onwards, though some schemes in subjects such as Photography, Audio Visual Studies and Technical Graphics, where substantial development work has already been undertaken, may be validated for students in the autumn of 1979.

The establishment of DATEC and its progress to date has been generally welcomed by the art and design world; for example, IRSCADE has given its blessing and James Holland, SIAD's Education Officer, has indicated that it has the Society's full support.[16] Although DATEC has stated that it welcomes submissions and participation in its discussions, so far it does not envisage regional involvement in its validation and assessment procedures. This has raised serious doubts in the regions that assessment in all its forms can be operated entirely from a London base. IRSCADE, for example, has recommended that the existing regional groups should continue to play a positive part in the new national structure and not be seen as a loose appendage.[17] This, indeed, they seem likely to do especially since some of the regions are pressing ahead with developments in this field: the West Midlands RAC, for example, is recommending that a scheme for non-advanced vocational courses in art and design be introduced into its colleges for the session 1980-1 and sees the forthcoming introduction of DATEC programmes as providing a unique opportunity to progress towards national standards with the maximum of regional participation. Indeed, following the RAC's initiative, discussions are taking place between DATEC and the regions about the establishment of regional liaison committees. Furthermore, the arrival of DATEC on the scene may well increase regional participation by providing an opportunity for regions which at present have no scheme to participate effectively in the devising of courses.

3 Degree courses

For little more than a decade, the high level qualification available to students seeking a first degree equivalent was the Diploma in Art and Design (Dip.AD). Set up in the early 1960s, it was a three-year full-time course with four broad areas of specialization; fine art, graphic design, three-dimensional design, and textiles/fashion. A national body, the National Council for Diplomas in Art and Design (NCDAD) was established in March 1961 to administer the award. The normal minimum entry requirement was five GCE O levels plus the successful completion of, or exemption from, a foundation course, though exceptionally talented students could be admitted without the minimum qualifications. Subsequently, a modest structure of post-diploma courses was created upon the basis of the Dip.AD. This consisted of a small number of NCDAD approved courses, comprising a one-year Higher Diploma in Fine Art, Graphic Design, Textiles/Fashion or a two-year Higher Diploma in Interior or Industrial Design.

Within a few years of the introduction of the Dip.AD, it became apparent that all was not well and discontent in some of the art colleges culminated in the so-called 'revolution' of 1968 which centred on the then Hornsey and Guildford Colleges of Art. The students and others were highly critical of the Dip.AD for a number of reasons, not all of them compatible: that it did not impart a sound technical training and failed to produce good design practitioners; that it was becoming so academic in content that it was losing touch with the market-place; that its status was popularly regarded as inferior to that of courses in other subjects which led to the award of degrees; and that instead of a network of inter-related courses imparting a wide range of studies, it offered only a small number of ladder-like disciplines. The integration of the specialist colleges of art into larger institutions like polytechnics also aroused apprehensions which added fuel to the flames. In response to this unrest, the National Advisory Council on Art Education (NACAE) and the NCDAD set up the joint Coldstream-Summerson committee to examine the structure of higher art and design education and suggest improvements. Its report, which appeared in September 1970, recommended that the structure of the Dip.AD be left relatively unchanged but that it be supplemented by the introduction of four-year sandwich courses, 'directed more specifically towards certain categories of industrial and professional design practice.'[18]

The government broadly accepted the Report's recommendations in July 1971 when it issued the long-awaited circular 7/71 which also announced the prospect of some small expansion of art and design courses. To that extent, the Circular received a cautious welcome in the art world,[19] but nothing very concrete occurred until three years later when, on 1 September 1974, the NCDAD merged with the CNAA. As a consequence, the Dip.AD and the Higher Diplomas in Art and in Design were replaced by the appropriate CNAA awards, but with no change required in entry qualifications. Thus, Dip.AD courses were subsumed by those leading to the award of a B.A. degree with honours and the one to two years' higher diploma courses to an M.A. degree. In general, however, the content and character of existing Dip.AD courses remained unaltered. Then, in 1975 and 1976, the CNAA's committee for Art and Design, which had been set up to monitor the existing provision, instituted a major review and renewal of approval of well over 100 B.A. honours courses. By 1977, the number of CNAA first degree courses in Art and Design had grown to 182, catering for some 13,350 students, of whom the great majority were to be found in the four Dip.AD specialist areas of Fine Art, Graphic Design, Three Dimensional Design and Textile and Fashion Design. However, a recent interesting development has been the introduction of multi-disciplinary courses such as that offered by North East London Polytechnic in Communication Design and by North Staffordshire Polytechnic in the history of design and visual arts with a chief study in ceramics. The latter also offers a multi-disciplinary design course. As yet, there is only a small number of multi-disciplinary courses on offer in England and Wales, but it is an important development which should be encouraged.

Another interesting development of the last year or two has been the introduction of courses in design, leading to the CNAA B.A., by a few of the former colleges of education with large craft resources, which are now part of colleges of higher education. It has been argued in some circles that permission has been given by the Council for these courses to operate without the normal validation by its Art and Design panel, because the colleges were previously concerned with degree work for the Bachelor of Education, and that this creates 'a dual standard within visual education'.[20] This concern, namely that the courses offered by the former colleges of education having different objectives from those

123

of the art and design faculties and colleges might be lacking in professional competence, highlights the problem of reconciling professional practice and standards with pedagogic demands in art and design education, an issue which is central to its future development. At present, of the 13,350 students undertaking CNAA first degree courses in art and design in 1977, fewer than 900 were doing so on a sandwich basis and none at all part-time. However, the percentage of students on sandwich courses has grown rapidly in the past few years, from 2 per cent of art students in Art and Design in 1975-6 to 7 per cent in 1977-8. One reason why the sandwich course is still relatively rare is that present arrangements for grant support effectively prevent work experience in small design practices and NATFHE, for one, is pressing that grant regulations be changed to enable students to be grant-supported during the sandwich period.[21] However, it is unlikely that this will come about during our current economic difficulties because of the implications for sandwich courses in other subject areas. It is also to be hoped that part-time courses in art and design will be developed as there would appear to be viable numbers of part-time students, including practising artists and designers, who would benefit from such provision.

As far as CNAA post-graduate studies are concerned, the Council undertook a searching review of its Master's degree courses in 1977. Some 18 courses were involved in the review which was headed by Mr David Bethel, Chairman of the CNAA Art and Design Committee, Director of Leicester Polytechnic and currently Chairman of the Committee of Directors of Polytechnic. The review was regarded as necessary because the change from NCDAD higher diplomas to CNAA master's degree programmes had resulted in substantial increases in the teaching in art and design courses and what some regarded as a difficult switch from a professional to an intellectual approach. One result of the review has been the withdrawal by the council of recognition from the M.A. course in fine arts at Birmingham Polytechnic and a recommendation that intakes to M.A. programmes in interior design and fashion at Leicester Polytechnic are suspended. Despite the recent growth in post-graduate courses, the provision is still very limited and NATFHE for one has strongly urged that it be increased.[22] However, two inhibitions on such an increase are the lack of suitably qualified and experienced staff as revealed in part by the CNAA review and the small number of bursaries available to suitable students.

Finally, art and design are increasingly a part of proposals for courses leading to the award of Bachelor of Education degrees and Diplomas in Higher Education, a development which poses the CNAA with problems in guiding and assessing both the content and standard of such courses. At the time of writing, it is in the process of establishing guidelines for their validation.

4 Teacher education courses

For the training of teachers in art, further education colleges have traditionally offered the one-year full-time post-graduate course leading to the Art Teacher's Diploma (ATD) or Certificate (ATC). For this purpose, nine institutions are currently recognized and approved by the DES. These are Birmingham, Brighton, Bristol, Leeds, Leicester, Liverpool, Middlesex and Manchester Polytechnics and the Cardiff College of Art, now merged into the South Glamorgan Institute of Higher Education. The nine centres together cater for only about 600 students, so that most of the courses are fairly small; in 1976, for example, the largest was Brighton Polytechnic with 147 students, while Leicester Polytechnic had 65. In recent years, however, following the merger of the colleges of education with polytechnics and colleges of higher education, a number of further education establishments are training art teachers for the school sector by such routes as a CNAA first degree course in Art and Design followed by a post-graduate Certificate in Education or a Bachelor of Education course in which Art and Design forms a substantial part. In addition, the Dip.HE may form the first two years of these course patterns. Thus the routes to becoming an art teacher have become more flexible, both in terms of the range of courses available and the stages at which students can choose a career as a teacher of art and design. In general, the merger of monotechnic colleges of art and colleges of education with polytechnics and colleges of higher education has, in the words of NATFHE, 'brought the education of art and design into a multi-disciplinary and multi-professional educational environment'.[23] Whether it is thereby improved is, of course, a matter of opinion.

5 Recreational courses

As we indicated in the introduction, we are mainly concerned in this book with courses that lead to recognized qualifications. However, recreational provision in the field of art and design education is exceptional in that it caters for some 80,000 students, many times more than those on courses leading to qualifications, and has always been at the centre of adult education. Most courses are held in the evening in evening institutes and include such subjects as drawing, design, painting, sketching, pottery, modelling, sculpture and photography. Clearly, art and design education of this sort can provide adults with a great deal of stimulus and pleasure, thereby enriching their lives. However, money for adult education in general has always been in short supply – as the 1973 Russell Report pointed out, only just over one per cent of LEA expenditure was devoted to it[24] — and art education is no exception to the general rule. Since then, due to the economic recession, recreational courses have been particularly subject to a series of expenditure cuts so that facilities have declined, courses have been curtailed or cancelled, and fees have been increased. Nonetheless, recreational courses in art and design continue to flourish in many areas and, as and when the economic climate improves, it is to be hoped that the colleges will be enabled to increase their provision.

It is in the very nature of the art and design world that differences of philosophy and emphasis make themselves felt. One such fundamental difference is that between fine art at one end of the spectrum and design at the other; this has been defined in terms of objectives, so that whereas in design one is working towards a defined goal with aims that are clear from the outset, in fine art there may be no defined goal other than satisfying the artist's inner demands.[25] Clearly, the distinction is not always so apparent; sometimes artists work as designers, and vice-versa. However, the differences are sufficient to make some lecturers feel that the linking of art and design is a marriage of convenience which would be better sundered, even to the extent of having separate departments. Fortunately, such a divorce is highly unlikely to occur and would, in any case, be undesirable, if only because art and design constitutes a single spectrum. The friction which has always existed between the two camps was made worse in the early 1970s when a number of colleges of art, some of them of considerable distinction, were swallowed up by polytechnics. This led to fears in some quarters that the polytechnics as tough, pragmatic and workaday institutions were unlikely to create a climate in which art and design could grow and flourish.[26] Such fears are probably misconceived and in the few years that have elapsed since the mergers took place there is no reason to believe that art education has suffered unduly at the hands of engineers and scientists in senior positions in the polytechnics.

The 1970s have also witnessed changes in the overall structure of art education courses. As we have seen, the CNAA validates courses at the highest level, with DATEC operating at the next level. In terms of validation, therefore, the only area of uncertainty concerns the foundation courses which still lack a national validating body. Thus, to a considerable extent, the pattern of courses in art and design has been 'rationalized' and brought more in line with the rest of further education. Whether this rationalization improves the quality of the courses, still less solves the problems of the art and design world, is another matter altogether. It will certainly do nothing to resolve the philosophical doubts of those who regard art and design as essentially different or yet others working in the art and design faculties of polytechnics who fear that the technological and scientific ambience of the institution is inimical to the needs and style of high-level art education. Indisputably, however, art and design education occupies an important place both in the life of the country at large and also in further education in particular, and its practitioners are only too well aware of the difficulties which they face. The future is not without hope, however, and developments such as the introduction of part-time courses leading to professional qualifications, a relatively neglected area of art education, may offer some promise of success.[27]

Education for Agriculture

For the most part, agricultural education — which includes education for horticulture, forestry, poultry husbandry and dairying — is carried on in specialist colleges of agriculture and horticulture, together with some general technical colleges. In November 1975, there were over 22,000 students taking agriculture courses leading to recognized qualifications in over 40 further education establishments in England and Wales; as in the further education sector at large, this represents a considerable increase in provision in recent years. The range of courses presently available, both advanced and non-advanced, has grown in piecemeal fashion, largely in response to the technological revolution which British agriculture has achieved over the last 25 years. At the non-advanced level, four main types of full-time course are available: the Ordinary National Diploma (OND), a three-year sandwich course in general agricultural subjects, designed to meet the needs of the 'technician'; the National Certificate, a one-year course for those intending to work as practical farmers, growers, or farm secretaries; College Award courses which vary in length and in standard and are often of a specialist nature such as flower-growing or farm secretarial work; and BEC Diploma courses which are being introduced by a small number of colleges. In addition, there is a substantial number of part-time courses at both craft and technician levels leading to awards of the CGLI and some of the Regional Examining Bodies. Indeed, most activity in agricultural education is on a part-time basis; in November 1975, for example, almost 15,000 students were taking day release courses. Although most of these are CGLI craft courses, as there is not the same clear-cut distinction between craft and technician functions in agriculture as there is in other industries, many of the Institute's schemes straddle the craft-technician boundary. For students possessing the necessary qualifications, there are two main categories of advanced full-time courses; degree courses offered by a number of universities; and Higher National Diploma (HND) courses offered by some of the

127

colleges of agriculture, which are science-based and concerned with the technological and managerial aspects of farming. In addition, five agricultural colleges offer full-time post-degree and post-HND courses, generally of one-year's duration, in such subjects as agricultural marketing, farm management and farm mechanization.[28]

As part of the general plan to reshape agricultural education to meet the changing needs of the industry and to bring it more in line with the rest of further education, the National Advisory Council on Education for Industry and Commerce appointed a committee late in 1970, under the chairmanship of Professor J.P. Hudson, Director of Long Ashton Research Station, University of Bristol, to examine and report on both the provision of full-time courses below that of OND and also all part-time courses in further education. In previous years, a series of reports had dealt with higher-level full-time courses, so that the Hudson Committee's work would complete the review of the whole pattern of agricultural education. The Hudson Report,[29] a very thorough and painstaking piece of work, was a long time in gestation; it was sent to the Minister towards the end of 1973 and was eventually published in July 1974. The report concluded that the pattern of courses and examinations below the level of OND lacked clarity and cohesion and that, consequently, there was a need to rationalize their provision so as to offer students a recognizable ladder of progression within clearly defined educational stages. To this end, it recommended the setting-up of an educationally independent national validating and examining body, serviced and administered by the CGLI, and composed of representatives of educational, industrial and training interests. It also recommended that new entrants to the industry should be encouraged to attend short induction courses providing practically-oriented instruction and information on opportunities in industry; and that craft education should be founded on two inter-related phases, normally completed within two or three years depending on whether or not full-time study is included, leading to a national craft qualification. In broad terms, our membership of the European Economic Community was likely to quicken the pace of technical and economic change in the industry, thereby causing a further contraction of the labour force and a further substitution of capital for labour, though at a slower rate than in the previous decade. It was necessary, therefore, for a higher proportion of an increasingly skilled work force to receive vocational education, with a need for management appreciation at all levels.

The Hudson Report received a general welcome from interested parties in agricultural education but, like reports on many other areas of further education, nothing happened for a long time. It was not until August 1976 that the then Secretary of State declared his intention of accepting its argument for a single, national, validating agency.

However, it was not to be autonomous, as the committee wanted; instead, discussions would be held with bodies such as TEC and BEC with a view to using existing validation schemes. This was not the most logical of arguments, it would seem, if only because the Hudson recommendations were concerned with craft courses, while TEC and BEC, the latter of which in any case was only likely to be peripherally involved, were supposed to be operating at technician level. However, the DES then began discussions with TEC, BEC, the CGLI, and a number of other unspecified bodies, as a result of which it issued, in March 1978, a consultative paper on 'future validating and examining arrangements for courses of agricultural education at craft level'. The document began by declaring that 'while BEC and TEC must be closely involved with the new arrangements, it would not be appropriate for these Councils to assume responsibility for levels of agricultural education which are not their proper concern'. Clearly, the intervening period since the Minister's statement of August 1976 had led to some clearer thinking. Accordingly, the document proposed the setting-up of a new Committee for Vocational Education in Agriculture. It would be established within the structure of the CGLI but would have a special relationship with TEC, BEC and other examining and validating bodies. Once established, the Committee's major task would be to devise a unified pattern of awards at the craft level, in accordance with the spirit of the Hudson proposals. For the Committee's guidance, the document attempted to define craft and technician education by suggesting that the dividing line between technician and craft courses should be fixed at a level below that of OND, so that National Certificate courses, for example, should become the responsibility of the new validating body.

The consultative paper was widely circulated and was received with mixed feelings. While there was near unanimity that there should be a single validating body, it was felt that it should cover all courses below degree level, including OND. The West Midlands RAC, for example, was typical in arguing that the attempt to differentiate between 'craftsman' and 'technician' was based on a misunderstanding of agricultural practice which did not distinguish between them; it therefore advocated the setting-up of a separate National Council with responsibility for establishing a unified structure of agricultural education below degree level. There was also widespread agreement on another major point, namely that the new committee should not form an integral part of the structure of the CGLI. The next and latest stage in this shifting argument occurred at the end of November 1978 with the appearance of a brief DES statement entitled 'Agricultural Education in England and Wales: Validating Arrangements'. Having taken on board the two main objections to its March 1978 proposals, the DES has reverted to its original proposal and in order 'to avoid multiple problems of interface with existing bodies', it considers it essential that the new Committee 'should be based within one of the major existing validating bodies' which, however, should not be the CGLI. It comes as no great surprise to discover that, in the Department's view, the new Committee 'could well function within the structure of the Technician Education Committee'. Having decided that since the CGLI is not really concerned with technician courses, it is inappropriate for it to be the validating body, it seems hardly logical to give the responsibility to TEC, which has no remit for craft courses. However, the DES draws a somewhat dubious analogy with art and design education and suggests that TEC should set up 'a completely new committee' along the lines of DATEC. TEC has, therefore, been invited 'to undertake this responsibility and open discussions with the other interests concerned, with a view to reaching agreement as quickly as possible'.

We are to conclude, therefore, that having pursued a somewhat tortuous course the DES has effectively come back to where it began, namely that all 'Hudson-type courses' shall be the responsibility of TEC. This has the superficial merit, apparently so attractive to bureaucrats, of ensuring a tidy system whereby vocational courses in technical subjects, in non-advanced art and design, and in agriculture become the responsibility of one body, TEC. Whether it is in the best interests of agricultural education, not to mention the spirit of the Hudson Report, is much more doubtful.

Whatever administrative arrangements are adopted, it is essential that they take into account two major differences between agriculture and the rest of British industry. First, it is for the most part composed of relatively small-scale and highly efficient enterprises employing limited numbers of men and women working in relative isolation from one another. It is no accident, for example, that agriculture is not included within the remit of the Manpower Services Commission. Second, as we have seen, the boundaries between the craftsman and technician in agriculture are shifting and difficult, if not impossible, to define.

Finally, an attempt to identify the major future training needs of the agricultural industry has been made by the Agricultural Training Board. In a recent report entitled 'The Years Ahead', it outlines a training programme for the 1980s based on a five-year 'rolling plan' devised by the Board in consultation with the agricultural industry. The programme envisages a great commitment to training by the training agencies, by the education service and not least by the agricultural industry itself, which is abjured to take on more apprentices and young entrants and to set up group training schemes.

Education for management

Education for management can be broadly defined as being predominantly concerned with the training of men and women for the higher-level supervisory and decision-taking posts. It thus differs from business education whose concern is mainly the teaching of the skills required for operating the technique of business administration, though of course there is a good deal of overlap between the two areas. It is convenient for our purpose to adopt the DES definition of courses in management education as being those which are post-graduate and post-experience.

A massive growth in management education took place in the second half of the 1960s, both in the further education and the university sectors. The present decade, by contrast, has been a period of consolidation and, in some instance, retrenchment within further education, but the principal management qualification continues to be the *Diploma in Management Studies (DMS)*. This qualification can be taken as either a post-graduate or a post-experience course and is equally relevant to a young graduate starting a career in management or to an older man with some experience of management, who wishes to bring himself up to date with the latest practice.[30] It aims to provide the student with a basic knowledge of the background to industry, to raise his general level of understanding of management processes, and to acquaint him with the tools and techniques of management. While the course leads to a national qualification, it is very flexible and can be studied on a full-time, sandwich, block release or part-time basis. Until a few years ago, the DMS was awarded to students satisfactorily completing a course at a college approved by the Committee for the Diploma in Management Studies or, in Scotland, by the Scottish Committee. However, the development of CNAA higher degrees and specialist management diplomas left the DMS in a somewhat isolated position and the two DMS committees decided to merge with the CNAA, a process completed by September 1976. Accordingly, the DMS has now become the Council's diploma level qualification in general management. At present, over fifty further education colleges offer courses leading to the award of the DMS, together with a number of extra-mural centres. Since the Diploma was introduced in its present form in 1961, probably more than 12,000 students have gained the qualification, making it by far the most popular post-graduate management qualification in the country. The numbers of the students taking the course have grown steadily over the years and in 1977-8, for example, there were 6,442 enrolled on 169 courses. Despite its popularity, the DMS has been subject to considerable criticism over the years, principally on the grounds that it was not of a sufficiently high quality.[31]

Indeed, this criticism was frequently levelled at management education in general and in her concern to ensure effective provision in the public sector institutions, the Secretary of State in March 1971 announced a plan for the creation of 12 Regional Management Centres (RMCs). These were to be based on a number of polytechnics and other further education establishments which already possessed strong departments of management and in some cases the designation related to a single establishment and in others to a grouping of two or more colleges. The RMCs would have four main functions: to develop advanced level work including post-graduate and post-diploma courses; to provide a wide range of management courses to meet the needs of industry, commerce and the public services; to meet the needs of industry and commerce through consultancy and applied research; and to act as resource centres for further education colleges in their regions.[32] In other words, the basic premise behind the establishment of RMCs was that they should be centres of excellence, performing a co-ordinating role for the provision of management education in their regions. As a policy of institutional innovation, based on national provision and designed to promote a single subject, the creation of the RMCs is unique in British further education.

The twelve RMCs fall into two broad groups, those consisting of one institution and those of two or more colleges. The first group consists of five RMCs: Kingston RMC based on Kingston Polytechnic; South West RMC on Bristol Polytechnic; Welsh RMC on the Polytechnic of Wales; North Midlands RMC based on North Staffordshire Polytechnic; and Yorkshire and Humberside RMC based on Sheffield City Polytechnic. The second group consists of seven RMCs: Anglian RMC based on Chelmer Institute of Higher Education, Chelmsford, in association with North East London Polytechnic; East Midlands RMC on Leicester and Trent Polytechnics and Derby Lonsdale College of Higher Education; London RMC on the Polytechnic of Central London in association with City Polytechnic, North London Polytechnic, Polytechnic of the South Bank and South West London College; Northern RMC on Sunderland and Teesside Polytechnics; North Western RMC on Liverpool Polytechnic and St Helens College of Technology; Southern RMC on Portsmouth Polytechnic, Farnborough College of Technology and Southampton College of Higher Education; and Thames Valley RMC based on Buckinghamshire College of Higher Education, High Wycombe, Oxford Polytechnic and Slough College of Higher Education. In some cases, the final shape of the RMC is different from that originally envisaged and some of them have taken as much as five years to come into existence.

Ironically, the development of many of them has been delayed by management problems, particularly those composed of a number of colleges who have had to negotiate a series of complex college mergers before they could start. Inevitably, the negotiations were beset by institutional rivalries and were, in some cases, made more difficult because the constituent colleges were of differing status and often miles apart. These negotiations have in some instances resulted in changes in the original plans. For example, in the case of the West Midlands RMC, which was originally to have consisted of North Staffordshire and Wolverhampton Polytechnics, it is now based only on the former; and, in contrast, the London RMC, which was originally to have been based on the Polytechnic of Central London, now encompasses four additional institutions. In some regions, difficulties were made almost inevitable by the DES change in policy; having originally decided to go for centres of excellence, the Department departed from that policy in order to give priority to achieving regional representation and co-ordination and in the process selected as constituent parts of RMCs institutions whose standards and status were not sufficiently high. There is little doubt that there would have been fewer teething troubles if they had been based from the start on single institutions of a status befitting the character of the subject and its clientele.[33]

Another problem that has beset the RMCs is that, instead of being financed from special, earmarked central or regional funds, they have had to derive the necessary resources from the parent institutions. Inevitably, this has brought them into competition for limited resources with the other activities of the polytechnics and colleges. As we have seen, the RMCs were designed to improve and co-ordinate the management education provided by a large number of neighbouring institutions in the regions, a role they have performed with mixed results. In some cases, like that of the Anglian RMC where the centre has deliberately adopted a low profile in its dealings with the associated East Anglian colleges and has given the larger ones a formal say in the running of the RMC itself, this function seems to be operating successfully. Elsewhere, however, management departments in technical colleges have been apprehensive lest their work and status should be eclipsed by nearby RMCs and have established a pressure group in the form of the United Kingdom Standing Conference of Management Heads (UKSC) to protect their interests.[34]

In the circumstances, it is hardly surprising that the implementation of the RMC policy has turned out to be somewhat disappointing, to say the least. This is not to say that it has not been withouts its achievements; among them, by all accounts, is the setting-up of the East Anglian RMC which is widely regarded as one of its few outstanding successes.[35] In addition to providing DMS courses, which form the staple diet of its students, the centre has developed in other directions, including specialist provision such as consultancy work in higher education management and specialized residential short courses.

Having perhaps come through their inevitable teething troubles, the RMCs should now be in a position to make a major contribution to the future development of management education. To promote their interests they have set up the Regional Management Centres Association (RMCA), which provides a forum for the expression of opinions by the Directors and senior staff of RMCs and associated colleges, who between them represent an increasingly large proportion of management education in the country as a whole. Certainly, the need to provide high-quality courses in management education remains as pressing as ever. As has been the case for years, one of the major difficulties in making such provision is the shortage of suitably qualified and experienced teachers. At the beginning of the decade, the Nind Report[36] concluded that the situation warranted urgent attention and recommended, among other things, a considerable development of in-service training. The RMCs were seen as perhaps the major vehicle for such provision and it is to be hoped that, within the next few years, their organizational and other problems can be sorted out so that they can make the substantial contribution to management education for which they were created. Certainly, one area of development in which they should be able to play a major part is in management education for further education staff along the lines envisaged in the third report of the Haycocks committee whose recommendations we describe in chapter 8.

7   Further education in Wales

While further education throughout the United Kingdom has changed rapidly during the last decade, Wales has been the scene of particularly dramatic developments. In addition to the changes which have flowed from the reorganization of the colleges of education, the work of TEC and BEC, and the initiatives sponsored by the Manpower Services Commission, Wales has been subject to two other particularly important developments. First, there was the government's decision to transfer responsibility for all non-university institutions of higher and further education from the Secretary of State for Education and Science to the Secretary of State for Wales, as from 1 April 1978. Second, there was, of course, the portentous issue of devolution which had it come about would clearly have had very considerable implications for the Principality. In this chapter, we shall concentrate on those features of change and development which are particular to Wales and, in the process, endeavour to identify the characteristics of the organization and administration of Welsh further education which distinguish it from its counterpart in England.

The transfer of responsibility for all non-university institutions of higher and further education to the Secretary of State for Wales which is, at the time of writing, twelve months old seems to have created no major administrative problems. However, it has inevitably led to a fundamental alteration in the relationship between the government and the Welsh LEAs. During this period, the Welsh Office has created a Departmental structure by which responsibility for Welsh education is vested in four divisions: Schools, Further Education 1, Further Education 2, and Educational Services, each Division being supervised by an Assistant Secretary. Further Education Division 1 is divided into two branches which are broadly responsible for all matters concerning teachers; and the planning and development of advanced further education, advanced course approval, and financial matters. Further Education Division 2 is divided into three branches concerned with further education and industrial training, vocational education and adult education respectively. Clearly, further education is now strongly

135

represented within the Welsh Office and the central authority in Wales is thus potentially equipped to give a firm lead to its future development.

As one would expect, there has been a substantial change in the pattern of further education establishments in Wales since 1972, particularly in respect of the provision of higher education. In response to DES Circular 7/73, 'The Development of Higher Education in the Non-University Sector', the Welsh Joint Education Committee (WJEC), which as we have seen constitutes a Regional Advisory Council for Wales, approved an outline plan for the Principality.[1] This plan was based on three major considerations: that in each of the new county areas stemming from the 1974 reorganization of local government boundaries, with the exception of Powys, there should be an institute of higher education incorporating colleges of education and major further education establishments, a proposal that was consistent with those submitted by the local authorities; that, with the exception of St Mary's College, Bangor, all the existing colleges of education should be incorporated into the proposed institutes, albeit with some change of functions; and that in order to strengthen the proposed institutes in Dyfed, Gwynedd and West Glamorgan, there should be a marginal redistribution of teacher training and advanced further education courses, involving also the transfer of student places into these areas from other areas.

In drawing up its outline plan, the WJEC was not content solely with commenting separately on the proposals made by its constituent local authorities but attempted to look at the needs of Wales as a whole, a procedure that was not always followed by the English RACs in respect of their regions. The plan included anticipated target figures for the teacher-training and advanced further education populations in 1981, of 4,800 and 8,800 respectively, which involved considerable give and take on the part of the individual authorities. Inevitably, however, the teacher training target has had to be adjusted downwards as the DES successively announced cuts in teacher training provision in England and Wales before, in July 1977, it finally settled on 2,900 places. Moreover, the decision to establish institutes of higher education in every county except Powys did not materialize wholly in the form proposed in the outline plan.

In Clwyd, for example, the North East Wales Institute of Higher Education was formed in 1975 from the amalgamation of three colleges: Kelsterton College of Technology, Connah's Quay; Aston Technical College, Wrexham; and Cartrefle College of Education, Wrexham. At one time, it was envisaged that the Yale Sixth Form College at Wrexham would also be incorporated into the Institute to form a comprehensive establishment catering for all those over the age of 16. However, this move was over-ruled by the Secretary of State for Wales on the somewhat nebulous grounds that it was important to allow the Sixth Form College to retain its identity. The neighbouring county of Gwynedd has as its establishment of higher education, Bangor Normal College; at present a monotechnic institution under the North Wales Counties Joint Education Committee offering only teacher training courses, it will give increasing emphasis to teaching through the medium of Welsh. The other college of education that was formerly located in Bangor, St Mary's College of Education, a church college, has been merged into the University College of North Wales.

By contrast with the North-east, Dyfed is not sufficiently industrialized to support an institution offering advanced vocational courses. Thus, as envisaged in the outline plan, its premier establishment is Trinity College, Carmarthen which, like its counterpart in Gwynedd, is a monotechnic teacher training institution. However, unlike Bangor Normal College which is maintained by the two North Wales local authorities, Trinity College is a voluntary college of the Church in Wales. As we shall see later, Dyfed also boasts two public sector national institutions, the Welsh Agricultural College and the Welsh College of Librarianship, both at Aberystwyth.

As in the north-east, both Gwent and West Glamorgan have established institutions of higher education by merging three colleges. Thus, the Gwent College of Higher Education was formed in September 1975 from Newport College of Technology, Newport College of Art and Caerleon College of Education; while the West Glamorgan Institute of Higher Education came into being in September 1976 from the merger of three long-established colleges in the city of Swansea: the College of Art, the College of Education, and the College of Technology.

As befits its largest city, Cardiff boasts the largest and most comprehensive institute of higher education in the Principality, with the exception of the Polytechnic of Wales at Treforest: the South Glamorgan Institute of Higher Education which was formed by the amalgamation of the Cardiff College of Food Technology and Commerce, Cardiff College of Education, Cardiff College of Art, and Llandaff College of Technology. In its original proposals, the City of Cardiff Education Committee envisaged that Llandaff College of Education (Home Economics) and the Welsh College of Music and Drama would also be incorporated into the Institute. However, as it was formerly part of the University and wished to revert to that status, the former has merged with University College, Cardiff – with the exception of its Social Work courses and its Higher National Diploma in Institutional Management which have been transferred to the South Glamorgan Institute – and the latter has remained a separate institution.

Finally, we come to the new county of Mid-Glamorgan, which inherited as its institution of higher education the Glamorgan

137

Polytechnic, at Treforest, Pontypridd. In April 1975, the Polytechnic was enlarged by being merged with the Glamorgan College of Education at Barry, 20 miles to the south in South Glamorgan, and was re-christened the Polytechnic of Wales. The merger was welcomed both by the DES and the CNAA who praised it as being a model of its kind.[2] The merger increased the student population of the Polytechnic by about 15 per cent and, perhaps more important, it represented a significant departure from previous practice in that, for the first time, the validation of teacher training courses in the Principality was to be vested in the CNAA. Indeed, by the beginning of 1977, the Polytechnic had already obtained CNAA validation for a Dip.HE/B.Ed. degree and five other similar courses flowing from the merger and was negotiating with the Council concerning a similar number of other awards. It came as a considerable shock, therefore, when, on 24 January 1977, the Chief Executive of the Mid-Glamorgan County Council received a letter from the Welsh Education Office of the DES stating the government's intention of removing courses of teacher-training from the Polytechnic as part of the overall plan to reduce the number of teacher-training places in the Principality to 2,850 by 1981. The plan also envisaged that the West Glamorgan Institute of Higher Education would lose all its teacher-training places. Not surprisingly, the Polytechnic's Governing Body reacted swiftly and within two days launched an all-out effort to persuade the government to change its mind. The Polytechnic's case for retaining teacher education was based on four main arguments: that it was the only public sector institution of higher education in the Principality which provided the full integration of teacher education with the remainder of the higher education system; that the proposals would leave the largest education authority in Wales employing the largest number of teachers, without involvement in teacher education; that the Polytechnic had already stopped recruiting for the Certificate of Education course, in line with the DES policy of seeking an all-graduate profession, and in September 1976 had attracted the largest number of teacher training students with a minimum of two GCE A levels in the Principality; and that the Polytechnic was being called upon to make a disproportionate sacrifice because it would have to drop its Dip.HE/B.Ed. programme which was a basic component of a newly developed integrated system of degree courses.

Despite the powerful case which it put forward, the Polytechnic failed to persuade the government to change its mind and the Welsh Office went ahead with its plans to remove teacher-training courses from the Polytechnic. The situation at West Glamorgan was, however, very different, as in the first half of 1977 the other Welsh teacher-training institutions mounted a rescue operation to save its courses. This operation proved successful and, in July 1977, the DES announced not only that teacher training would continue at Swansea but also revised teacher-training figures for Wales whereby the number of places in 1981 would be increased by 50 to 2,900. These 50 places would be allocated to West Glamorgan, together with another 250, consisting of 50 to be taken from the quotas of Gwent, South Glamorgan, Bangor Normal, Llandaff and St Mary's Bangor.

This decision, to cease teacher training at the Polytechnic while allowing it to continue at West Glamorgan, seems to have been based on political rather than educational considerations. According to Dr D.W.F. James, the then Director of the Polytechnic of Wales, the government's decision was a reflection of its desire not to rock the boat and was connected with arguments about the Welsh language, arguments which had already saved Bangor Normal College from merging with the University College of North Wales so that it could develop as a Welsh medium teacher-training college.[3] It may also have been the political considerations involved which led both the WJEC and the University of Wales to remain silent throughout the argument. The summary way in which teacher education was disposed of at Barry also contrasts strongly with what happened in North East Wales: here, there was much lobbying to prevent teacher training based on Cartrefle College of Education, now merged into the North East Wales Institute of Higher Education, from contracting further; it is indeed ironical that on the same day, 26 July 1977, that Gordon Oakes, Minister of State at the DES, declared that Cartrefle should be spared the axe, predominantly on the basis of its geographical location, he should pronounce a death sentence at Barry.

Now that the dust has settled on these major institutional changes, the effect has been to reduce the number of further education establishments in Wales from 53 to 47, while the number of local authorities has been reduced from 13 to 8. The 47 institutions are made up of the Polytechnic of Wales; three national institutions in the shape of the Welsh College of Music and Drama, at Cardiff, and the College of Librarianship of Wales and the Welsh College of Agriculture, both at Aberystwyth; 6 colleges or institutions of higher education; and 37 other establishments (Figure 6).

On the other hand, in the past few years the number of students in further education colleges in Wales has increased very considerably. For example, in the six years between 1969 and 1975, the number of students on full-time and sandwich courses in Welsh establishments rose from 12,390 to 19,587, an increase of over 60 per cent. The position concerning part-time students is very different, however; in the same period, their numbers only increased from 54,843 to 56,528. Moreover, it remains a cause for considerable concern that the number of youngsters in the 16 to 19 age range who attend day release courses in Wales is proportionally one of the lowest in England and Wales.[4]

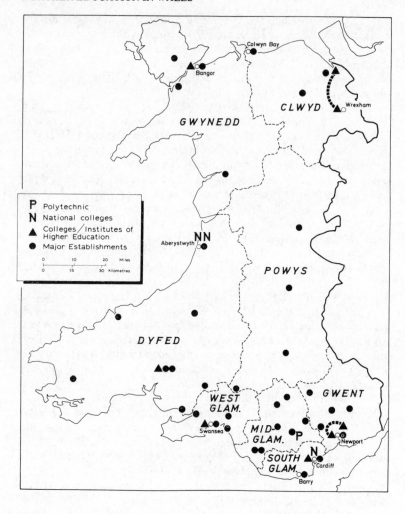

Figure 6   *Further education establishments in Wales*

As we have been at pains to emphasize, it is important to formulate a general policy of provision for the 16 to 19 age group as a whole and it is encouraging, therefore, that in the last few years the WJEC has been closely examining the situation in Wales with a view to identifying needs. A Working Party was first established by the Technical Education Committee of the WJEC in 1976 but it soon became clear that its membership was too limited to cover so broad a field. Consequently, a broadly based panel was set up including representatives of local education authorities, teachers in further education colleges and in schools (including Yale Sixth Form College and the tertiary college at Cross Keys), members of the careers service, and representatives of industry and the Manpower Services Commission. Following a residential workshop held at Ferryside, in Dyfed, in May 1978, an interim report was published which, at the time of writing, is under discussion by the constituent local education authorities.[5]

Having identified three main areas of priority which it defines as curriculum, organization and structure, and guidance and counselling, the Report turns its attention to the provision of vocational training. While acknowledging the reasonable working relationships that exist between the colleges, employees and the industrial training boards in Wales, it nevertheless deprecates the fact that there does not appear to be a full understanding of the role of the Manpower Services Commission. It urges, therefore, much closer co-operation between the DES and the MSC to integrate courses provided by the latter into the total provision of education and training. Certainly, the MSC has initiated a number of interesting developments in the Principality, among them the establishment in Clwyd of two training workshops which operate under the auspices of the North East Wales Institute of Higher Education. The workshops are designed eventually to train and employ up to 150 young people in activities varying from the repair of furniture to the manufacture of sailing dinghies for the Sports Council.[6]

The Report is also concerned with the divide between the school provision of essentially non-vocational courses and that of the further education colleges whose main role is to provide vocational courses. While recognizing that this is an inescapable fact, it nevertheless hopes that in special cases, for example in the remoter parts of the country where no convenient further education colleges exist, vocational courses might well be introduced into the schools. In this respect, and in others, the Report is a stimulating and worthwhile document and it is to be hoped that some of its recommendations will be implemented before too long. It certainly adopts a broader approach than the recent Welsh Office Report, 'Sixth Form Education',[7] which discusses the future organizational and curricular needs of school sixth forms with little or no reference to the requirements of the 16 to 19 age group as a whole.

141

The WJEC has also represented the views of the Principality concerning the development of technical education following the setting-up of the Technician and Business Education Councils. A few years ago, it was decided to go in with TEC and BEC rather than argue for separate Welsh councils, on the grounds that the time was not opportune. It therefore abrogated any examining function in the new courses and, instead, set up a co-ordinating panel, responsible to its Technical Education Committee, to ensure co-operation between colleges in phasing out old courses and in the curriculum developments associated with the new ones. As a consequence, examinations in the existing corresponding courses are being phased out and will cease completely from 1980.

The WJEC also has firm views on the teaching of courses through the medium of Welsh which in general it supports. However, it is opposed to the concentration of Welsh medium higher education courses in any one centre because it regards such a move as 'neither desirable, nor practicable', at the present time.[8] As will be readily appreciated, one of the major developments in Wales in recent years has been the increasing use of the Welsh language, presently spoken by an estimated one in five of the population, in schools and colleges, in public administration, and in the mass media. This has resulted in a growing demand for courses in business studies and public administration which relate to the vernacular and, in particular, for Welsh-medium secretarial courses at all levels, from those for youngsters who have left school at 16 to those for university and college graduates. This process has been facilitated by the introduction of a now well-established Welsh shorthand notation, which was developed almost exclusively by further education staff, and an extensive vocabulary of Welsh business office terms produced by staff from the Faculty of Education at the University College of Wales, Aberystwyth, together with the Principal of the Aberystwyth College of Further Education.[9] Another interesting development has been the publication of a Welsh language office magazine called *Swyddfa*, the Welsh word for 'office', published by the North East Wales Institute of Higher Education with the help of financial support from the Midland Bank. Other courses which have developed in response to public demand include those for Welsh translators and interpreters and a wide range of short courses on Welsh language and culture designed to help people who do not speak Welsh to play a fuller part in the life and society of the Principality. Additionally, at the time of writing it is anticipated that there will be candidates in at least 4 colleges and institutes of higher education offering Education through the medium of Welsh as part of the B.Ed. degree.

Establishments

As we have seen, there are now 47 further education establishments in Wales consisting of the Polytechnic of Wales, 3 national institutions, 6 colleges and institutes of higher education, and 37 major establishments. The last group, the 37 major establishments, include colleges of technology, technical colleges, colleges of further education, colleges of agriculture, a college of horticulture, a college of art which has just moved into a new purpose-built building, and one tertiary college, Cross Keys College, Gwent, which opened in September 1976.[10] These establishments are very largely concerned with the provision of non-advanced vocational courses and courses of general education, similar to those available in England.

Apart from the debacle over its teacher-training courses, the *Polytechnic of Wales* has grown very considerably during the present decade. When it was designated as Glamorgan Polytechnic in 1970, it had about 800 full-time and sandwich students. At the time of writing, the college, renamed the Polytechnic of Wales in 1975, has over 2,400 full-time and sandwich students and about 1,200 part-time students. More than two-thirds of its students come from the highly industrialized areas of South Wales and another 10 per cent come from Central and North Wales. It is therefore, in terms of its student population, very much an indigenous institution, in marked contrast to most of the constituent colleges of the University of Wales who draw many of their students from England. Despite this fact, the Principality itself is still reluctant fully to recognize the importance of the Polytechnic's contribution to advanced vocational education and to accord it the status it merits. This may be due partly to the fact that, compared to the University of Wales, the Polytechnic is very much a new arrival on the higher education scene, and partly because of the Welsh tendency, even more marked than in the rest of the country, to regard technological education as less prestigious than that in pure science and the humanities.

In its outline plan for the future development of higher education in the non-university sector in Wales published in 1974, as we have seen the WJEC envisaged a growth in the number of students on advanced courses, other than teacher-training, to 8,800 by 1981, of which almost half, 4,300, were expected to be in the Polytechnic. It seems unlikely, however, that these targets will be achieved. In the meantime, the Polytechnic has made considerable progress and has continued to develop a wide range of degree, sub-degree and professional courses. It has also played a central part in promoting management education in Wales: in 1977 it was designated as the Regional Management Centre for the Principality, it is already acting as a focal point for developing management education across the country, and the MSC Committee for

Wales has agreed that its Training Services Division and the Polytechnic should continue to develop an integrated approach to management training in the Principality, and should give a regional dimension to those national developments that the MSC will be promoting in the future. Finally, it has established a wide-ranging programme of research within the institution and has maintained a proportion of its staff working for higher degrees.[11]

The future of the Polytechnic and its development in the next decade is, inevitably, difficult to foresee. Under its first Director, Dr D.W.F. James, it has become the premier institution of higher education in the maintained sector in Wales. Moreover, since the transfer of responsibility from the DES to the Welsh Office in April 1978, it has occupied a unique position in that, compared to England with its large number of polytechnics and to Scotland with its 3 central institutions which are analogous to polytechnics, it is the only polytechnic in Wales. However, it will inevitably be subjected to considerable competition over the next decade from the newly established colleges and institutes of higher education, who to a large extent command support from the WJEC. The Polytechnic has recently appointed as its new Director, Dr John Duncan Davies, previously Principal of the West Glamorgan Institute of Higher Education and, before that, Dean of Civil Engineering at University College, Swansea. Despite his wide experience of higher education in Wales, his task of guiding the destinies of the Polytechnic in the nineteen-eighties will be far from easy.

The three national colleges in Wales are, as we have seen, specialist institutions concerned respectively with music and drama, librarianship, and agriculture. The *Welsh College of Music and Drama* which occupies impressive new buildings in the Castle Grounds at Cathays Park, Cardiff, was designated as a National Institution in 1970 and is now well established. A relatively small college with some 250 full-time and 900 part-time students, it is administered by the South Glamorgan Education Authority and has a Governing Body which includes representatives of all the Welsh local education authorities, the University of Wales, the Welsh Arts Council, the Welsh National Opera Company, the BBC and Harlech Television. As we have shown, it remained a separate establishment following the reorganization of public sector higher education in Wales and it is now widely recognized as a National Institution offering full-time and part-time courses for professional performers of Music and Drama, together with honours B.Ed. courses and Graduate Diploma courses for would-be teachers of these subjects. The four-year honours B.Ed. courses in Music and Drama, which as a condition of the College remaining separate are arranged in conjunction with the South Glamorgan Institute of Higher Education, are the only courses in Wales designated to train teachers of these subjects for secondary schools. Among the one-year graduate Diploma courses is one in drama which is unique in that the Welsh language is the medium of instruction. All these courses are validated by the University of Wales.

The College's courses for professional performers, unlike those for intending teachers, do not qualify for mandatory awards, a situation which may change before long. In the wider scene, it is possible that training for music and drama throughout the United Kingdom will be reorganized in the form of a small number of specialist centres, in which case it is likely that the Welsh College of Music and Drama will be one of those to be so designated.

The College of Librarianship of Wales, at Aberystwyth, was established as a separate institution in 1964 and is the only one of the schools or departments of Library and Information Studies in the United Kingdom which has such status, all the others being parts of universities, polytechnics, or colleges. Under an instrument of government made by an Act of Parliament, Dyfed County Council is the College's maintaining authority. It, in turn, delegates responsibility for the direction of the College, subject to its approval of financial estimates, to the Governing Body. Although it is therefore clearly part of the maintained further education sector in Wales, the College has also developed very close working relationships with the nearby University College of Wales, Aberystwyth. Thus, at the undergraduate level, the College offers a joint honours degree in conjunction with the University College leading to the Bachelor of Librarianship of the University of Wales, whilst suitably qualified librarians may undertake advanced study or research at the College, leading to a Master of Librarianship degree of the University or Fellowship of the Library Association. The College has some 400 students, all of whom are full-time; like those in the nearby Welsh Agricultural College and Aberystwyth College of Further Education, and indeed the University College, they are all members of the Aberystwyth Guild of Students. This situation is probably paralleled elsewhere in the United Kingdom only by the position at Loughborough where students at the University of Technology and the nearby College of Art and Technical College are all members of the Loughborough Students Union. These relationships, which cross the boundaries of the binary line between the maintained and autonomous sectors of higher education in Wales, give the College of Librarianship a unique flavour. It has also developed something of an international character; not only does it attract a proportion of its students from overseas, but it also has strong links with overseas institutions. In addition, it runs an Annual International Graduate Summer School which offers courses in aspects of modern librarianship, set in a world-wide context.

The contribution which the College makes directly to the development of librarianship and allied subjects in the further education sector

145

in Wales is however limited, if the evidence of the research interests of the staff and the published list of student projects are anything to go by. If this is indeed the case, it is to be regretted. For example, one valuable task to which the College could turn its hand is the gathering together and classification of material relating to further education in Wales. Our own experience in writing this chapter has confirmed our previous experience that this material is in short supply and widely dispersed, and some of it will disappear altogether if it is not soon collected. It would undoubtedly be of great benefit to future scholars working in this field if the College were to create a central repository of classified material on a sector of education of which it is, after all, a not insignificant part.

The third specialist further education establishment in Wales, the *Welsh Agricultural College*, is also in Aberystwyth. When it opened its doors in 1971, it was the realization of a long-desired wish to provide Wales with a comprehensive system of agricultural education whereby a high-level institution would be added to the existing colleges of agriculture and horticulture. As a truly national institution, the College has on its Governing Body representatives, in equal numbers, of all the Welsh local authorities. The smallest of the three specialist colleges, it has just over 150 full-time students, of whom about half come from Wales. The main courses presently being offered by the College are Higher and Ordinary National Diplomas, the specialist areas being animal production, crop production, farm mechanism, agricultural engineering, and farm business organization and management. An important feature of these courses is detailed consideration of the role of British agriculture in the European Economic Community. In addition, the College runs a one-year post diploma degree course in beef and sheep production and marketing. Thus, the major part of the College's activities can be described as intermediate in level between those of a typical college of agriculture and a university department of agriculture offering degree-level courses.

The College maintains close and constant links with the other seven Welsh colleges which run courses in agricultural education and students who obtain a National Certificate in Agriculture at one of them can transfer to the Welsh Agricultural College onto an Ordinary National Diploma course. The fact that the College is situated in a campus-like setting alongside two other further education colleges not only reduces the isolation which is characteristic of the great majority of agricultural colleges, but also enables it students to share residential, recreational, and sporting facilities and membership of student societies both with the College of Librarianship and the Aberystwyth College of Further Education and also with University College, Aberystwyth. The link with the University College is further strengthened because the present

146

Principal of the College, Dr David Morris, also holds the appointment of Professor of Agriculture at University College, Aberystwyth. This dual role, which must surely be unique, is a most welcome example of co-operation between a university and a further education college.

Reference has already been made to the two colleges of education within the Principality. *Trinity College, Carmarthen* is an Anglican Foundation, dating back to 1848, and has been fortunate in not having its student numbers substantially reduced during the recent re-organization of teacher education. The College offers a variety of initial and in-service teacher-training courses, including Dip.HE., B.Ed. and PGCE programmes. All courses are validated by the University of Wales and a small number of B.Ed. candidates study Education through the medium of Welsh each year. Currently the College is seeking to diversify its offerings and approval is being sought for three new BA degrees in the areas of the humanities, studies in the rural environment, and the arts and their administration.

The *Normal College, Bangor*, which was established in 1863, is also an institution which has made an important contribution to teacher education in Wales. Maintained by the North Wales Counties Joint Education Committee, consisting of Gwynedd and Clwyd, it offers initial and in-service courses for teachers including Dip.HE., B.Ed. and PGCE programmes all of which are validated by the University of Wales. At the time of writing, the College is awaiting approval for three new BA degree courses in the areas of communication, administration, and outdoor education with environmental studies, which will be available both in English and through the medium of Welsh. Clearly, these proposals have a dual importance for the College: firstly, they represent an extension of the Welsh medium and bilingual provision, an important aspect of the work of the College; and secondly they are part of the diversification process which is vital to the continued existence of an institution which presently has one of the lowest teacher-training targets in England and Wales. Furthermore, the Normal College is geographically adjacent to the University College of North Wales, Bangor, which offers similar courses of teacher-training and, in some respects, competes with it for students. Moreover, as the University validates the Normal College's courses, it would seem to us that whatever the pros and cons of retaining a local authority based teacher-training institution in Gwynedd, a much more sensible long-term solution would have been to integrate both the Normal College and St Mary's College into the University College of North Wales when that opportunity arose after 1974.

As we have seen, the establishment of the four *Institutes of Higher Education* has been one of the major developments in Welsh further education in recent years. With their creation, the institutional pattern is settled and seems likely to remain so for some years to come. However, the viability and success of the colleges and institutes of higher education is much more open to question. Taking the most optimistic view, it seems unlikely that the 6 colleges and institutes together will have more than 6,000 students on courses of advanced further education, including teacher training, by 1981. In that case, only two institutions Gwent and South Glamorgan, will have more than 1,000 students on high-level courses. For all of them, much of their work will be of a non-advanced character, a fact of life which is not reflected in their titles. As we have pointed out previously, they would in our view be more accurately described as institutes of further and higher education. In this context it is interesting to note that in 1976 the DES informed the WJEC that it was customary to use the title 'College or Institute of Higher Education' only for establishments where the advanced courses represent 60 per cent or more of the total provision, which is certainly not the case in all the Welsh colleges. The DES was somewhat curtly informed that this was a matter for the LEAs concerned.[12] In the meantime, the colleges themselves are trying very hard to develop high-level courses, partly for the reasons of 'academic drift' we have discussed in chapter 5, and are supported in this endeavour by the LEAs, who regard them as their prestige institutions, and by the WJEC. However, it seems unlikely that in the foreseeable future they will attract sufficient students to make them viable as institutions predominantly offering courses of higher education.

The training of further education teachers

Another area in which Wales differs clearly from practice in England is that of teacher-training for further education. As we have seen, in England this is very largely concentrated in the further education sector in the colleges of education (technical) and in a number of polytechnics and other colleges. In Wales, however, as a result of a request made by the WJEC in 1968, the major centre for such training is University College, Cardiff, in conjunction with the University of Wales Institute of Science and Technology. This centre, therefore, provides a range of courses both in-service and pre-service. The former, which are open to full-time lecturers in further education establishments in Wales, lead either to the Post Graduate Certificate in Education (Further Education) or to the Certificate of Education (Further Education) and consist of two periods of eight weeks' attendance at the Faculty of Education of the University College, interspersed with one year's supervised teaching and tutorial sessions in the students' own institutions. All students are required to forgo four weeks of their vacation for each of the two eight weeks in-college sessions. A new course is mounted every other year and both awards confer qualified teaching status for further education. Pre-service provision consists of a separate one year full-time PGCE (FE) course for mature entrants. As the syllabuses and teaching methods devised for the in-service PGCE course are also used on the equivalent full-time course, the latter has been accepted by the General Nursing Council as a recognized route for the training of nurse tutors.[13]

Teacher-training for further education has, however, begun to extend beyond its base in Cardiff as the University has recently approved a scheme for the introduction of courses based on institutes of higher education. The first of these courses began in 1978 when, in June and July of that year, a group of students from further education colleges in North Wales attended an eight weeks' session at the North East Wales Institute of Higher Education. The course has been organized in colla-boration with the staff of the Faculty of Education at Cardiff and is identical to the one offered there.

Up to the present, the Cardiff-based in-service course has attracted over 100 staff to each of its bi-ennial intakes, but in future the course will cater for an intake of around 60 every two years. The Welsh course has adopted a 'systems' approach, based on behavioural objectives, which is becoming increasingly acceptable in further education; as we have seen, the new Technician Education Council courses use this approach to a large extent. While further education staff who are trained by these methods thereby become well-versed in the techniques required by the new courses, it is to be hoped that they will not uncritically accept what is after all a major curriculum development which has yet wholly to prove itself.

It will be seen, therefore, that teacher training for further education in the Principality revolves almost entirely around the University of Wales, which also validates all courses for the professional training of teachers, including those for primary and secondary schools. We have already described the removal from the Polytechnic of Wales of teacher-training courses which were obtaining CNAA validation and therefore outside the University's orbit. It seems unfortunate, to say the least, that the premier public sector institution, in terms of the number of students on advanced courses, should, for a variety of historical and political reasons, be denied any share in teacher-training. The Polytechnic must find it all the more galling that a situation is developing whereby newly established institutes of higher education are becoming sub-centres of the Faculty of Education at Cardiff for training further education teachers, a role that is denied to the Polytechnic because it has lost its involvement in the professional training of teachers.

FURTHER EDUCATION IN WALES

The devolution debate

At the time of writing, the debate over the Labour Government's proposals for devolution for Wales has been temporarily stilled by the very substantial majority which voted against devolution in the referendum of 1 March 1979. However, it is unlikely that we have heard the last of the matter and, in any case, the prolonged debate that preceded the referendum provided a unique forum which illuminated clearly some of the major issues underlying the organization and provision of Welsh education, in particular post-compulsory education.

The government's proposals for devolution for Scotland and Wales were fully outlined in the White Paper, 'Our Changing Democracy: Devolution to Scotland and Wales', published in November 1975.[14] The most important of these was the establishment of an elected Welsh Assembly which would be responsible for all educational matters, including all further and higher education with the exception of the university. Predictably, the appearance of the White Paper sparked off a lively debate in educational circles which revolved around three broad issues: the wisdom of excluding the university from the Assembly's area of responsibility; the role of the WJEC *vis-à-vis* the Assembly; and the effectiveness with which an elected Assembly would be able to overcome the inherent weaknesses in Welsh educational provision.

On the first issue, as one would expect, the protagonists broadly lined up on either side of the binary line. Thus, university staff, together with some Welsh Nationalist (Plaid Cymru) opinion, for the most part argued that Assembly control of the university would result in undue government interference and would place the University of Wales in an anomalous position in regard to its membership of the University Grants Committee. The Labour Party in Wales, on the other hand, opposed the exclusion of the university on the grounds that the present injustice of the binary system could be rectified by bringing together all higher education under the control of the Assembly. It, therefore, made two alternative suggestions: either the establishment of a Welsh University Grants Committee with direct responsibility to the Assembly or that the Assembly should have the right to appoint an assessor to the existing UGC to deal with matters of special interest to Wales. Plaid Cymru, by contrast, advocated the setting-up of a new Welsh university consisting of both the present University of Wales and the Polytechnic of Wales, the newly formed institutes of higher education and the remaining independent colleges of education to become constituent colleges of the enlarged university. The Nationalists also envisaged that the new university would validate the award of all advanced certificates and diplomas, at the same time ensuring comparability with existing awards. A less far-reaching proposal was that of

150

NATFHE Welsh Region which was to establish a comprehensive system of higher and further education in the Principality of which the University would be an integral part,[15] a proposal which was strongly supported by NUS Wales in its submission on devolution.[16] Finally, a variety of other views were put, including that of Dr D.W.F. James, at a time when he was Director of the Polytechnic of Wales, namely, that the arguments for excluding the university from the Assembly's remit could also be applied to the Polytechnic.[17] When one considers that the links between an individual polytechnic and the other polytechnics and the Committee of Directors of Polytechnics are not unlike those of a university with the UGC and the Committee of Vice-Chancellors and Principals, then clearly there was force in his argument.

The second major issue of public debate was the relationship of the WJEC to the Assembly after devolution. The White Paper itself was silent on the matter, either because it had not given it any thought or because it thought it politic to say nothing. Needless to say, the WJEC itself had strong views on the subject, views which may be summarized under three heads. First, having been established under the 1944 Education Act as an agent and instrument of Welsh local government and financed entirely by its constituent authorities, it did not consider that its consultative procedures should be subject to the decisions of an Assembly made up of 72 members elected to represent parliamentary constituencies. Second, it was, and is, concerned to maintain its existing links with national bodies such as TEC and BEC, the Council of Local Education Authorities, and the Standing Conference of RACs, links which might be damaged under the new Assembly. And, third, it argued that unless the Assembly was given some responsibility for the planning of the whole of higher education including the universities, particularly in respect of student numbers, then the public sector institutions would be likely to suffer at a time when resources are scarce. Its attitude may be summed up in its firmly stated belief that, if its function were taken over by an Assembly council, the traditional balance of power between central and local government would be undermined.[18] In addition, of course, the officers of the WJEC are worried and uncertain about their own future, just as are many of the staff of the other Regional Advisory Councils in the wake of the Oakes proposals.

Perhaps the most important issue which the devolution proposals threw up is the third one, namely the fundamental question of whether the Assembly was the right body to ensure that Wales is provided with an effective educational system. As previously indicated, a considerable measure of devolution has already taken place with the handing-over to the Secretary of State for Wales, on 1 April 1978, of responsibility in the Principality for all non-university institutions of higher and further education; public libraries; the youth and community services, and adult education.[19] While this is a logical follow-up to the transfer to the Welsh Office in November 1970 of responsibility for primary and secondary education, it further underlines the somewhat anomalous position of the University of Wales in the context of further education. As we have seen the University validates all teacher training courses in Wales and itself has a virtual monopoly of the training of teachers for further education. Moreover, it validates the great majority of the Dip.HE and degree courses in the public sector institutions; indeed, other than the Polytechnic of Wales, only two establishments — the Gwent College of Higher Education and the South Glamorgan Institute of Higher Education — offer CNAA-validated courses, and those are in the Art and Design field. In these ways, the University has a considerable involvement in the maintained sector of higher education. While there is nothing necessarily wrong with these arrangements — indeed they seem to work reasonably well — it is understandable that the Welsh Region of NATFHE, for example, in its comments on the proposed transfer of responsibility to the Welsh Office[20] should have reaffirmed its view that the exclusion of the University of Wales from the Assembly's sphere of responsibility would prevent the establishment of a comprehensive system of further and higher education in Wales.

Undoubtedly, the organization of education in Wales is a highly complex matter which throws up problems requiring careful and detached consideration if they are to be resolved. In the prevailing circumstances, it was natural, if regrettable, that the devolution debate should have been dominated more by self-interest than detachment. Thus, the University was, and still is, anxious to preserve its interests and independence, while the Association of University Teachers was opposed to devolution in general because it wanted to secure national negotiating machinery on behalf of all university teachers in the United Kingdom. One of the few outspoken critics of the university viewpoint from within its own ranks, as it were, is Hywel D. Lewis. A retired university professor with substantial experience both within and without the Principality and a member of the Court of the University of Wales, he argued that the University should break away from the UGC and become responsible to the Assembly.[21] The WJEC is anxious lest it should cease to have a viable future, and NATFHE is concerned to promote the interests of the public sector institutions in which its members work. These reactions, while natural enough, do not help to create a reasonable consensus of opinion. One interesting suggestion, however, was that put forward by Sir Goronwy Daniel, then Principal of the University College of Wales, soon after the publication of the White Paper.[22] He envisaged the setting-up of a Welsh Assembly Education Committee which would delegate authority to a group of four joint committees responsible for the schools, the colleges and institutes of higher education, adult education, and the university, respectively. While this idea was not without its merits, as it left the ultimate responsibility for Welsh Education with the Assembly, it did not, however, resolve the doubts about that body's fitness to assume such a role.

The government itself subsequently gave the matter some further thought and in a supplementary statement to the White Paper, published in August 1976,[23] it suggested the establishment of an education council within the Assembly which would be a forum for the discussion of all post-school education in Wales, though it would not include the university in its area of responsibility. However, the government proposed to take into account the views of the Assembly in making appointments to the UGC which would have been asked to revise its terms of reference to take thorough account of the Welsh education system outside the universities. In the government's view, this would have involved having advisers from the Welsh administration at all levels of UGC business. On the face of it, this would appear to have been only a minor concession to the views of those who oppose the exclusion of the university from the Assembly's area of responsibility.

The next development in this complicated story was the appearance, in March 1978, of the Oakes Report which, as we have seen, recommended the establishment of a national body to oversee the financial management of higher education in the public sector. In a separate section devoted to Wales, the Report, while acknowledging the complicating factor of the WJEC's existence, saw no reason why the proposed arrangements should not apply to Wales during the pre-devolution period.[24] After devolution, it would be for the Welsh Assembly to consider what new arrangements would be made.

During the months following the appearance of the Oakes Report, the government gave further thought to the arrangements for administering higher education in Wales and crystallized its views in the shape of a Consultative Document, entitled 'The Management of Higher Education in the Maintained Sector in Wales', published by the Welsh Office in August 1978. The document began by stating that the government was considering establishing from the outset a separate National Body for Wales. While such a body would operate broadly along the lines of its English equivalent, there would be two important differences: first, there would be no need for a Welsh RAC as the national body itself would exercise its functions; and, second, the proposed national body would also subsume the functions of the separate forum for the discussion of all post-school education in Wales proposed in the Supplementary Statement on Devolution. The Consultative Document then suggested a broad remit for the Welsh national body, including a general oversight of the development of maintained higher and further

153

education and its cost-effectiveness; the fulfilment of certain functions envisaged for RACs in England, particularly in relation to the initial, induction and in-service education of teachers; and in addition acting as a forum for discussing the future development of all post-school education in the Principality. Finally, it outlined a possible member-ship of the national body and invited comments from interested parties.

It would seem that these proposals gave insufficient thought to their implications for the WJEC which, on the face of it, would be excluded from meaningful involvement in the provision of higher education in the maintained sector. It was hardly surprising, therefore, that having sounded out opinion in the Principality, the government had second thoughts about its proposals. As a result, the Welsh Office came up with a new and fascinating solution to the problem of the WJEC which it put forward in a second Consultative Document, issued in November 1978 under the same title as the first. The document stated that con-sultations had revealed a wide measure of agreement on two broad matters: that while there should be separate arrangements for Wales, these should not diverge too widely from those applying in England. The document then recapitulated the elements of the situation in Wales which necessitated a special solution, namely the existence of the WJEC which functions as the RAC for the Principality, the Oakes recommendations concerning the establishment of new RACs, and the prospect of the new post-devolution council for Welsh post-school education. Taking these factors into account, a solution was proposed which the document claimed would both avoid the wasteful prolifera-tion of bodies in the field of higher and further education in Wales and also preserve the identity of the WJEC. If agreement to the proposals were forthcoming, they would be incorporated into a new Education Bill which promotes the establishment of two new bodies, to be known as Advanced Further Education Councils (AFEC), one for England and one for Wales.

The scheme proposed for the establishment of the AFEC for Wales is ingenious indeed and the broad particulars are as follows. First, the WJEC would be invited to appoint a new committee which, in the words of the Consultative Document, would 'reflect the balance of membership envisaged for the AFEC for Wales'. The Secretary of State would then appoint the members of the new committee to be members of the AFEC. In other words, the non-statutory WJEC committee would become a statutory body to carry out the duties defined in the Oakes Report and embodied in the proposed legislation. Second, the WJEC would also be given additional functions, on a non-statutory basis, to act both as a new RAC for Wales and also to be a forum for the discussion of Welsh post-school education as envisaged in the

Supplementary Statement on Devolution. Finally, the WJEC would be asked to provide a secretariat and staff for the new body.

The reactions to these proposals were generally favourable and were typified by the Local Authorities Committee of the WJEC which gave its approval in principle to the establishment of an AFEC/RAC. In doing so, however, the Committee assumed that non-advanced further education would remain the joint responsibility of the WJEC and the local authorities. In particular, there was understandable concern that nothing should be done to prejudice the continuance of 'free trade', that is the transferability of courses and qualifications between institutions in England and Wales, and the links which exist with major further education bodies outside the Principality. Subsequently, the proposal to create a Welsh AFEC, alongside a similar body for England, was incorporated into an Education Bill which was well into its Committee stage in the House of Commons when it became a casualty of the dissolution of parliament at the end of March 1979.

At the time of writing, it is uncertain whether or not the Welsh AFEC will come into existence. However, whatever the outcome, it is to be hoped that, eventually, administrative machinery will emerge which is both effective in providing for the needs of Wales in its entirety and is also capable of exercising a co-ordinating function over the whole of post-school education in the Principality.

Our review of the further education sector in Wales reveals a situation which has changed considerably during the present decade. As we have seen, higher education in the Principality has assumed a quite different form from that which existed in 1970 so that we now have 10 institutions of higher education made up of the Polytechnic of Wales, 3 national colleges, and 6 colleges and institutes of higher education. The number of students on advanced further education courses has grown steadily since the beginning of the decade and will probably go on doing so, albeit on a more modest scale. The likelihood is that by 1981 the public sector institutions will have some 12,000 students on advanced courses, close on three-quarters of the 16,500 who are presently accommodated by the University of Wales. During the period under review, there has also been some growth in the number of students on non-advanced courses and in 1977, for example, there were almost 12,000 entrants to WJEC technical examinations as compared with 9,338 candidates for at least one GCE Advanced level examination.

Had the referendum resulted in a sufficient majority voting in favour of devolution for Wales, then the Welsh Assembly would have come into being and would have assumed responsibility for the administration of all Welsh education outside the university. While this would have

155

allowed of a broader view to be taken of the educational needs of the Principality, it would still require the willing co-operation of the University of Wales to be fully effective. As we have seen, the University occupies a unique position in the educational system of the Principality in that it validates all teacher-training courses as well as almost all the other advanced courses offered by the institutes of higher education, and it has a big stake itself in teacher-training, including a virtual monopoly of the training of teachers for further education. It has acquired this position for a number of reasons including the fact that historically it was essentially the creation of the people of Wales themselves and has made a major contribution to the educational needs of the nation. However, like Welsh national consciousness itself, the University has emphasized the cultural, linguistic and academic aspects of the country's life at the expense of the vocational and technological. The latter have lacked an effective spokesman partly because the Polytechnic of Wales which, in other circumstances, might have been able to give a lead, is in an isolated position, being the only one of its kind in the Principality. It is, therefore, unfortunate, if understandable, that the University has devoted relatively little attention to the needs of Welsh further education, despite its over-riding position in the training of further education teachers. Given its powerful influence over the whole of Welsh education, until and unless the University shows a greater interest in and awareness of the importance of further education to the Principality, it will not be able to flourish properly.

Yet that it should do so is vital to the well-being of the Principality as a whole. The last few years have witnessed an unprecedented period of economic depression for Wales such that by the end of the financial year 1977-8, when 8.3 per cent of the employee population were out of work, unemployment had reached its highest level for nearly 40 years. Although the severity of the problem varied between localities, in general the construction and engineering industries were depressed throughout 1977-8 and only tourism saw any significant expansion of employment.[25] In many ways, therefore, the revitalization and reshaping of Welsh industry and commerce is seen by many to be the single most important problem facing the country, alongside which issues like preserving the best of Welsh culture and fostering the Welsh language are less urgent. If this revitalization is to be accomplished then the further education colleges have a vital role to play and it is encouraging to note, for example, that in 1977-8 they provided almost half of the 5,421 places available under the Training Opportunities Scheme (TOPS) of the Manpower Services Commission.[26] Indeed, the MSC is giving a lead in this respect and its Training Services Division has recently initiated a number of interesting developments such as the agreement with the Gwynedd LEA to build an extension to Gwynedd Technical

College, Bangor, to house TOPS courses and the development of strong links with the Polytechnic of Wales to foster high-level TOPS courses in management. The work of the MSC Committee for Wales, which was put on a permanent footing in November 1977, is central to these developments and it is to be hoped that the educational service will encourage further similar initiatives.

Finally, as we indicated at the beginning of this chapter, the importance of the further education sector in Wales is now clearly recognized in the way in which the Welsh Office is organized. However, while the central authority is thus well placed to give a lead to future development of this sector, its well-being depends also on the contribution of the WJEC and, perhaps most of all, on the initiative of the further education colleges themselves. It is imperative that they continue to develop those vocational, and non-vocational, programmes which are essential to the needs of the Principality, a task more suited to their real strengths and the country's real requirements than the pursuit of ephemeral academic prestige.

8 Teacher education and staff development in further education

As we have seen, the number of full-time teachers engaged in further education has grown enormously in the last thirty years, from just over 4,500 in 1946-7 to almost 77,000 in 1977 (Table 2). The numbers of part-time staff have grown in proportion so that in 1977 there were about 130,000 part-time teachers in further and adult education employed by local authorities. As the further education sector has expanded its provision so its character has become more complex and varied and the demands upon teachers in the colleges have grown. For those teaching the 16 to 19 age group, for example, the development of vocational training in recent years following the establishment of the Manpower Services Commission, the changing pattern of technician education as a result of the creation of TEC and BEC, and the growth in GCE work in the further education colleges have all placed new demands on them, including additional curriculum development and course assessment duties.[1] Higher education within further education has also grown apace and has taken the form of both vocational and non-vocational provision following the creation of the polytechnics and the merging of the colleges of education into the further education sector. The number of mature students returning to study after years of work or undertaking retraining programmes in the colleges has grown and is likely to continue to do so. Moreover, students in colleges encompass a wide age range and exhibit very varying academic abilities and communication skills. All these factors are increasing the complexity of the work of further education teachers of whom, at present, well under half of the full-time staff, and even fewer of the part-timers, are trained in the sense that they have successfully completed a full programme of professional teacher-training leading to qualified teacher status. While teachers in further education are not required to have 'qualified status', that is to have successfully completed a professional course of teacher-training recognized by the DES, it is nonetheless highly desirable that they should have done so. The need for teacher education and staff development for further education is therefore urgent and is the subject of much debate and not a little progress. We

158

Table 2
Full-time teachers in grant-aided further education establishments,1977

	Poly-technics	Other Major Establishments	Evening Institutes/ Divided Service	Total
Principals	30	635	107	772
Vice-Principals	105	532	53	690
Other heads of departments	664	2,573	94	3,331
Readers	47	7	1	55
Principal lecturers	2,772	3,619	9	6,400
Senior lecturers	7,757	12,229	38	20,024
Lecturers grade 2	3,832	17,572	261	21,665
Lecturers grade 1	222	23,573	214	24,009
Totals: All grades	15,429	60,740	777	76,946

(Based on provisional figures at 31 March, 1977, supplied by DES.)

shall now proceed to examine these two aspects of the problem in detail.

Teacher education and training for further education

At present, the training arrangements for further education teachers are concentrated mainly in five specialist centres. Four of them are in England: Bolton College of Education (Technical); Garnett College, London; the former Huddersfield College of Education (Technical), now part of Huddersfield Polytechnic; and the former Wolverhampton Technical Teachers' College, now part of Wolverhampton Polytechnic. These colleges have concentrated mainly on providing initial training courses leading to a certificate in education, which take three forms: a one-year full-time pre-service course for graduates, similar in structure to post-graduate courses which train teachers for schools; a four-term sandwich course for practising teachers; and a two-year part-time course incorporating short periods of full-time attendance, also for practising teachers. In Wales, training is provided jointly by University College, Cardiff, and the University of Wales Institute of Science and Technology who provide one-year full-time courses and sandwich courses. In all, these courses in the five centres cater for fewer than 2,000 students a year. In order to increase the availability of their training programmes, three of the English colleges and University College, Cardiff, have also developed a network of extra-mural centres which, effectively on a day release basis, offer two-year courses leading to a certificate in education;

in all there are about 1,000 students on these courses. Thus, the provision made by the five institutions, some 3,000 places in all, is relatively small in proportion to the size of the further education teaching force.

In addition to this provision, another major route to teacher-training is provided by the City and Guilds of London Institute through its Further Education Teacher's Certificate schemes, Course No. 730, which does not, however, lead to a professional qualification conferring qualified teacher status. Although the scheme was devised for part-time teachers, it is increasingly taken up by full-time teachers who regard it as a basic or induction course. In all, some 3,000 candidates take the course each year, of whom about one-third are full-time. In addition, the Royal Society of Arts offers somewhat similar Teacher's Certificate courses in Office Arts and in the Teaching of English as a Foreign Language and the College of Preceptors operates a relatively small programme leading to its Associateship and eventually to its Licentiateship, a qualification which is recognized as degree equivalent.

This totality of provision, which has grown in an *ad hoc* fashion, is quite inadequate to meet the needs of teachers in further education and has long been recognized as such. Back in 1966, the Russell Report on the Supply and Training of Teachers recommended that, by 1969, a professional training requirement should be introduced for all new entrants into the further education colleges, a recommendation that was never implemented because of the urgent need for teachers at the time and the shortage of money. By the early 1970s, however, the situation looked more favourable; the re-organization of teacher education following the 1972 White Paper and the run-down of initial teacher-training made it seem feasible to redeploy resources to raise the quality of the teaching force in further education.[2] In October 1973, the recently established Advisory Committee on the Supply and Training of Teachers set up a sub-committee, under the chairmanship of Professor N. Haycocks, to 'consider and advise the main Committee on policy for the training of teachers in establishments of further education in England and Wales'. Twenty months later, in June 1975, the sub-committee submitted its first report on the training of full-time further education teachers, known popularly as the Haycocks Reports, to the Secretary of State. For various reasons, of which the most compelling was probably the financial constraints which existed at the time, the DES did not officially publish the report until the end of 1977, though inevitably its contents were widely known to interested parties by then. Having recognized the urgency of the problem – that, as we have seen, there is no pre-service teacher-training requirement for new entrants to the colleges and well under half of the existing teaching force have a professional teaching qualification – the report made six main recommendations.

First, all new entrants to full-time further education who have not had pre-service training and with less than three years' teaching experience should take a systematic induction training course. This would consist of day release throughout one academic year together with a four-week period of block release and should become a requirement before 1981, if possible. Second, about one-third of untrained new entrants should have the opportunity of an additional year's training on the same scale as they receive in their first year; together these might lead to a formal qualification. Third, new entrants who have completed a full-time one-year pre-service course should be required to undertake an induction programme equivalent to one day's release a week for one term. Fourth, opportunities for further in-service training should be more generous for further education teachers than for those in schools and, in any event, they should be at least on the same scale. Fifth, release for in-service training should be increased to five per cent of the further education teaching force at any one time as soon as resources are available. And, sixth, each further education college should have at least one professional tutor who would normally be a member of the full-time staff. In order to facilitate progress, the report recommended that regional bodies be asked to draw up and submit plans for their areas for the organization of in-service courses.

The DES accompanied the report with Circular 11/77, 'The Training of Teachers for Further Education', in which it declared the Secretary of State's support for the proposals in principle, together with the hope that an early start would be made on their implementation, 'so far as this is possible within existing resources'. The Circular considered that it should be possible to introduce the report's recommendations for induction training gradually and also to make some progress towards in-service training, but with a target of three per cent of staff released at any one time, rather than the recommended five per cent. Even then, it was doubtful if these recommendations could be fully implemented by 1981. In the circumstances, priority should be given to the institution of systematic induction arrangements for teachers without previous training or experience. Significantly, however, the Circular ignored the recommendation that opportunities for further in-service training should be at least as generous for teachers in further education as those in the schools. Regional Advisory Councils were asked to draw up plans and report progress on their plans to the DES by September 1978. In the light of these and subsequent reports, the Government would give consideration to the recommendation that induction training be made compulsory by 1981.

As far as the institutional structure was concerned, the report called for a rationalization of the present pattern to be based on a network of centres in each region, including an important role for the colleges of education (technical), particularly in developing pilot schemes for professional tutors, of whom there should be at least one in every further education college. The setting up of a programme of staff development, including an introduction for all new staff to their role in the establishment, should be a normal activity of every college. At the regional level, an appropriate body in each region, either a college or a committee, should secure the co-ordination of arrangements for validation and, at the national level, a forum should be established for consultation between those concerned with validation. These latter were envisaged as being the CNAA and the universities. In short, the report sensibly placed the emphasis on decentralization and on making the most effective use of existing resources, a sentiment echoed in the accompanying Circular.

Although the report provides much food for thought, with its proposals for a pattern of continuous training throughout the career structure,[3] it does have one important omission, namely it fails to get to grips, perhaps deliberately, with the curricular implications of its recommendations. For example, although it comments in passing that some staff teaching the 16 to 19 age group need to have an understanding of both further education institutions and the secondary schools,[4] it nowhere identifies the need to devise an appropriate training course for teachers of this age group in the light of such developments as those being initiated by the Manpower Services Commission in the field of vocational training and the emergence of tertiary colleges. It declares, perhaps rightly, that it would be inappropriate to provide detailed guidance on the curriculum, on the grounds that this might be regarded 'as presumptive and thus inhibit reasonable and appropriate variations to suit local circumstances'.[5] However, it then provides by way of illustrative example a detailed account of an induction course for newly-appointed teachers which is in many ways a reflection of a traditional post-graduate certificate in education course with a strong educational theory component.

The report tackles head-on the difficult problem of certification and validation and recognizes the need for a unitary system providing all teachers with a common base in the form of an induction course to which can be added another year's programme leading to certification. In its discussions, the committee identified the problem of devising an induction course whose primary purpose is to provide an effective programme for new teachers while at the same time being sufficiently rigorous to be acceptable to validating bodies as the first year of a two-year programme leading to certification. To reconcile these two requirements may not be easy. The report also touches upon the delicate subject of professional tutors who it considers will form a key element in the implementation of its proposals. It makes the valid point that many of the experienced staff in the colleges, upon whom the new entrants will have to rely for support, have themselves received no professional training, a position quite different from that in the schools. Hence, it recommends that the colleges of education (technical) should develop pilot schemes to examine further the role of professional tutors in further education. Whether this goes far enough or will quickly bring into being a properly-founded programme of training for professional tutors is open to question.

As was to be expected, the report received a general welcome though NATFHE, for example, reflected educational opinion at large in expressing its disappointment that no firm date had been set in the Circular for the introduction of the training requirement envisaged in the report. It also took issue with the report's statement that the additional year's training will only be necessary for one-third of untrained new entrants offered the opportunity, believing that the number should be greatly increased. Above all, it expressed dissatisfaction with the Secretary of State's announcement that the report's proposals be implemented 'so far as this is possible within the limit of existing resources', on the grounds that while physical resources may be adequate for a start to be made, additional resources will clearly be needed to provide for the release of the appropriate staff.

More specifically, NATFHE in its Draft Policy Statement, an interesting document worthy of careful study, builds upon the Haycocks' proposals by advocating the need for an all-graduate further education teaching profession. It points out that this has become an increasingly desirable objective, particularly since the movement towards an all-graduate profession in the schools sector means that, from 1983-4, existing professional teacher education will no longer give further education teachers qualified teacher status for the purpose of teaching in schools.[6] Accordingly, it advocates the eventual introduction of a system of four-years' full-time education and training, or its part-time equivalent, with appropriate credit recognition for previous qualifications and experience. While this would, in general, be a welcome development, it is not likely to come about in the foreseeable future. Nor may it be entirely appropriate for all teachers in further education, for example those teaching non-advanced vocational courses in such areas as secretarial, catering and craft courses, many of whom might not be able or willing to undertake graduate studies but who are nonetheless admirable teachers of their subjects.

The policy statement sensibly urges the development of forms of teacher education to meet specific and short-term needs, such as those of the young unemployed in the current Youth Opportunities Programme and in the field of remedial and compensatory education. Its approach to the curriculum is essentially pragmatic in that it advocates a teacher-

163

training course oriented towards the achievement of professional competence, rather than what it calls 'merely the academic study of education'.[7] Hence, the basis of the course must be classroom experience and the ability to cope with rapidly changing curricular problems. The use of the word 'classroom' in this context, rather than 'lecture-room', is interesting in that it is a tacit acknowledgment that the further education college is, or should be, a place where the emphasis is placed on teaching rather than lecturing. Finally, in respect of courses of training leading to professional qualications, the statement affirms that as the majority of students on such courses will be serving teachers, the identification of pedagogical needs and the achievement of terminal standards are more important criteria than formal entry qualifications, a policy which, as we shall see, has not proved wholly acceptable to the CNAA in drawing up its guidelines for courses leading to certification. Although the statement makes some reference, therefore, to curricular needs, it is, like the Haycocks Report, much more concerned with advocating the creation of an organizational structure for providing effective teacher-training for further education. While this is understandable, and perhaps inevitable, it should not disguise the fact that no structure will be effective until and unless a firm curricular foundation is established on which to base it. Unfortunately, as we shall see in chapter 9, that foundation does not exist. To give but one example, effective programmes of training require the provision of sound textbooks written specifically to meet the needs of further education teachers and, unfortunately, very few such books exist.

Undoubtedly, the deliberations of the Haycocks committee and the eventual publication of its first report have stimulated a flurry of activity and initiated a number of welcome developments in teacher-training for further education. As we have seen, the Regional Advisory Councils were asked to draw up plans for their areas and report progress on them to the DES by September 1978. The RACs seem to have responded with alacrity and no doubt their progress reports are presently sitting in an in-tray on an important desk in the Department. An interesting reaction has been that of the London and Home Counties RAC which set up a Working Party, under the chairmanship of Professor W.D. Furneaux of Brunel University, to prepare for its consideration a document commenting upon the Haycocks Report. In so far as it probably expresses a fairly typical RAC view, the working party's report makes most interesting reading.[8] It deals in a comprehensive and realistic way with the many issues arising out of the Haycocks Report as they relate to a major geographical region which contains about one-fifth of all the full-time teaching staff in further education institutions in England and Wales.

First, it takes issue with the Haycocks recommendations that perhaps one-third of untrained new staff with less than three years' teaching experience, having undertaken a one-year induction course, might move on to a further year's study leading to a professional qualification. It points out that, in the London and Home Counties area, current practice in the colleges, strongly supported by the teaching staff, is for release for a full two-year Certificate in Education course. Taken to its logical conclusion, this would mean making the induction year an integral part of the certificate course for all new staff. Second, the RAC report draws attention to the fact that many teachers in polytechnics believe that existing courses leading to the Certificate in Education are of little relevance to them and expect courses to take account of the differing needs of those teaching mainly advanced courses as compared to those teaching mainly non-advanced courses. This sentiment is likely to be echoed throughout the country and while it would not be fair to criticize the Haycocks committee for concentrating mainly on teachers of non-advanced courses, it does identify an area of further education teacher training which requires special consideration. In this regard, the activities of universities and indeed a number of the polytechnics may provide useful examples.

But perhaps the most significant finding of the Working Party, which in the course of its deliberations carried out a survey of full-time teachers in the region, is that there was already in existence in the London and Home Counties region a very considerable training capacity consisting of courses leading to Certificates in Education for further education teachers. It also considers that the Haycocks Report was mistaken in its belief that the teaching force in further education required by 1981 is likely to be 90,000; the rate of increase in the region has been so small that it concludes that, in fact, there will be *no* major increase in the further education teaching force by 1981. These two factors taken together lead it to believe it entirely feasible to consider a far higher level of release for a second-year programme than the one-third envisaged by Haycocks and that the original Haycocks recommendation of a five per cent target for in-service training is more realistic than the three per cent proposed by Circular 11/77. It seems very likely that the other RACs will concur with these sentiments. As we shall see, a number of RACs have been engaged in providing some form of teacher-training, especially for part-time staff in further education colleges; the significance of Circular 11/77, however, is that it requires *all* the RACs to examine closely full-time provision in their regions. It would seem, from the first reports of the plans submitted by the RACs, that each region is likely to designate one or two independent centres as the main providers of in-service courses, together with a number of subsidiary centres.[9] A major problem, however, which has surfaced in the deliberations of at least one RAC, is that its

165

local authorities and Principals have hitherto normally recommended for release for in-service training only those teachers who have had a minimum of four or five years' service. If the emphasis is to shift to new entrants to the colleges, as Haycocks would have it, then clearly it may bring about a conflict of interests.

Another important development following the Haycocks Report has been the introduction of a number of new courses specifically for further education teachers, under the aegis of the CNAA. In order to monitor and facilitate this process, the Council set up a Working Party on Teacher Training in Further Education which, among other things, produced a set of guidelines, which have been formally approved by the Council, for colleges submitting courses for approval. The guidelines include a list of entry qualifications which for the most part are similar to those granting entry to the Council's teacher-training courses for would-be school teachers; in that respect, they do not accord with NATFHE's belief that formal entry requirements are less important than the achievement of terminal standards. Certainly, a case could be made for granting entry to *all* full-time teachers in further education, who if they do not possess formal qualifications at least almost invariably have considerable industrial or business experience.

In recognition of the growing volume of work, the Council in 1978 transmogrified its Working Party into a Further Education Board, which by the end of the year had already approved two-year part-time Certificate in Education courses at three English polytechnics; a three to four years' part-time Bachelor of Education course at one of the colleges of education (technical) and a three-year full-time B.Ed. at another; and courses involving options dealing with further education or the 16 to 19 age group in three polytechnics and one college of higher education. More significantly, perhaps, the Board is anticipating, at the time of writing, submissions principally for part-time Certificate in Education courses from a growing number of polytechnics and colleges of higher education. This development is significant for two reasons: it increases considerably the national provision of courses for further education teachers leading to a professional qualification; and it gives the polytechnics and colleges of higher education a large and growing stake in an enterprise that has hitherto been very largely confined to the colleges of education (technical). The former have moved into this field partly because, with the publication of the Haycocks Report, the time is ripe, but also partly because in many cases, having absorbed colleges of education whose role in initial teacher-training for schools has greatly diminished, they wish to redeploy the resources into further education teacher-training. Such a redeployment is not, however, easy, as few of the former colleges of education staff have had much experience of further education and may not be fully tuned to its needs, particularly in respect of curriculum development.

We have dealt at some length on the First Report of the Haycocks committee and its aftermath because of the relative importance of full-time teachers to the further education colleges. However, as we have seen, they are outnumbered by part-time teachers and it was to their more diverse and complex problems that the Haycocks committee next turned its attention. It was in March 1978 that it issued its second report, on 'The Training of Adult Education and Part-time Further Education Teachers'; it is perhaps significant that, whereas the first report was sent out with a DES circular, this one was issued only as an ACSTT paper, endorsed by the Advisory Committee as a whole and over the signature of the Chairman of the Sub-Committee. The report begins by identifying the 130,000 part-time teachers in further and adult education employed by local authorities; thus there are nearly twice as many part-time as full-time staff employed in this sector, though, of course, their teaching commitment in terms of hours of work is much less. Nonetheless, they constitute, and will continue to do so, a very important element in the teaching force, of which they make up about one-quarter in terms of full-time equivalent teachers. Various types of training are available for part-time teachers of which by far the most widespread scheme is, as we have seen, the CGLI Further Education Teacher's Certificate Course No. 730 which, each year, attracts some 3,000 candidates. In addition to this course and those run by two other national bodies, the Royal Society of Arts and the College of Preceptors, some local authorities and RACs operate their own schemes. These have become increasingly important in recent years and include courses which have been operated or are planned in Yorkshire and Humberside, Glamorgan, the North-West region and the East Midlands, and directly by such authorities as Oxfordshire and Leicestershire.

As this provision caters for only a small proportion of part-time further education teachers and, with very few exceptions, leads to no formal qualification, it in no way constitutes an adequate or unified system of training. To rectify this state of affairs, the report recommends a unified scheme, on a regional basis, within which both common and specialized units would cater for the various needs of part-time teachers. To meet these needs, a three-stage pattern is anticipated: a first or induction stage, providing a brief initiation into basic teaching skills, which all part-time teachers would be expected to undertake; a second stage involving more advanced training in pedagogical skills, which the majority would be encouraged to complete; and a third stage, for those anticipating more substantial service, which would lead to the award of a Certificate in Education. In addition, suitable arrangements

---

should be made for new part-time staff joining the further education service to have some introduction to their place of work, and further training should be provided to enable experienced part-time teachers to upgrade their subject knowledge and skills. Special provision should be made for the 2,000 or so full-time adult education staff, including LEA organizers, along the lines suggested in the first Haycocks Report. The RACs should again be asked to draw up and submit plans to meet the needs of part-time teachers in their regions. Finally, the national forum recommended by the first Haycocks Report should perform the same function for courses for part-time teachers. In this context, it is interesting to note that, despite demands from various sources that a national body should be established forthwith, the DES has contented itself with the very cautious statement that it is considering how best to proceed at national level.

The reactions to the second Haycocks Report have, on the whole, been favourable although, in some quarters, there has been a strong feeling that it fails to get to grips with the needs of adult tutors; by assuming that they are similar to those of part-time teachers, it fails to recognize the large managerial element in their work. However, at the time of writing, the DES has yet to follow the report up with any positive action and, until it does so, we are not likely to obtain an effective scheme providing coherent courses of training for part-time teachers. Such a scheme should link closely the pattern of part-time training to that of full-time teaching; it should eschew unnecessary distinctions between 'vocational' and 'non-vocational' course provision; and make full use of the resources and experience already available in colleges throughout the country. In order to ensure proper and economic use of resources, which are unlikely to be lavish, a degree of co-ordination is essential; the RACs would seem to be the obvious focal point for this co-ordination and therefore the main agencies of development.[10]

The third and final product of the Haycocks committee's deliberations appeared in August 1978 in the form of a discussion paper on 'Training Teachers for Education Management in Further and Adult Education'. The paper was circulated to interested organizations for discussion and comment and, at the time of writing, that process is still going on. The paper begins by reviewing present provision which is made by a wide variety of bodies including the Further Education Staff College, the only institution which is exclusively concerned with education management training for further education staff; by universities; by further education colleges, including the Regional Management Centres and the colleges of education (technical); by individual local education authorities; and by other national and regional bodies like the RACs, the CGLI and the Local Government Training Board. Having identified what it describes as 'a number of sound developments in this field', the paper then concludes that there is a need to improve both the quality and quantity of education management and suggests various ways in which this might be done. Thus, the subject should be given particular emphasis within programmes of post-initial in-service training for further education teachers; consideration should be given to the possible inclusion of an element of introduction to the subject at the initial teacher-training stage; and emphasis should be given to the provision of short courses. Finally, RACs should be asked to consider what the paper inelegantly describes as 'resource availability and future co-ordination in respect of training for education management', and consideration should be given to setting up a national advisory and consultative group.

Although the paper is a thoughtful and stimulating document, it seems the least likely of the Haycocks committee's three reports to be followed by concerted action, at least in the short term. For one thing, as the paper itself demonstrates, a good deal of provision, albeit in a somewhat unco-ordinated fashion, is already made and, for another, there is a certain amount of scepticism of the value of management courses as presently constituted which will have to be overcome before wholehearted support is forthcoming. In any case, there is first much work to be done in the regions, for some of which this is a relatively new matter for consideration, to identify management needs and resources. Moreover, the problem of who should be the primary agent of provision will need to be resolved. Both the RACs and the Regional Management Centres can lay claims to this role; however, in our view, whoever makes provision must take as their major criterion the needs of the educational service and must have a knowledge of the further education sector as a whole.

In conclusion, our review of the present state of teacher education and training for further education leads us to deduce that, hopefully, we are on the verge of witnessing a very considerable expansion of provision. Given that, hitherto, this has been a largely neglected area, this development is greatly to be welcomed. However, it will not give a major impetus to the improvement of teaching in the further education sector – which, after all, is or should be the main object of the exercise – unless, and until, soundly-based courses of teacher-training are devised to meet the pedagogic and curricular needs of further education teachers. The situation is complicated by the fact that changes are about to take place in initial teacher-training for schools which will undoubtedly have repercussions for further education.

The DES announced in July 1977 that the last general entry to non-graduate initial Certificate in Education courses would be in the academic year 1979-80 and that, thereafter, all would-be teachers would have to become graduates. In addition, all those expecting successfully to complete a course of initial training leading to qualified teacher status at the end of the academic year 1983-4 will, on entry to the course, be expected to provide evidence of competence in English language and mathematics equivalent to GCE O Level. However, the Circular outlining these decisions[11] expressly states that the provision of Certificate courses designed for training teachers for further education is not affected by these changes, except in one respect. There is, at present, an arrangement whereby non-graduate teachers who have completed a Certificate course successfully, in one of the Colleges of Education (Technical) for example, may be accepted by a local authority as school teachers in shortage subjects such as craft, design and technology, and business studies. In all, about 200 non-graduates a year have been entering schools in this way. This route whereby non-graduate further education teachers of these specialist subjects can teach in schools will be closed after 1983-4. These complex arrangements point up the differences which still obtain between the school and further education sectors in respect of teacher-training requirements, differences which it will not be easy to resolve.

Finally, the Warnock Report on Special Educational Needs[12] has drawn attention to the implications for teacher-training arising from the increasing numbers of handicapped students in the colleges and has specifically recommended that a special education element be included in all initial training courses for further education teachers and that a one-year full-time course or its equivalent leading to a recognized qualification be available to further education teachers specializing in teaching students with special needs. A number of RACs have considered the Warnock Report[13] and one at least is urging the DES to ascertain the present national provision of training for specialist teachers.

Staff development in further education

Staff development, as the term connotes, is concerned with the professional and personal development of the staff of the further education sector, whether they are engaged in teaching, administrative or ancillary duties. Although the concept of staff development, as a major responsibility of the colleges and the employing authorities, is comparatively new in this country, it has nonetheless become widely and rapidly accepted and a large number of establishments have adopted a formal policy. In some colleges, this applies only to the teaching staff, and in some of those only to the full-timers, while in others it is extended to embrace administrative and ancillary staff. To implement their staff development policies, some colleges have appointed staff development officers, usually at principal or senior lecturer level; some have assigned the duties to a senior member of staff, such as the vice-principal; some have delegated the task to lecturers teaching education courses; and yet others have appointed professional tutors from among existing members of staff either as alternative to or, occasionally, in addition to a staff development officer.

The very considerable growth in interest in staff development among the further education colleges is also reflected in the establishment of organizations to stimulate staff development and related areas. It was thought impracticable to set up a national scheme and so, after a DES conference in Oxford in 1976, it was decided to establish two networks, one in the south and one in the north, to promote workshops, seminars and conferences, to exchange information, opinion and ideas, and to further the concept and practice of staff development. The southern network, which came into being in 1976, is an informal organization which publishes an interesting and informative bulletin, *Staff Development Newsletter*, which emanates from the Ealing College of Higher Education. The northern network seems to be less well organized and functions through occasional meetings at Bolton College of Education (Technical). More recently, a communications network has been started in the Midlands, based on the Faculty of Education at Wolverhampton Polytechnic, and has established two regular study groups, one concerned with staff development, the other with in-service training. Another body concerned with staff development is the Standing Conference on Educational Development Services in Polytechnics (SCEDSIP) which was formed in June 1974 by a group of polytechnic lecturers to plan co-operative activities and share resources. Although membership of SCEDSIP is limited, at present, to polytechnics, it encourages individuals from other institutions to participate in its deliberations and seeks active collaboration with the staff development networks. It issues a number of publications, including the *SCEDSIP Bulletin*, and organizes a bi-annual conference.

A somewhat similar body is the National Association for Staff Development set up in 1977 to represent the special interests of what it calls 'staff development officers and other teachers concerned with staff development and in-service education'. It has members in a wide range of further education establishments and issues a publication, *NASD Journal*, which first appeared in March 1979. At the time of writing, it is hoped to publish two or three issues a year.

Finally, another group of activists in the field of staff development recently established an organization called the Association of Professional Tutors, to formalize the role and functions of the professional tutor and to foster an awareness of his work. It is currently organizing a series of one-day conferences in various regions and issues

171

a newsletter, appropriately called *Apt Comment*, from the South Downs College of Further Education, Havant. However, it is indicative of the plethora of acronyms which nowadays besets further education that confusion has arisen because of the similarity of the initials of the Association and that of the Association of Polytechnic Teachers. The former has, therefore, decided to call itself the Institute of Professional Tutors and is currently looking for a new — and doubtless equally apt — title for its newsletter.

A number of individuals and groups have also made valuable contributions to the debate on the nature and importance of staff development including G. Tolley, the Rector of Sheffield City Polytechnic, G.E. Wheeler, the Director of the FE Staff College, and a joint working party of the Association of Colleges in Further and Higher Education and the Association of Principals in Technical Institutions.[14] Much to its credit, the DES has also organized a number of stimulating and valuable short courses on staff development as, of course, has the FE Staff College, in the form of study conferences. A number of institutions have spearheaded developments in this field and polytechnics, like some universities, have been particularly active, notably Manchester Polytechnic through its Staff Development and Educational Methods Unit.

If we consider the specific needs of the colleges in respect of staff development, these operate at two levels. First, there are the staff of colleges of further education who principally teach non-advanced courses; they chiefly need professional pedagogic training, including an element of curriculum development, in the form of induction courses and programmes leading to professional qualifications. As we have seen, they are being catered for by the provision of induction courses within individual institutions and by teacher-training courses in various establishments such as polytechnics and colleges of education (technical). As the recommendations of the Haycocks first report are implemented, so these forms of provision will grow. Second, there are the staff of the colleges and institutes of higher education whose needs are predominantly academic; for the most part, they are seeking higher degrees, partly to enhance their career prospects and partly because, in some cases, their institutions are seeking to develop higher degree courses which, in turn, generally require the staff teaching them to have higher degrees. The first example of the latter approved by the CNAA, in November 1978, is the course leading to the Master of Education degree to be run at Worcester College of Higher Education; similar courses are coming forward to the Council for approval and a number have already secured validation by universities. At present, the great majority of the staff of the colleges of higher education who are working for higher degrees are doing so by courses and research programmes in the universities. As far as both groups are concerned, and especially the senior staff among them, they often have major administrative and organizational responsibilities and would benefit, therefore, from appropriate managerial training.

From our survey of teacher education and training for further education as it presently exists and is likely to develop in the next few years, it is possible to draw a number of general conclusions. First, we would wish to re-emphasize our conviction that there is a pressing need to devise carefully constructed courses, specifically oriented to the needs of further education teachers, rather than to rely on existing programmes which, to varying degrees, reflect the needs of the school sector. Thus, their pedagogic content must be relevant to the requirements of further education staff, particularly those teaching non-advanced vocational courses. A good example of what can be done in this respect is provided by the Further Education Teachers' Study Groups which the Southern Regional Council has been organizing for almost two decades. These are concerned with specialist subject areas such as Mechanical Engineering, Construction, Plumbing, and Motor Vehicle Studies and their increase over the years has required the RAC to appoint a part-time Research Organizer who acts as a link between the groups.[15] The Study Groups meet regularly to discuss experiences and new approaches to teaching and assessment, they organize conferences, and publish useful reports on teaching schemes, project work, syllabuses, and the like. There is no doubt that these activities have provided much of practical benefit for many of the staffs of the colleges in the region.

Second, it is apparent that, although teacher-training for further education has hitherto been concentrated mainly in the colleges of education (technical), which are specialist institutions to a large extent outside the mainstream of teacher education, that situation is beginning to change. Polytechnics and colleges of higher education are increasingly taking a share in this activity and, as they have mainly trained teachers for primary and secondary schools, which will continue to be their main function, they may lack the necessary knowledge of further education to make proper provision, especially for staff teaching non-advanced vocational courses. On the other hand, the development of further education teacher-training by the faculties of education in the polytechnics and colleges of higher education does at least place it in a setting which encompasses the whole spectrum of education and so helps to break down its former isolation. These developments have considerable implications for the colleges of education (technical) who will have to adapt to a changing role. They possess a valuable and much-needed concentration of further education pedagogic expertise which can be put to good use in providing in-service training along the lines suggested by the Haycocks Report. For example, the extra-mural centres which they have established could be built up to provide an expansive induction programme[16] and they are the obvious focal points for the provision of training courses for professional tutors. They have, hitherto, made perhaps too small a contribution to research and post-graduate work, but that situation is beginning to change: for example, Huddersfield Polytechnic is proposing to build what it calls 'a comprehensive array of courses' to meet the needs of all further education staff, including higher degrees; Garnett College offers a two-year part-time M.A. in Further Education, validated by the University of London; Wolverhampton Polytechnic is seeking CNAA validation for a range of courses for further education teachers; and Bolton College of Education (Technical) has recently secured approval from the University of Manchester for a similar Master of Education degree. Research into further education has also developed in these colleges in recent years, through, for example, the work of Garnett College's ILEA Research and Development Unit. It is in these fields of activity that the four colleges should be able to carve out for themselves a distinctive and successful role.

As far as staff development is concerned, as we have seen, this is a considerable growth area which does, however, labour under a number of difficulties. First, there is no clear consensus as to what precisely staff development consists of and this problem of identity has caused its growth to be confused rather than coherent. Second, as staff development tends to mean different things to different people — it can, for example, be seen as harmonizing the interests and wishes of the individual, or promoting the needs of the institutions or, most commonly, as reconciling the two — so it becomes difficult to formulate a coherent policy for the future. The present position has been well described in the following terms: 'In general, staff development, of some stature now but still in its youth, is uncoordinated, unsure of its own nature, and uncertain of its proper direction'.[17] Third, if staff development is to forge ahead, then substantial resources will need to be devoted to it, a somewhat unlikely contingency for some years ahead at least.

However, the future is by no means entirely bleak. The local authorities are under pressure from the DES to increase the provision they make for the release of staff for in-service training, a provision which they acknowledge is in the best interests of their colleges but which shortage of money has inhibited in the last few years. If, hopefully, the economic situation of the country improves and money becomes available for this purpose, the LEAs will certainly send more and more of their teachers on in-service courses. However, it is to be hoped that they will not concentrate their resources unduly on courses which lead to the award of a professional qualification but will also heed the advice of the first Haycocks Report and release staff from their colleges of higher education and the like who wish to obtain a higher degree in a subject area.[18] The polytechnics have for some years been expanding their research activities, despite the low priority accorded to this activity in the 1966 White Paper, and they are increasingly being joined in their endeavours by the colleges of higher education; for this development to be well-founded, it is necessary to deploy staff who, through the training provided by higher degree courses, are themselves well versed in research. Nor must the vocational concerns of further education be ignored: these must reflect areas of dynamic growth and recent developments in such diverse areas, for example, as the para-medical field and electronics. The changes in the colleges flowing from the work of TEC and BEC and the Manpower Services Commission also have important implications for staff development. In these respects, further education is subject to considerably more change than the school sector and the only way the teaching staff in the colleges can keep abreast of such changes is through an adequate programme of teacher education and staff development.

9 Research and curriculum development in further education

Educational research in general may be characterized by three main objectives: it should advance the body of knowledge of disciplines which form the subject matter of education; it should contribute a stream of information to educational decision-makers; and it should improve the teaching and learning processes and other practices within the educational system.[1] In this chapter, our concern is with research *into* further education, wherever undertaken, and not, therefore, with technical or scientific 'subject' research which is being undertaken within the further education establishments themselves. Neither shall we be considering those aspects of educational research which, although being conducted within the further education sector, are essentially concerned with schools or with the theoretical aspects of education. In other words, our interest lies in those aspects of educational research which are relevant to the further education sector as distinct from the school sector and the universities. Thus, we shall also be interested in research into relevant vocational training, wherever it may be conducted, for example by the Manpower Services Commission or by an industrial training board.

Curriculum development, in the context of this chapter, is precisely what the term implies, namely the development of curricula for use in the further education sector. A considerable body of work in this field is now going on, not only in further education establishments and in a few universities, but also more recently under the auspices of the examining and validation bodies and the newly established Further Education Curriculum Review and Development Unit (FEU). Indeed, it is most heartening that both research and curriculum development in further education have grown considerably during the past decade. Ten years ago, relatively little research into further education was being conducted and curriculum development was virtually non-existent. However, although the position is improving steadily, the further education sector still lags substantially behind the school sector in both respects.

176

Research into further education

When considering the growing range and variety of research into further education, it is necessary to consider a number of factors, of which perhaps the most important is the problem of overlap with other areas of the educational system and with training for industry and commerce. As we have seen, the last decade has witnessed an enormous expansion of advanced course provision within the further education sector. As a result, research into topics like the methods of teacher-training for further education and staff development in polytechnics and colleges of further and higher education are within our remit. In addition, there is a great deal of overlap between further education on the one hand and secondary schools and adult education on the other. Consequently, there is much research activity that is relevant to all three sectors of the educational system and it is important to be aware of what is going on in contiguous fields. Finally, education and training is a continuous spectrum of activity and, as a good deal of research work is going on in such bodies as the Manpower Services Commission and the Industrial Training Boards, it is necessary to be conversant with it in so far as it is relevant to the work of the further education colleges.

Our first task is to survey those major research activities which have been completed, or are still in progress. In order to compile an accurate picture of this work one has to turn to a variety of sources. Firstly, there are a number of *reviews* including those by ourselves and by W. van der Eyken.[2] Under this heading come the Coombe Lodge Reports issued periodically by the Further Education Staff College and the recent extremely comprehensive report of a research workshop on the transition from school to work held in Bruges in July 1977 under the auspices of the Institute of Education and Cultural Foundation of the Council of Europe.[3] In this context, the work of the Further Education Research Association (FERA) is particularly significant. Set up in 1973, largely thanks to the efforts of Willem van der Eyken, its membership has grown to embrace more than 70 colleges. It publishes the *FERA Bulletin* which is an important source of up-to-date information on current educational research into further education, and from time to time issues surveys of educational research among its members. Still in a formative stage, FERA meets regularly in London and more recently established a northern branch which meets in Manchester. In this way, it enables the staff of the member institutions to come together to discuss individual research projects as well as to undertake collaborative research. Its significance lies in the fact that it is the only indigenous research association thrown up by the further education colleges themselves. Although at present only one in ten of them belongs to it, that number is likely to grow in proportion to the increase of research activities within the establishments.

Other important sources of information on research into further education are *Registers* and *Abstracts*. Among the more important of a growing number of registers are the Register of Educational Research in the United Kingdom, published by the NFER, and the Training Research Register issued by the Training Services Division of the Manpower Services Commission (MSC); informative abstracts include Higher Education Abstracts published by Kingston Polytechnic Library; Technical Education Abstracts; and Training and Development Abstracts published by the Education Resource Information Centre (ERIC). Useful *bibliographies* include those issued by the British Association for Commercial and Industrial Education (BACIE), and those on Vocational Education by the Council of Europe. In addition, a growing number of *theses* and *dissertations*, produced mainly by staff and research students of universities, polytechnics and other further education establishments, are available; lists are published in the ASLIB Index, in the Register of Research in Adult Education of the University of Manchester, in a 1976 Survey issued by FERA, and in compilations issued by the Colleges of Education (Technical), for example, the Research Abstracts produced by the Educational Research Unit at Bolton College of Education (Technical). Another important source of information is provided by a wide range of *journals*. Among the most useful are the *BACIE Journal*; *Education and Training*; *Industrial and Commercial Training*; *Journal of European Industrial Training*; *NATFHE Journal*; *Technical and Vocational Education*, published by the Council of Europe; the recently-established *Educa*, a digest for technical and commercial education; *The Vocational Aspect of Further Education*; and the *Journal of Further and Higher Education* (see Appendix 3).

In addition, there is a very wide range of other bodies and organizations engaged in developing research projects on areas and subjects which spill over into the legitimate concerns of the further education colleges. One such topic is, of course, industrial training and here the Training Services Division of the MSC (formerly the TSA) and the industrial training boards are particularly active. One particularly important exercise, for example, being undertaken by the MSC is the building-up of a pack of easily understandable descriptions of skill and knowledge, transcending individual jobs and occupations, as an aid to increasing occupational mobility and assisting vocational preparation.[4] Among the most active of the industrial training boards in research is the Engineering ITB which has produced a substantial number of Research Reports.[5]

A wide variety of national examining and validating bodies is also engaged in research of one kind or another, including the CGLI, TEC and BEC. The CGLI has been sponsoring research for a number of years, both in universities and polytechnics. In 1974-5, for example, it financed a computer analysis by a research unit at Reading University of traditional examinations and a comparison of student performance in the different examination papers; and in 1975-6 it supported a Brunel University research project into the teaching of mathematics for vocational purposes.[6] In connection with its Foundation Courses, the CGLI sponsored the development of pilot schemes by the staff of the Faculty of Education of Huddersfield Polytechnic under whose aegis groups of teachers have worked over the past few years to produce suitable curricula. More recently, it has set up a new department to provide testing services both in support of its own courses and examinations and for industrial purposes. We have already referred to the somewhat belated setting-up by TEC of a sub-committee to study research and development projects, including evaluation. BEC, on the other hand, established a Research and Monitoring Committee from the outset and gave it the task of advising on possible research requirements and of supervising research on a range of topics including the nature, potential, and cost of BEC courses and methods of monitoring standards.[7]

Only a few years ago it was estimated that of the money spent on educational research in general, only a pitiful 4 per cent went into research into further education.[8] Although the situation today is rather better, it still scarcely reflects the vitally important contribution of the further education sector to our educational system as a whole. Until comparatively recently, the DES itself had done very little in this regard; at long last, however, there are signs that the Department is beginning to play a part in stimulating research into further education by financing a variety of projects. The establishment of the Further Education Curriculum Review and Development Unit (FEU) and the work being undertaken by the Centre for the Educationally Disadvantaged which is based in Manchester are important examples of such initiatives. Furthermore, of great value to those undertaking research into further education are, of course, the volumes of statistics published by the DES. Hitherto, those concerning further education have had to be obtained by the DES through the RACs, a procedure which inevitably resulted in considerable delay. Now, however, the statistics are currently being fed directly into a central DES computer and it is to be hoped that they will more speedily be made available. In this context, it would be helpful if the DES established a common basis for its statistics of the school and further education sectors by, for example, relating them to a similar calendar year instead of having one set based on age or 31 December in a given year and the other on 1 January the following year.

Among the more important national bodies engaged in promoting educational research are the National Foundation for Educational

Research (NFER) and the Social Science Research Council (SSRC). Although the NFER is mainly concerned with school work, in the last few years it has begun substantially to extend its activities into the further education sector, particularly in the area of overlap with secondary schools, of which a good example is Dean and Choppin's work on education provision for the 16 to 19 age group.[9] In addition, the NFER has sponsored two projects concerned with handicapped students in further education.[10] Moreover, much of the research undertaken by the NFER into the education of older secondary school students is clearly of considerable relevance to many further education teachers. The SSRC has, hitherto, been very largely concerned with fostering educational research within universities and, although it has been anxious to extend its sponsorship into the public sector institutions, the latter have been relatively slow in taking up the opportunity. However, there are now encouraging signs that staff both in polytechnics and in colleges of higher and further education and colleges of technology are responding to the challenge, an interesting example being a recently completed SSRC sponsored project on the work of the CNAA, by M.C. Davis of Lanchester Polytechnic. In this context it is to be hoped that the absorption of the Colleges of Education into the further education sector does not result in a further bias towards school as distinct from vocationally-related issues. Clearly, the pressure on the staff in the new Institutes of Higher Education to undertake research together with their lack of experience of vocational courses within further education will tend to lead them to develop research projects in those areas, namely the schools, with which they are most familiar.

Other national bodies, with more specialist interests, are also active in sponsoring research: two good examples are the National Institute of Adult Education and the Catering Education Research Institute. The former is particularly active in publishing reports on research into adult education both in the British Isles and also on developments in Western Europe of particular interest to this country, such as Paid Educational Leave. Given the very considerable amount of adult education that takes place within the further education sector, the Institute's work is clearly of considerable interest and relevance. The Catering Education Research Institute (CERI) under its full-time Director, Mr John Williams, is located at Ealing College of Higher Education. CERI sponsors research into catering education, in a wide variety of public sector institutions as well as at least one university, and publishes a list of reports on latest developments.

Among the regionally-based organizations which occasionally sponsor research into further education are the Regional Advisory Councils and the Regional Examining Boards. The role of the RACs has varied considerably from one to another and most perhaps have not considered the encouragement of research an important part of their remit. Although, inevitably, they have been inhibited by shortage of funds, a few RACs and REBs have sponsored research projects over the years. These include one on project work by the Department of Educational Studies at Aston University sponsored jointly by the West Midlands RAC and the SSRC, one on the use of case studies in technical teacher training undertaken by a Research Group of tutors under the aegis of the Southern RAC, and a third on current practices and future developments of the Certificate of Secondary Education within the East Midlands by Professor G. Bernbaum and M. Galton of Leicester University sponsored by the East Midlands Regional Examining Board.

Finally, there is a group of national bodies whose interests are not primarily in further education but who have, on occasion, funded projects concerning some further education activity. These include charitable trusts like the Nuffield and Leverhulme Foundations, and bodies like the Council for Educational Technology, all of whom are empowered to make funds available for this purpose. Whilst the small number of projects funded by such bodies may in part be the result of too few worthwhile submissions, it may also be that they have yet to be convinced that research into further education should be given priority in the allocation of funds. In this context, it is encouraging to learn that, at the time of writing, the Council for Educational Technology is appointing a Project Co-ordinator for a project designed to develop guidelines for resource provision and management in institutions of further education. Another national body of significance is the Scottish Council for Research in Education, to which the Scottish Education Department is a major contributor of funds. It, too, sponsors occasional research projects into aspects of further education though generally, it gives priority to research into the school sector.

Within individual institutions research activity is, inevitably, related closely to studies being undertaken by individual members of staff many of whom are following diploma or postgraduate programmes on a part-time or full-time basis. Many of these diploma courses are provided by the colleges of education (technical) and their general orientation is towards the improvement of the candidate's professional ability as a teacher rather than as a researcher. Undoubtedly, the most research-oriented of the colleges of education (technical) is Garnett College, London which has for many years housed the ILEA Research Unit. Among its recent publications is the Garnett Adult Multi-Aptitude Test[11] for use by researchers working with further education students, a test which is now being closely monitored by the Unit's director.

As far as the polytechnics are concerned, although they have developed a great deal of research activity overall, specific projects concerned with the further education sector itself are relatively few in number. Among them are the work of the staff development unit at Manchester Polytechnic where research into mathematical developments under TEC is being undertaken in conjunction with FERA; the pilot studies into the development of curricula for CGLI Foundation Courses carried out by the Faculty of Education at Huddersfield Polytechnic; and the various projects undertaken by the Centre for Institutional Studies at the North East London Polytechnic. The latter include studies on the government and financing of the polytechnics,[12] some of which have made a significant contribution to discussions on the future of higher education in the public sector. Mention should also be made of the steady growth in postgraduate studies leading to higher degrees under CNAA regulations, a number of which are concerned with topics of general relevance to the further education sector.

As far as the universities are concerned, their involvement with research into further education is of two kinds. First, a significant number of university tutors are supervising staff from further education colleges who are working for higher degrees either by research or through a taught course which includes a dissertation. Many of the latter understandably select a research area within further education relating to their own experience and expertise; however, as university tutors frequently have relatively little knowledge of the further education sector, this occasionally results in inadequate supervision. Second, there is a small number of universities which are actively engaged in stimulating research into further education: these include Keele, where research projects in co-operation with both the FEU and CERI are being undertaken and where students on higher degree programmes can choose to specialize in courses on further education; Lancaster, which has established a specialist Institute for Research and Development in Post-Compulsory Education under Professor Gareth Williams; Lancaster, Leicester, and Loughborough, which offer the study of further education as optional courses in their higher degree programmes; and University College, Cardiff which has a unique position in Wales in the training of teachers of further education. John Heywood, now Professor of Education at the University of Dublin, and his team have carried out a number of major studies into the education and training of professional engineers, some aspects of which are described in their recently published book on job analysis.[13] Of considerable interest, too, is the work of the Industrial Training Research Unit, which is supported mainly by a grant from the Training Services Division of the MSC. The Unit under the direction of Dr Eunice Belbin is conducting research into the problems of industrial selection and training, a subject of importance to further education particularly in respect of apprentices, and is also undertaking work commissioned by the FEU.

This brief survey of organizations and institutions interested in developing and sponsoring research into further education is a clear indication of a growing volume of activity. However, it remains the case that much of this activity is the work of a small number of dedicated individuals many of whom find it very difficult to obtain funds to develop their research further. It is regrettably true that there has been relatively little growth in the amount of money available for research into further education, with the exception of the area of industrial training where the Department of Employment is able to deploy some of the considerable sums available to it.

From an examination of the position described above, it is possible to draw a general picture of the major current areas of research into further education. Perhaps the most popular subject for examination is that of student selection and performance, including the effectiveness of teaching methods and forms of assessment. Another popular subject concerns student and staff attitudes in further education colleges, including factors which affect student choice of courses and the social background of students. The sociological aspects of further education inevitably provide a fertile field for research and in recent years a number of Conferences on the Sociology of Further Education have been held at which researchers into this particular area have described and compared their activities. The philosophy of further education, particularly its relationship to industry, and comparative further education, including overseas education, are also quite widely studied. There is a growing interest in curriculum development and course design and also in careers guidance and counselling: of particular note is the Careers Guidance Integration Project which the National Institute for Careers Education and Counselling (NICEC), based at Hatfield Polytechnic, is undertaking under the joint auspices of the DES and the EEC and which involves both schools and FE colleges in some five local education authorities. However, although there is a number of studies of the organization of higher education within further education, such as those by Tyrell Burgess and John Pratt, and Michael Locke,[14] very little research has been undertaken into the administration and organization of the further education sector as it relates to non-advanced course provision.[15] In short, although the volume of educational research in the further education sector is increasing, largely perhaps because of the merger of colleges of education with further education colleges, the amount of research into further education itself is still relatively minute as compared to the total amount of educational research sponsored by the university and school sectors.

A major inhibiting factor is undoubtedly the difficulty in obtaining access to the relevant literature. This is partly because, as we have seen, a very wide range of organizations is issuing reports and bulletins of relevance to further education and partly because of problems of library classification. Developments in further education have been taking place so rapidly that library classifications have been unable to keep up with them. Moreover, the multiplicity of classification systems, of which the Dewey and Library of Congress systems are the most common, result in some dubious classification of relevant material. For example, one major university library defines higher education as 'provision for the over-18s' and further education as 'courses, usually of a vocational nature, for youth and adults in local education authority colleges'. While confusion of this sort is understandable, it undoubtedly makes the task of the further education researcher unduly difficult. Nor is his burden lightened by the fact that access to many relevant journals is often extremely difficult; although educational journals are commonly taken by university and polytechnic libraries, for example, the publications of such bodies as the industrial training boards are often conspicuous by their absence. That being said, it must be acknowledged that libraries are almost invariably helpful in obtaining, by one means or another, relevant materials. Here again, there are signs that the position is improving; for example, the Engineering Industry Training Board has recently published a Thesaurus to help those engaged in information-handling in training, education and manpower areas[16] and its author Elizabeth Orna is currently working on a similar document for the Further Education Curriculum Review and Development Unit. Another important growth point is the development of computer-based information retrieval systems. Thus, the EEC is developing its EURONET system[17] to provide on-line access to various bibliographic bases and data banks including the British Library Automated Information system (BLAISE). In addition, the now well-established American abstracting service based at Washington, D.C., on the Educational Resources Information Centre (ERIC),[18] with its growing output of data on areas such as vocational education, is also becoming progressively more accessible to researchers in the United Kingdom.

Meanwhile, the picture we have painted of current research into further education inevitably prompts the question 'Are we directing our research activities to the right targets?' Our answer to this question must regrettably be in the negative and we would suggest that instead more attention should be focused on four major areas of critical importance. The first is the need to make suitable educational provision for the 16 to 19 age group as a whole. While the full-time education of this important sector of the population is receiving substantial attention at the hands of researchers, their interests are far too often directed towards the 'new' sixth former, that is the youngster who stays on at school for only one year after school-leaving age, as illustrated by the work being undertaken by the Schools Council.[19] As we have seen, there is also much attention being devoted to the problem of providing adequate industrial and commercial training for young people, particularly those who are unemployed. What is lacking, however, is a major programme exploring the various ways in which the further education colleges can contribute. It is for this reason that the FEU has commissioned some studies in this area; however, not only is the funding available to the unit quite inadequate to meet the needs, but also its main concern is with curriculum development rather than research. Important topics which require urgent attention include the problems of developing school-college links, the difficulties which arise in the colleges when teaching student groups of very heterogeneous backgrounds, and fundamental studies identifying the strengths and weaknesses of the British system which is based on separating education and training as compared with alternative systems, particularly those practised in Europe.

A second major topic we should be exploring is to identify the knowledge which is required to achieve a satisfactory job performance. Given that the most distinctive, and perhaps the most important, aspect of the college's role lies in the provision of vocational courses, it is regrettable that hitherto insufficient attention has been paid to the content of the theoretical basis of such courses and its relationship to practice. Although there are some encouraging developments, such as the MSC Training Services Division's research into the identification of common skills, the HCIMA survey into 'Tomorrow's Managers', individual studies such as that of Tyrell,[20] and some aspects of the work of the TEC and BEC, it is imperative that much more be done if we are to achieve a satisfactory marriage between theory and practice. A welcome initiative along these lines is that presently being undertaken by the Manpower Services Commission and the Inner London Education Authority, in association with Ashbridge Management College. They are engaged in a two-year project of detailed skills analysis among a sample of fairly common occupations and trades in the inner London area. The resulting data is being used to improve understanding of the wide range of skills required in the competent performance of these occupations, including the extent of skills-commonality among them, and to modify curriculum in a number of work-preparation courses which are being operated experimentally under the MSC's special programmes arrangements.

A third important area which has as yet received relatively little attention is evaluative research. There have been a few important studies such as Susie Kaneti-Barry's evaluation of CGLI Craft Studies courses and the NFER Colleges of Education Curriculum Evaluation Project.[21] In addition, there are at least three current studies relating to TEC developments: the Manchester Polytechnic-FERA evaluation

185

of TEC Level 1 Mathematics; the Garnett College, London, evaluation of TEC Engineering courses; and the FEU evaluation of the impact of TEC on curriculum development processes in the colleges.[22] Another heartening development has been the joint planning by the Society for Research into Higher Education and FERA of a major conference on 'The problems in the Development and Evaluation of Technician Education', held at Garnett College, London, in January 1979. However, this amount of activity is still only a very small proportion of the evaluation research being carried on into developments in the school sector and much remains to be done before further education is properly served in this respect.

Finally, as the success or failure of the work of the colleges depends, in the last resort, upon the quality of the teaching, it is to be regretted that, hitherto, relatively little attention has been paid to the distinctive needs of teachers in this sector, though in some measure the colleges of education (technical) have made a useful contribution. We have described the expansion in staff development programmes now taking place, particularly within the polytechnics and colleges of higher education, but much of the content of those programmes is derived from the practice relevant to schools rather than to further education. Although the problems facing the further education teacher are in some ways comparable with those of his colleagues in the school sector, especially since changes in relation to the education of the 16 to 19s progressively necessitate a common approach, in other respects he has to cope with quite different circumstances. Firstly, the staff recruitment pattern is much more varied and such professional training as is available is likely to be 'in-service' rather than 'pre-service' and, secondly, the students will be much more heterogeneous, for not only will they be of mixed ability but they will be attending courses covering a complete spectrum ranging from vocational to non-vocational. Now that we are on the verge of a considerable expansion of professional training for further education teachers, following the recommendations of the Haycocks Report, research into teacher education is all the more imperative. Garnett College, London, has recently initiated a major review of existing course provision,[23] which could provide a useful starting point for such research.

Curriculum development in further education

As with research into further education, curriculum development has expanded considerably in recent years and there is now a growing number of agencies contributing to curricular change. In respect of higher education within further education, the CNAA has been, and remains, a potent force for promoting curriculum development; by requiring polytechnics and other colleges to construct, submit and justify new courses, it has had a substantial and, on the whole, beneficial effect on the quality of degree courses in the further education sector. At its best, the CNAA approach combines curriculum development with staff development in that it requires the teachers concerned to provide a rationale for their courses which is then worked out in the curriculum design. This is an approach which differs substantially from that of most other further education programmes which are based essentially on 'implementation'. The role of the TEC and BEC has already been referred to in detail in chapter 4, and so will not be dealt with further here. At the non-advanced level, the CGLI has long played an important part in devising curricula and, in recent years, it has ventured into the field of curriculum development on a significant scale. During 1976-7, for example, it operated in collaboration with a number of colleges a pilot scheme to determine the viability of a programme of Communication Studies to run in parallel with its schemes for Craft Studies. Having established the viability of the scheme, work has now begun on a comparable scheme for Numeracy. As we have seen, the CGLI has introduced schemes for Foundation Courses, which are coming increasingly to be appreciated by both educational and industrial interests. Finally, the Institute, having circulated widely a consultative document containing proposals for a comprehensive framework for progression in a career and for the recognition of attainment in both technical education and industrial training, has recently introduced a new policy for its certificates and other awards based upon these principles. It is illustrative of the complexity of provision at this level that the CGLI has felt it necessary to provide in its own words, 'a better "map" to show the public how people attracted to City and Guilds schemes can "navigate through the further education jungle" '.[24]

The Further Education Staff College at Coombe Lodge has also made an important contribution and, indeed, its collection of papers on 'Curriculum Development in Further Education'[25] was one of the first attempts to deal with the application of theoretical principles to curriculum development within the sector. Finally, individual establishments are also involved: for example, the Further Education Centre at Trent Polytechnic is running a project assigned to assist teachers of General and Communication Studies with their curriculum design problems,[26] Wolverhampton Polytechnic offers a course leading to an Advanced Diploma in Curriculum Development, and Bolton College of Education (Technical) offers a taught course on Curriculum Studies in Further and Technical Education leading to an M.Ed. degree of the University of Manchester.

A long-awaited and most welcome development was the establishment by the DES in January 1977 of the Further Education Curriculum Review and Development Unit (FEU). The Unit was set up to act as a focal point for curricular matters in further education and to promote a more co-ordinated and cohesive approach to further education curriculum development in England and Wales. Given that FEU has only a small staff and very limited funds, this is a very tall order. Broadly speaking, the Unit is charged with four main tasks: to review the range of curricula offered by the further education service, identifying overlap, duplication and deficiencies; to determine priorities for action to improve the total provision; to assist in the general development of further education curricula by carrying out specific studies; and to disseminate information on the process of curriculum development. The Unit is financed by the DES on the basis of annual estimates submitted and approved in advance but its policies and programmes are independent of the Department. To this end, its policies are guided by a Board of Management representative of local authorities, teachers, industry and government agencies.

FEU's first Director is Mr Geoffrey Melling, seconded from HM Inspectorate, and its Chairman is the Rev Canon George Tolley, Principal of Sheffield City Polytechnic. During 1977, the Unit acquired a number of full-time staff, including three development officers, and a very modest research budget. Sensibly, therefore, it has decided to limit its activities by giving first priority to curricula for the immediate post-school stage of education, particularly relating to the interface between education and work. Accordingly, it has developed three major initiatives: assisting schemes of Unified Vocational Preparation; working on the further education elements of the Youth Opportunities Programme; and examining the curricular bases of one-year full-time courses for young people who enter further education without a clear vocational or academic commitment. In addition, the Unit has commissioned a series of major studies including an investigation by the Industrial Training Research Unit into the learning styles of young people, an inquiry by Youthaid into alternative further education curricula for those groups most affected by long-term structural unemployment, a survey of the dissemination of curriculum information in further education by a group of staff at Blackpool College of Technology, and a review of the major styles of curriculum design in further education under T.J. Russell at Coombe Lodge. More recently, it has commissioned an analysis of selected curriculum developments within the school and higher education sectors in terms of their styles and strategies, in order to identify the relevance of the lessons learnt for further education; this particular study is being directed by Professor R.F. Kempa and I.F. Roberts at the University of Keele.

Finally, in conjunction with the West Midlands Regional Advisory Council, it has set up a Regional Curriculum Unit to support curriculum change in the colleges. In essence, this is a pilot scheme designed to link the Unit with the RAC, the further education establishments and teacher education both in the public and university sectors. If the scheme is successful, additional regional development officers will be appointed so that it can be extended to other regions.

Given the very modest sums of money available to the Unit, this is a realistic programme of work and one which, if it comes to full fruition, will be of enormous value in making more effective some of the most crucial work presently being undertaken by the further education sector. In the short time it has been in existence it has already produced a number of useful reports, including 'Experience, Reflection and Learning', 'A Postal Survey of FE Provision for the Young Unemployed, 1977', and a 'Review of Research into Aspects of the Education and Training of the Young Part-time students' by Marjorie Holt, (also published in Guy Neave, *op. cit.*) all of which were published in 1978. Much of the credit for the FEU's work must go to the drive and initiative of its Director, Geoffrey Melling. However, if it is to make a more considerable impact on the further education sector, the FEU, once it has established a reputation for effective curriculum development, must be provided with much more money to widen the scope of its operations.

Another agency at work in matters of curriculum development relevant to the further education sector is, of course, the Training Services Division of the MSC and reference has already been made to its work in identifying common skills which transcend specific jobs and occupations. More widely, funds deriving from our membership of the Common Market have become available to sponsor a number of curriculum development projects. For example, the DES acts as an agent for a major EEC programme on the transition from school to work costing some three-quarters of a million pounds; in London, five further education colleges and eight schools are trying out a two-year bridging course for low achievers during the last year at school; and in Sheffield, three comprehensive schools are closely co-operating with further education colleges, the career service and other social services in trying out ways of improving what they offer to low achievers in the last two years at school. Another example of co-operation is that of a grant to Buckinghamshire College of Higher Education to develop joint business administration courses between institutions of higher education in member states of the EEC by which it is planned that staff at Buckinghamshire will work with similar institutions in Osnabruck and Clermont Ferrand.

A small number of individuals have been at work, some of them for years, in the field of the theoretical bases of further education curriculum development. From time to time, they publish the results of their work in learned journals; for example, three useful and informative articles published recently are those by Professor J. Heywood on the classification of objectives, by B.M. James on the relationship of course design to occupational needs, and by I. Clements on the Education and Training of Technicians.[27]

Finally, although local education authorities have had little direct involvement in curriculum development, one notable exception is the Inner London Education Authority whose Curriculum Development Project in Communication Skills has for some years now been stimulating lower-level courses in further education.[28] A communication workshop was set up in the then City College in 1971, which led to the establishment of similar workshops in most other ILEA colleges. A wide range of teaching materials has been developed by teachers and these materials, together with appropriate teaching methods, are used in a variety of courses. Students who have followed an agreed course and achieved a satisfactory standard in appropriate assignments can obtain a CGLI certificate in elementary communication skills. Curriculum development has also been stimulated by some of Her Majesty's Inspectors who organize short courses and gather together local and regional groups of further education teachers to work on materials and teaching approaches.

Despite the encouraging recent increase in the amount of curriculum development activity in further education, it is clear that the sector still lags behind the school sector in this respect. There are a number of reasons for this unsatisfactory state of affairs, perhaps the principal one being that, until the creation of the FEU, further education has had no equivalent body, even on a small scale, to the Schools Council. Moreover, because the emphasis has traditionally been on the provision of vocational courses, the colleges have lacked both trained teachers and also expertise in the theory of curriculum development. Nor has the complexity of further education provision, with the multiplicity of agencies involved and the sometimes conflicting needs and objectives of courses directed towards both education and training, made the task any easier. During the last few years, however, under the spur of such developments as the need to devise appropriate TEC and BEC courses and to respond to initiatives emanating from the MSC, the further education sector has begun to awake from its long sleep and to catch up with the schools sector in developing new curricula and in identifying objectives upon which to base them.

From our survey of research and curriculum development across the further education sector, a number of conclusions clearly emerge. First, it is apparent that if further progress is to be made, then the overriding problem to be faced is that of too few personnel who are experienced and expert in the fields of research and curriculum development and who also have an intimate knowledge of the further education sector and, in particular, of vocational course provision. Whilst research experience can be obtained 'on the job', the most effective means of increasing the availability of suitably qualified researchers is to provide suitable research training programmes. However, as has already been shown, not only is the number of post-graduate programmes allowing specialization in aspects of further education very few and predominantly restricted to the university sector, but also the expansion of such provision is restricted by the shortage of staff with experience of further education and the continuing reluctance of university departments and schools of education to recognize the importance of further education. We must therefore look primarily to the polytechnics and colleges of higher education to put research into further education high on their list of priorities, particularly since they are currently developing post-graduate work. Given that most of these institutions derive their departments and faculties of Education largely from the merger of colleges of education whose staff have hitherto had little or no experience of further education, this will be no easy task.

Another factor inhibiting research and curriculum development in further education has been the relative lack of money available for this purpose, certainly when compared to the funds made available to school-based research, through the aegis of the Schools Council, for example. This is partly because the funding bodies have not been sufficiently educated to the importance of the educational needs of the further education colleges and partly because, given the lack of suitably qualified researchers, the claims on such funds as are available have been very limited. As we have seen, there is a plethora of bodies with an interest in further education, spanning the whole spectrum of education and training, and while many of them, such as the MSC, the industrial training boards, and the RACs, have an interest in promoting a measure of research activity, there is a tendency for them to work in isolation with too little reference to what is going on elsewhere.

Nor have matters been helped by the seeming reluctance of the DES to give as strong a lead as it should. Some years ago, it began to develop an interest in further education research which led it to set up the Further Education Group at Brunel University, under the direction of Willem van der Eyken. However, the grant which was for a five-year period from 1968 to 1973 was not renewed and the group was disbanded. As we have seen, it required individual initiative on the part of van der Eyken and others to establish FERA which, despite the fact that it is the major forum for promoting knowledge of and interest in further

191

education research, receives little or no help from the DES.

The same is true of the Inner London Education Authority's Research and Development Unit in Further Education at Garnett College, London. Established as a Research Unit in 1962, following the recommendations of the Oliver Report of 1960 that research into the content, methods and organization of further education could best be encouraged by concentrating it in the colleges of education (technical),[29] the Unit is responsible to the ILEA Advisory Committee on Research in Further Education. Its remit is to promote research both at Garnett College itself and also at further education establishments in and around the London area. As part of its work, it provides an advisory service for research workers, maintains an index of research in progress, and is developing a research library. In recent years, it has initiated a survey into the backgrounds, abilities and attainments of students in further education and has been examining the working day, timetable and workload of new entrants to further education teaching. However, it obtains only a very small amount of financial support from outside bodies, receiving a mere £1,000 a year from the Social Science Research Council during the period 1975 to 1978. There has been some uncertainty about the future of the Unit, particularly concerning its relationship to the ILEA; however, the recent appointment of Dr I. McCallum to direct it and its retitling as the ILEA Research and Development Unit in the summer of 1977 are clear indications that its valuable work will now continue.

Finally, we believe that both the SSRC and the CNAA should be persuaded to play a major role in encouraging research and curriculum development in further education. Through its Educational Research Board, the SSRC should give priority to research which meets the needs of the further education sector and in addition should consider ways of increasing the number of awards available to institutions capable of providing the right type of research training. Similarly, the CNAA should foster the development of appropriate postgraduate programmes and also lend its weight to make sure that the local authorities and governing bodies of the institutions concerned provide adequate resources for such developments.

No account of research and curriculum development in further education would be complete without acknowledgment of the contribution of the Further Education Staff College at Coombe Lodge in Somerset. Opened in 1963, its purpose is to improve the efficiency of establishments of further education and to provide facilities for education, training and research in all branches of further education. Essentially, the College sees itself as providing a setting where senior staff and others from the further education service can meet one another, as well as people from industry and elsewhere, to exchange information, ideas and experience. The method used by Coombe Lodge, under its director, Mr G.E. Wheeler, is the residential 'study conference', normally of one-week duration, though in addition a number of both shorter and longer conferences are provided. From time to time, it has held Research Conferences, for example, in 1968, 1970, 1973, and 1976, and has published useful reports of the proceedings.

Inevitably, the influence of Coombe Lodge is limited, partly because of restricted finance due to its reliance on funds derived from the Department of Environment which in turn deducts the money from the Rate Support Grant paid to local authorities. Recently, its financial plight has worsened as the Association of Metropolitan Authorities and the Association of County Councils, acting on behalf of the local authorities, have cut its financial allocation by about fifteen per cent. As a conference centre, Coombe Lodge depends very substantially on the syndicate approach which is in turn dependent on the contribution of the participants, many of whom will lack sufficient knowledge or adequate preparation. Its library resources are inevitably limited and the problems of following-up conferences in sufficient detail and of ensuring continuity are almost insuperable. All that being said, however, the College has played a substantial role over the years in the analysis, evaluation and development of the further education system and Coombe Lodge Study Conference Reports have for some time been an important element in the resource materials available to the researcher. Of late, their remit has become wider as they include references to activities in the fields of education and training taking place in Europe. Indeed, the College is anxious to carve out for itself a major role as a centre for feeding European ideas into the British education debate, and for transmitting to education officials in Western Europe analyses of developments in British further education.[30]

The National Foundation for Educational Research (NFER) is another body which, like the Further Education Staff College, has made a contribution to research and curriculum development in further education but which is operating under severe financial constraints. In addition to undertaking a major evaluation of the Colleges of Education Curriculum Project arising out of developments following the 1972 James Report on Teacher Education and Training, the NFER has recently extended its work into the non-advanced further education sector, including an independent evaluation of the unified vocational preparation schemes. However, like all the other bodies engaged in research of this kind, it is dependent upon securing sufficient funds and, perhaps more difficult, recruiting staff with the necessary experience of research and with an adequate knowledge of the further education sector. As we stated at the beginning, this is the biggest single factor inhibiting research and curriculum development in further education.

Finally, looking to the future, one can discern a new dimension which is being added to research into further education, namely its European context. Following Britain's membership of the European Economic Community, it has become more and more important to be informed of cognate developments in Western Europe; this is by no means an easy task as there is an enormous variety of material available, the problem of communication is not readily overcome, and there is a tendency to think of further education in England and Wales in insular terms. However, there is a growing realization that we can learn much from continental practice and thanks to the activities of such bodies as the FEU, FERA and Coombe Lodge our horizons are becoming wider.[31]

10   The future of further education

As we have seen in the course of this book, further education is a highly developed sector covering a field of considerable diversity. It comprises a wide range of establishments including the polytechnics, colleges and institutes of higher education and many other colleges with various titles such as colleges of further education, technical colleges, colleges of technology, colleges of art, colleges of agriculture and evening institutes. In addition, there are a few specialist colleges which receive a grant direct from the Department of Education and Science and a number of independent establishments such as specialist secretarial and correspondence colleges. The great majority of further education colleges are, however, maintained or assisted by the local education authorities. This bewildering range of institutions comprises a very flexible system whose chief glory is, perhaps, that it provides an opportunity for everyone, whatever his or her capabilities in whatever time may be available, to follow a course of education or training. There are no upper age limits and qualifications can be acquired for their own sake or as a means of entry into more advanced courses.[1]

It is hardly surprising, therefore, that the boundaries of the further education sector are not easy to define. At one extreme, it encompasses a very considerable degree of higher education, comparable in standard to that provided by the universities: not for nothing have the polytechnics been dubbed 'the state universities'. At the other, the degree of overlap between the colleges offering non-advanced courses and the secondary school sector is growing all the time, reaching its apogee in the tertiary college. As a sector which has always been distinguished by its provision of vocational courses, its remit extends into the area of industrial and business training, one which has been much affected in recent years by the activities of such bodies as the Manpower Services Commission and the Technician and Business Education Councils. Catering as it does for students of all ages beyond 16, the further education sector purveys a considerable amount of what might otherwise be described as Adult Education; it is also the chief vehicle in this country for the dissemination of Recurrent or Continuing Education.

Like the educational system as a whole, it provides for the education of the disadvantaged who may be said to fall into three main categories: ethnic minorities, girls and women, and the handicapped. Perhaps more than any other sector, because of its concern with the needs of industry and business, it has been strongly influenced by the economic and educational developments that have flowed from our membership of the European Economic Community.

Finally, the variety and diversity of further education are reflected in a complex administrative framework which is subject to a wide variety of influences at all levels, local, regional and national. It is our purpose in this final chapter to examine critically the broad issues we have enumerated above and to suggest how they are likely to develop in the decade that lies ahead.

The provision of higher education in the public sector has, as we have seen, changed substantially during the 1970s as the colleges of education sector has virtually disappeared and the former colleges have for the most part been merged with polytechnics and other further education establishments. To that extent, therefore, the so-called binary line, the division between the public and university sectors of higher education, has become more firmly delineated. In other respects, however, the distinctions between the public sector institutions, particularly the polytechnics, and the universities have become more blurred. In the thirteen years since the binary line was established, with the 1966 White Paper announcing the Government's intention of creating polytechnics, these institutions have undoubtedly come to resemble universities more closely. They are today more and more concerned with degree-level work, their full-time provision has increased, they increasingly draw students from the country as a whole, the social composition of their student body is increasingly like that of the universities, they have developed a range of research activities, they have built up faculties of humanities and social science, and they have established a number of links with international bodies and institutions. On the other hand, it would not be fair to minimize the differences between polytechnics and universities: for example, the polytechnics' orientation is predominantly vocational; their emphasis is much more on teaching than research which in 1976-7, for example, only accounted for 1.2 per cent of polytechnic expenditure as compared to 12 per cent of university income; they have a much smaller stake in post-graduate work; they are not self-validating institutions; and, perhaps most important, they offer a very substantial number of both full-time and part-time sub-degree courses. These are healthy differences but whether they constitute a distinct ethos which clearly distinguishes them from the universities, as is claimed by Mr David Bethel, the Chairman of the Committee of Directors of Polytechnics,[2] is open to question. In any

196

case, as we have pointed out earlier, it is as dangerous to generalize about the polytechnics as a homogeneous group of institutions as it is about the universities.

Looking ahead into the 1980s, we would expect the binary line to become more blurred and the universities and polytechnics to become yet more like one another, though this process will result as much from significant changes in the universities as in the public sector. Higher education increasingly faces the problems of a chronic shortage of resources and the challenge of demographic change, and to meet these problems successfully the universities will have to move away from the exclusive and somewhat limited concept of their function which has hitherto reigned supreme. In the next decade, they are likely to be subject to greater direction nationally, and perhaps regionally, and also to develop much more part-time provision. The polytechnics, on the other hand, assuming the National Bodies recommended by the Oakes Report come into being, will obtain greater room for manoeuvre in the planning and financial management of their own academic programmes and some of them at least should obtain a measure of self-validation in respect of the courses they offer. In all these ways, the universities and polytechnics are likely to move closer together.

What is not to be expected, however, is the disappearance of the binary line altogether. There are those, of course, like Professor Robin Pedley of the University of Southampton, who somewhat romantically advocate comprehensive universities embracing the whole range of post-18 provision, others, like NATFHE, who talk in rather vague terms about the need for a comprehensive system of higher education, and even the editorial column of *The Times Higher Education Supplement* which has suggested the extension of the university sector to include most of the present polytechnics.[3] None of these somewhat radical proposals looks at all likely to come about, for two cogent reasons. First, the existence of the binary system enables the local authorities to be involved in the provision of higher education and its removal, in one direction or the other, would substantially alter the balance of central and local government responsibilities.[4] Second, in our debate on the future role of the polytechnics *vis-à-vis* the universities and vice versa, we must not forget the increasingly important part being played in higher education by the new colleges and institutes of higher education. The binary system provides them with a 'ring fence' within which they can establish their new courses on a sound and professional academic basis and they are not likely happily to acquiesce in its disappearance.[5]

Collaboration has, of course, developed across the binary line in a number of ways. At the local and regional levels, universities and polytechnics are collaborating in respect of courses and research projects and,

197

as we have seen, many colleges of higher education still retain university validation for their courses. One hopes, and expects, that this collaboration will grow during the next decade. If, as seems likely, a national information service on credit transfer comes into being, then transfer between institutions both among those on either side of the binary line and also within the public sector itself will become more common. In administrative terms, the Oakes' AFECs, if they come into existence, will give the public sector institutions organizations similar in some respects to the University Grants Committee and it would be desirable if the three bodies could begin to develop the joint planning of student numbers in higher education.[6] As some would have it, the next logical step would be to amalgamate them along the lines of the Australian Tertiary Education Council, with its responsibility for overseeing the whole of further and higher education. It appears that Scotland is about to go some way along this road by creating a Council for Tertiary Education to advise the Secretary of State on the whole field of post-school education, including universities. However, in England and probably even in Wales, such a development still seems some way off.

Within the public sector of higher education, the relationships between the polytechnics and the new colleges and institutes of higher education are presently working themselves out. The new colleges face an uncertain future: with the anticipated decline in the number of students moving into higher education in the next decade, the disappearance of the Certificate of Education as a route into higher education for students without 2 GCE Advanced level passes or their equivalent, and the problematical future of the Dip.HE, some of them look very vulnerable. Like the polytechnics before them, they are in search of a role and an identity and, in the present harsh climate, they cling together for safety. To these ends, as we have seen, they have established the *Standing Conference of Directors and Principals of Colleges and Institutes of Higher Education*, which has been asking for direct representation on the Oakes' National Body and also requesting a clarification from the Government of their status and role. This will not easily be forthcoming because their future is so uncertain; however, we would reiterate our belief that they do have a distinctive contribution to make, in two important respects: they offer excellent focal points for the local and regional development of recurrent education; and some can uniquely span the divide between non-advanced and advanced further education by providing courses at all levels, thereby becoming institutions of both higher *and* further education. They also contain within their ranks a number of colleges which are wholly or partly administered by the churches and these have come together to form the *Association of Voluntary Colleges*. Representative of 30 establishments, this body was established in May 1978 to advance education in the voluntary colleges and to protect their interests; it is anxious, for example, to clarify its relationships with the Oakes' proposed AFECs. In these ways, the 'third force' in higher education, the newly-established colleges and institutes of higher education, represent a link between the polytechnics and the lower-level further institutions and between the local authority institutions and those administered by the churches.

Another important issue facing the public sector institutions in the next few years is the nature of their relationship with the Council for National Academic Awards. As we have seen, relations between the polytechnics and the CNAA have been strained by the Teesside Polytechnic affair and many of the colleges of higher education have found that measuring up to the validation procedures of the CNAA has been a traumatic business. Although changes in CNAA validation procedures are likely to come about, it is doubtful if they will go as far as the recent suggestion of the Chairman of the Committee of Directors of Polytechnics that individual polytechnics should, like universities, acquire Royal Charters which would enable them to award their own degrees, but with the difference that each degree course would be accredited by the CNAA.[7] If the future role of the CNAA is somewhat unclear at the moment, there seems little doubt that it will survive. Its existence is necessary for two very important reasons: first, as higher education becomes more diverse and accessible, so co-ordination and concern for standards become more, not less, necessary; and, second, it is unlikely that any government would permit wholesale self-validation if only because it would weaken its powers over the general direction of higher education and create a free market in which resources might be wastefully dissipated.[8]

If the future of higher education is, to say the least, somewhat obscure, then the DES has at least tried to cast some light into the prevailing darkness with the publication in February 1978 of its discussion document, 'Higher Education in the 1990s'. The paper is concerned with likely demographic changes during the next twenty years and how best to cope with the anticipated rise, and subsequent fall, in the higher education population between now and 1995. As the basis for discussion, it postulates five possible models representing alternative policy approaches. Of these the one which has attracted most support and attention is Model E which would compensate for the fall in student numbers by drawing on untapped supplies of students by, for example, encouraging more participation by children of manual workers and by developing recurrent education.

In the year or so since the publication of the document, the discussion which it has engendered has significantly shifted its ground. Initially, the discussion was largely concerned with the demographic issues raised in the paper; more recently, however, it has centred around the educational policies to be adopted to meet the likely needs of the 1990s and the institutional changes that will be required. This change of emphasis has been brought about by two major factors: firstly, the growing realization that manpower planning is an extremely imperfect science and that the DES projections about future student populations are largely hypothetical; and, secondly, the increasing indications that the anticipated demand for higher education is not materializing and that, therefore, the public debate on the future of higher education will have to be recast. This is coupled with a growing emphasis, understandable in times of economic recession, on the desirability of providing more vocationally-oriented higher education. Such provision which has, of course, always been a major function of further education, necessarily requires some degree of manpower planning, however imprecise it may be. Moreover, this kind of educational planning cannot function effectively unless it takes into account the manpower requirements of industry and business as a whole as, for example, postulated by a body like the MSC in formulating its training programmes.

When determining the future character and shape of higher education provision, it is clearly essential that it should not be allocated resources at the expense of the rest of further education but that this should be made as part of an overall plan.[9] Quite apart from anything else, higher education can only flourish if there is a sound basis of provision for students who are at an earlier stage in the education system. Among the great virtues of the further education sector are that, uniquely, it caters for the whole post-school age range and also spans the divide between non-advanced and advanced provision. However, as we have seen, this latter fact is not always reflected in the institutional pattern which has developed, with some establishments concentrating almost exclusively on non-advanced and some on advanced course provision. Moreover, due to the process of 'academic drift', the advantages of retaining a continuity of post-school provision within a given institution tend either to get overlooked or, on occasion, not even discussed.

In administrative terms, non-advanced further education has been regarded historically as the responsibility of the LEAs alone, while advanced courses have been rationalized predominantly through the Regional Advisory Council machinery. In recent years, however, the RACs have taken a more global view by considering also non-advanced provision, realizing that more often than not the two areas are interdependent so that it makes little sense to consider them in isolation. The problem is essentially one of securing the correct balance of local and regional interests. Although, administratively, therefore, the situation is changing somewhat at the present time, and in the right direction, one still occasionally gets the feeling of an uneasy truce between those colleges devoted to the cause of non-advanced provision and those concerned very largely with higher education. The antagonisms which exist are exacerbated by the process of academic drift and by the fact that, under Burnham further education salary arrangements, the teaching of advanced courses attracts greater awards than lower-level courses. In general, the dichotomy between advanced and non-advanced further education is not always meaningful and sometimes positively harmful, and likely to become more so in the future as part-time courses and recurrent education are more fully developed. It constitutes a problem, therefore, which will have to be tackled more effectively than has hitherto been the case.

Another vital area where attitudes are changing concerns the relationship between education and training. The traditional British approach has been to regard them as essentially separate, the former provided by the further education colleges and the latter by industry. This approach contrasts sharply with that adopted by many continental countries which include vocational training within the school system and link it closely with education. While further education establishments in England and Wales have, of course, always played an important part in training for industry and business, with the advent of developments such as the MSC-inspired Youth Opportunities Programme and the introduction of Unified Vocational Preparation schemes, they have become more and more involved with the education and training of young school-leavers. These developments have helped to bring the education and training interests closer together leading, for example, to the creation of the Training and Further Education Consultative Group.

The activities of the Manpower Services Commission, with the very considerable sums of money at its disposal, have inevitably generated some friction and apprehension within the education service and, indeed, fears have been expressed that the MSC is more and more dominating the further education sector. More specifically, it has been criticized for failing to involve teaching staff in its decision-making process or, when it has done so, bringing them into the discussions too late. However, the MSC itself has acknowledged the justice of this criticism and has recently improved its procedures accordingly. Some further education colleges have been worried that a number of Skill Centres have provided not just vocational training but also associated educational courses. However, they seem to be very few in number and, if the TOPS schemes are anything to go by, it is patent that a large number of students are following courses of both education and training in the colleges. Finally, there is concern lest some students following

201

non-advanced full-time courses in further education might be tempted to give them up in favour of MSC programmes because of the financial assistance which the latter carry. At the time of writing, some disagreement has been generated between the MSC and the CGLI concerning the latter's intention of developing a national 'employment preparation award' for the Youth Opportunities Programme, in response to requests from colleges and some MSC regional organizations. Similar to the CGLI award for the unified vocational programme, it will be based on the assessment of project work and is intended to provide young people with an incentive to do their best on such programmes. However, the MSC is at present refusing to recognize the award on the grounds that it would be wrong to establish a leaving certificate based on the assessment of performance, particularly for youngsters many of whom have consistently failed within the traditional educational system; instead, it intends to issue its own certificate to everyone completing the programme. Whatever the rights and wrongs of this argument — and there is much to be said on both sides — it arises from one of the fundamental dilemmas of education and training for young school-leavers, how to motivate and encourage them without inducing, for some at least, a sense of failure.

The 'Holland-type' developments initiated by the MSC pose a major challenge to many further education colleges now having to meet the needs of large numbers of young people, many of whom will not be well-motivated towards study. One of the central problems facing those devising courses is how much time should be devoted to vocational training and how much to education in the form of imparting 'social and life skills'. If the programmes are to be successful, then the right balance of education and training must be secured. Moreover, it is important that the courses are taught by the staff best qualified to do so. Some will argue that such teachers are craftsmen and the like who have themselves successfully made the same kind of transition from school to work and have experienced the kind of jobs for which the students are being prepared.[10] It does not, of course, follow that such people are the best teachers and best able to establish good relationships with their students. On the other hand, the traditional teachers of general and liberal studies who in many ways are best suited to teach social and life skills, as far as training and temperament go, may lack credibility with young people because they generally have had little or no experience of the kind of work situation in which the students are involved. This is inevitably a matter of great concern to teachers in the colleges who are presently responsible for General Studies. Perhaps the way ahead is not to try to identify the characteristics of the perfect tutor for the new programmes but to bring together a team of teachers who will contain the sum of the characteristics necessary to teach them successfully.[11]

All in all, the challenge is a very considerable one and, to be met properly, will require the colleges to be given a great deal of help both in matters of curriculum and also pedagogy. In the former area, the contribution of the Further Education Curriculum Review and Development Unit (FEU) is crucial and, as the Unit's first experiences have shown, the colleges depend heavily upon it for guidance in constructing suitable courses. Given the relatively limited resources at the disposal of the FEU, the burden resting upon it is very considerable. As far as pedagogy is concerned, it is important that, in order properly to motivate young people, teaching staff adopt the sort of experiential student-centred approach characteristic of much of general studies teaching. As this approach is very different from that which is traditional in vocational further education, it will involve a substantial change of attitude on the part of many staff, a change which would be facilitated by the provision of appropriate in-service teacher-training.

In the meantime, it would be short-sighted to consider education and training only in the context of the 16 to 19 age group for, if young people are successfully to bridge the gap between school and work, then we require a co-ordinated approach which extends to the education and training of students in their last two years of compulsory schooling and so we need to think rather of the 14 to 19 age group.[12] Certainly, this is the approach adopted by the Engineering Industry Training Board in its recent far-reaching proposals for the reform of engineering craft apprenticeships. At the end of March 1978, the EITB issued its Information Paper 49, 'Review of Craft Apprenticeship in Engineering', in which it proposed a completely new structure of training. This would consist of three parts: first, schools would develop two-year pre-apprenticeship courses for 14 to 16 year-olds, possibly through links with further education colleges, in mathematics, applied mechanical and physical sciences, technology and craft practice; second, on leaving school, young apprentices would spend one year off-the-job on full-time training and associated further education; and third, trainees would then spend at least one year in industry practising their crafts with appropriate further education. At the end of the final period, trainees who reached the necessary standards and were over 18 would qualify for the Certificate of Craftsmanship. The essence of this system is that it would enable apprentices to reach defined standards in the minimum necessary time, which would vary between individuals, instead of a fixed term of apprenticeship as at present, when the Certificate of Craftsmanship is awarded after three or four years' training which usually begins from the age of 16.

The implications of this scheme for both schools and colleges are very considerable indeed. For the former, it would mean the introduction of a pre-apprentice course in practical engineering which would not only pose problems of facilities and staff for many schools but also raise fundamental issues concerning the role of the school in vocational preparation. However, it is interesting to note that Dutch lower technical schools, for example, have for some years offered what is probably the nearest equivalent and their experience, with all the attendant drawbacks and difficulties, suggests it is worth undertaking.[13] Colleges would have to introduce a new pattern of first-year courses for apprentices and to change the part-time engineering craft studies provided for the later stages of training. Predictably, the reactions to these proposals from the education service have been mixed. The NUT, for example, has suggested that if there is to be a vocational course for pupils in the last two years of school, it should be broadly based so as to provide a foundation course for a range of industrial apprenticeships, not just for engineering, and NATFHE, having initially given the proposals a cautious welcome, has since expressed similar reservations and concern that opportunities for career choice at the age of 14 and 16 are not restricted and that further education and the schools should be fully consulted before any curricular changes are agreed. In any case, the new scheme will not be cheap to run, the cost to fall partly on the MSC and partly on the employers. In the meantime, consultations are continuing and it is still to be seen if the proposals are generally acceptable. If nothing else, however, they will have brought further education, the schools and industry together to discuss the education and training needs of a section at least of 14 to 19 year-olds. This process should be further extended and developed so that the needs of this age group, and the teacher-training requirements of the teaching staff involved, are identified and catered for.

This process should be made easier by the fact that, as we have seen, a growing degree of overlap between further education and the secondary school sector has developed in recent years. It should gather momentum in the next few years as demographic changes lead to a reduction in the size of the 16 to 19 age group and so necessitate a rational use of provision both in the secondary schools and the colleges. As we have suggested, one consequence of this may be that tertiary colleges become an increasingly attractive solution to the problems which many LEAs will face of concentrating provision for 16 to 19 year-olds in a limited number of institutions. As far as GCE A Level provision is concerned, it may be possible to bring school and further education courses together in the shape of the community college, as developed by Leicestershire and a number of other local authorities.[14] This sort of development would be greatly facilitated if the DES would direct its attention to reducing the discrepancies between regulations governing the schools and further education sectors respectively.[15]

Finally, the secondary schools and further education share one major responsibility in common, namely that of ensuring that young people are enabled to bridge successfully the gap between school and work. Sadly, we are one of the few major industrial countries in the world lacking a policy for a smooth transition from school to work. As in many other areas, we rely instead on an *ad hoc* approach to the problem in which both the secondary schools and the further education colleges have key roles to play. It is all the more important, therefore, that co-operation between the two sectors is close and effective. It would be wishful thinking to suppose that this is everywhere the case at present and much could be done both by LEAs and teachers' unions to bridge the gap between them. In this respect, the 1978 NUT Conference on the Education and Training of the 14 to 19 age group marks a useful step forward.

As we have already indicated, another major area of overlap is that which exists between further education and what is generally described as adult education, not least because the further education colleges offer courses of education and training to very substantial numbers of adults. Traditionally, adult education has been regarded as the provision of non-vocational education of a recreational or cultural nature. The main agencies involved in this provision are the further education colleges, the extra-mural departments of universities and organizations such as the Workers' Educational Association. Of the three, the further education sector is by far the biggest provider and in November 1976, for example, about 1,800,000 students were enrolled by LEAs at their adult education centres and evening institutes on a very wide range of recreational and cultural courses, from handicraft, dressmaking and cookery to art, archaeology, and foreign languages. These courses are offered mainly on an evening-only basis, but in response to a demand from housewives and others who have day-time leisure, a growing number of centres offer courses during the day.

There is, however, a newer concept of adult education which takes the form of recurrent or continuing education and it is significant of the growing impact which this concept is making that the Government chose to give its 1977 Advisory Council responsibility for Adult *and* Continuing Education.[16] In general terms, recurrent or continuing education is based upon the principle that individuals should be able to return to education throughout their lives, alternating or accompanying periods of organized educational study with other activities, especially work. This concept is particularly well-established in Western Europe where it is sometimes described as 'éducation permanente'. Clearly, our educational system already contains substantial elements of recurrency,[17] with the further education sector as the main vehicle of provision.

Apart from the recreational provision described above, perhaps the largest amount of recurrent education in Great Britain occurs in the form of part-time day release. Virtually restricted to 16 to 21 year-old apprentices, it caters only to a small minority of the age group: in 1977-8, for example, about 268,000 young people under the age of 19 years, representing only just over 18 per cent of those not in full-time education, were attending day release courses in colleges of further education in England and Wales, consisting of about 29 per cent of the boys of this age and only 7 per cent of the girls. Dissatisfaction with this state of affairs has led to repeated demands for the introduction of compulsory day release, the latest being that from NATFHE, in May 1978. However, as we have indicated, the introduction of compulsory day release is not in our view a practical proposition, partly because we lack the resources to carry it through and partly because it is doubtful if such an obligation could be enforced on youngsters who were unwilling to attend the further education colleges. More practicable, and heartening, is the undertaking given by the Secretary of State to a conference organized in June 1978 by the National Union of Teachers on the education and training of 14 to 19 year-olds that the Government considered the expansion of day release to be 'the next big step forward'.[18] Mrs Williams made it clear that substantial difficulties would have to be overcome, such as the possibility that if employers were obliged to offer their young employees day release – though the latter would not be under an obligation to take it up – it might cause conflict between them and make young people relatively less attractive to employers with a corresponding rise in youth unemployment. Subsequently, discussions have been taking place with the Department of Employment about the form which an extension of day release might take. While any extension is very welcome, it is perhaps in order to regard the Government's pledge with some scepticism; after all, a direct promise to introduce compulsory day release was included in the 1974 Labour Party manifesto, only to be dropped like a hot cake after the election.

In the meantime, we look forward to the day when the education and training of the 16 to 19 age group is thought of as a national responsibility and not merely as a matter which is seen in the context of the current economic recession or the short-term manpower needs of industry and business. Some form of national scheme is required which is educationally satisfactory, capable of implementation with our limited resources, and likely to be reasonably attractive to the youngsters concerned[19] – admittedly, a tall order.

In more general terms, part-time day release can be seen as part of a larger principle, namely Paid Educational Leave (PEL), that is a system of educational leave of absence from employment without loss of income. The movement to PEL has gathered force in Western Europe in recent years and was the subject of a general conference of the International Labour Organization, held in Sweden in 1974, which adopted a convention that it should be provided through voluntary action and collective bargaining between the two sides of industry, with encouragement from central government. The United Kingdom was a signatory to this convention and endorsed its commitment to PEL in a subsequent White Paper (Cmnd 6236). When it comes to provision, however, we lag behind other countries in Western Europe[20] and, given the current economic climate, we are unlikely to witness much extension of PEL in the near future. However, a major research project into PEL is currently under way, funded by the DES and the MSC, and its findings should help to stimulate parallel research and, eventually perhaps, greater provision.

Of course, part-time provision is not restricted to day release and PEL, and an increasing number of part-time degree and other advanced courses are available in the further education sector. In 1976-7, for example, CNAA part-time first degree courses increased to just over 15 per cent of all their courses as compared to 12.5 per cent in the previous year, and student numbers rose to over 6,750 as compared to just over 4,500 in the previous year. In addition, the Council is planning to alter its regulations to allow students on specific courses to follow a combination of full-time and part-time study, a development which is likely to increase the number of mature students on CNAA programmes. In general, the further education sector has made far greater provision for part-time students than the universities who, with the exception of the Open University with its 55,000 students all of whom are part-time, have a relatively small commitment in this area. The Open University has also been one of the main agencies promoting the interchangeability of credit, that is the willingness of institutions and examining bodies to accept the value of each other's courses and facilitate the transfer of students from one institution to another. In 1977, it reached an agreement with the CNAA whereby, under certain conditions, Open University students can transfer to CNAA courses at polytechnics and colleges of higher education, and vice versa.

Both bodies have been active in pressing on the Government the need to set up a major agency to oversee credit transfer arrangements in higher education throughout the country. Some transfer of students already goes on, for example, from a two-year Dip.HE programme in a college of higher education to a third-year course in a polytechnic leading to a degree. However, such transfers are made on an informal basis and are relatively limited in number. Credit and transfer schemes are, by contrast, common-place in the United States and, if they could be developed in this country, would help to promote the growth of recurrent education. It is encouraging, therefore, that the DES has set up a working party to study all aspects of a national credit transfer agency. The first major product of the working party is a feasibility study being conducted under the direction of Peter Toyne of the University of Exeter to see whether it is practicable to establish a national information service to provide comprehensive information on credit transfer arrangements. Mr Toyne is due to make an initial report in Summer 1979 and it is to be hoped that he will find that it is indeed practicable to establish a national agency. If so, it will mark another stage in the gradual erosion of the academic exclusiveness which has hitherto made it so difficult for students to transfer from one institution to another. Looking further afield, one may envisage credit transfer not just within the United Kingdom but between the countries of Europe, an eventuality to which the Council of Europe's committee for higher education has been giving thought in a series of monographs on the problems of student exchange between institutions of its member nations.

In the meantime, there seems every likelihood that the next decade will witness an expansion of recurrent education, particularly on the basis of part-time higher education. Developments in this field figure prominently in the plans which many polytechnics and colleges of higher education are making for the 1980s.[21] There are a number of reasons why there is likely to be a healthy demand for part-time, advanced courses, particularly those leading to awards. First, there is a growing demand for training and staff development from large groups of people, among them, as we have seen, teachers of further education themselves. Second, the establishment of the colleges of higher education has put an institution offering advanced work within reach of the great majority of the population, a development which in itself is likely to encourage part-time study. And, third, and perhaps most important, the number of colleges offering or aspiring to offer advanced courses is increasing faster than the demand for full-time study; as the number of 18-year-olds declines into the 1980s, the colleges will increasingly see their salvation in the provision of recurrent and continuing education.

The likely expansion of part-time students will, however, call for a major re-adjustment by the staff of the colleges in terms of curriculum development and teaching methods. While part-time students, on the whole, make fewer demands on conventional teaching resources, they do require a range of other learning materials, college support services and liaison with sponsoring employers.[22] Moreover, something will have to be done at the national level to rectify grant regulations which discriminate against part-time students and those who are not following an orthodox academic route. The awarding of discretionary grants, for example, has become increasingly arbitrary and capricious as LEAs have sought to cut back on local government spending and the successive increases in tuition fees by the Open University and other bodies have made the lot of the part-time student more and more difficult. The present grant structure was designed very largely for a higher education system in which the great majority of students study on a full-time basis; if we wish to encourage greater provision of part-time courses, then we need a thorough overhaul of the present regulations for student support.[23]

One of the major features of further education in recent years has been the growth in provision for the educationally disadvantaged. Although it is not easy to designate those who are 'disadvantaged', they fall broadly into the four categories identified by the Centre on Educational Disadvantage: ethnic minorities, women and girls, underachievers, and special school-leavers, particularly those designated Educationally Sub-Normal. We shall concern ourselves with three groups — ethnic minorities, girls and women, and the handicapped — who, although they are defined by different criteria, are all disadvantaged in various ways and, indeed, individuals may fall into more than one category.

The major ethnic minorities may be broadly defined, in the words of the Office of Population Censuses and Surveys, as people of New Commonwealth and Pakistan origin. They numbered 1¾ million in Great Britain in 1976, of whom 353,000 were in the age group 15 to 24. They live mainly in the four English regions of Yorkshire and Humberside, the Midlands, the North West and the South East and they tend to be further concentrated into inner-cities with all their social and environmental problems. Although ethnic minorities resident in Great Britain are composed of immigrants, and descendants of immigrants, from many differing cultures and races, they face in common a number of difficulties.[24]

It seems that a disproportionate number of immigrant school-leavers find themselves in the lower academic groups in schools and therefore find job seeking more difficult and are less likely to move on to further education than their white contemporaries. Many recent young immigrants, particularly those from Asia, who have obtained most of their schooling overseas, may have a limited knowledge of the English language. And, as we have seen, because of the pattern of immigrant settlement, young people from ethnic minorities are disproportionately affected by inner-city problems. It is therefore not surprising that, since the beginning of the present recession at the end of 1973, the number of young unemployed people from the ethnic minority groups has grown faster than the rate of the total of young people unemployed.

It has long been an established feature of our educational system to identify and assist youngsters with special educational needs, a tradition in which the further education colleges play an important part. In addition to special programmes related, for example, to the learning of English as a second language, the further education colleges, especially those in the inner-city areas, provide a means of obtaining recognized educational qualifications and training eagerly sought after by many young people from immigrant groups. This is particularly true of the Asian community with its cultural tradition of staying on in education as long as possible. A very difficult problem, however, is that of the significant numbers of young blacks who, enmeshed by poverty, homelessness and unemployment, are alienated from the official agencies which should be helping them. However, further education which traditionally has responded sympathetically to changing needs and demands is uniquely placed to provide them with not only a 'second chance' but also genuine equality of opportunity.[25]

In recent years, the growing problem of long-term unemployment among young people, especially of young blacks who are disadvantaged because of their colour and background, has led the Manpower Services Commission to recognize its special responsibility to them. Its earlier schemes, such as the Job Creation and Work Experience Programmes, attracted a considerable degree of participation from young people from ethnic minorities. In developing its Youth Opportunities Programme, the MSC is sensibly seeking the help of organizations representing racial minorities, recognizing that, to a considerable extent, the success of its programmes will depend on taking their interests fully into account. As we have seen, YOP includes a larger educational component than its predecessors, with a special emphasis on Communication and Life and Social Skills. As we have already emphasized, the provision of this component and also of appropriate vocational elements will pose a considerable challenge to the further education colleges. They will be faced with a greatly increased number of short courses, with students, many of them from ethnic minorities, coming and going at all times of the year, and with a demand for extra accommodation. Consequently, there will be a need for rapid in-service training and curriculum development of an imaginative kind, designed to appeal to a wider range of interests and abilities than ever before.[26]

The Government's concern for the educational needs of ethnic minorities was expressed in the White Paper of August 1974, 'Educational Disadvantage and the Educational Needs of Immigrants' which, among other things, recommended the establishment of an information centre 'concerned with giving advice on curriculum, teaching methods and good practice generally relevant to the education of the disadvantaged'. This recommendation led to the setting up of the Manchester-based Centre on 'Educational Disadvantage which began work in January 1976. The Centre provides an information and advice service and operates through a team of field officers. It also publishes a bi-monthly Newsletter, *Disadvantage in Education*, and a variety of other publications.

While the Centre is doing a very useful job, its scope is clearly limited and if the ethnic minorities are to be more fully provided with educational opportunities, then the further education colleges must respond effectively to the challenge. In 1976, the then Community Relations Commission published a booklet entitled 'A Second Chance: Further Education in Multi-Racial Areas' which contained a number of recommendations to LEAs, RACs, further education colleges and others, designed to promote proper multi-racial education and provision. The booklet recommended, among other things, the provision of appropriate courses and of suitable staff training, the appointment in every further education college in a multi-racial area of a full-time member of staff with special responsibility for ethnic minority students, the adoption of an appropriate language policy, the establishment of close contacts with minority communities, and the provision of special admissions and counselling services. While some of these proposals have considerable financial implications, others could be implemented without undue expenditure given the necessary determination. If nothing else, however, they provide a useful starting point for the further education sector to consider the role it can play in the promotion of proper and effective multi-racial education.[27]

An examination of the statistics of students on courses leading to recognized qualifications in the further education sector reveals the extent to which women and girls are disadvantaged. Thus, of the total of about 1,212,000 in November 1975, fewer than one-third were women. Within these global figures there are even greater differences, for although women are in the minority in every category of study the disparity is particularly great in part-time day release where there were only 104,000 women to some 450,000 men. The present provision of further education courses for women is still very largely in the 'traditional' occupations of teaching, nursing and secretarial work. The same is true of relatively highly-qualified women, for as the September 1974 White Paper on 'Equality for Women' revealed, some three-quarters of all women with qualifications at GCE Advanced level and above are employed in the health and educational fields. It remains to be seen whether the current reduction in teacher-training places and the consequent needs for girls who would formerly have entered teaching to consider alternative careers will encourage a greater diversification of roles. At present, however, it is depressingly true that, 'Women, like Cleopatra, may display infinite variety, but their career choices are notoriously predictable'.[28]

There are a number of obvious reasons both for the smaller percentage of women than men undertaking courses of higher education and also for their limited choice of employment. As a recent EEC survey illustrates, chief among them are family commitments, male attitudes and occupational attitudes.[29] Nor, in many cases, have women themselves helped their cause; it would appear, for example, that many girls at the stage of making career decisions have relatively low aspirations while mature women often undervalue themselves and their potential.[30] Social changes like earlier marriage and the decline in the birth rate suggest that more married women will return to work after only a few years at home in which case the further education colleges will clearly have an important part to play if they are to be retrained in jobs which will match their potential.

In the meantime, if experience in the London region is anything to go by,[31] there has been a steady, if unexciting, growth in recent years in the percentage of women of all students enrolled on further education courses. Doubtless, this increase has been partly stimulated by social factors and partly by recent legislation such as the 1975 Equal Pay and Sexual Discrimination Acts, and the setting up of the Equal Opportunities Commission. Certainly, there has been a number of encouraging developments such as the recent expansion of TOPS courses which in the year ending March 1978 provided over 43,000 training places for women although, regrettably, these were mainly in the traditional sphere of office work. On the other hand, the Equal Opportunities Commission has accused higher education of failing to provide adequately for women despite their growing demand for places; indeed, the Commission sees the current planning debate, centering around the report, 'Higher Education in the 1990s', as a golden opportunity to redistribute the benefits conferred by higher education and so remedy the relatively disadvantaged position of women.

However, despite the fact that virtually throughout further education the enrolments of women students are increasing both relatively and absolutely, the rate of improvement is slow and, even if it continues, it will be another thirty years before the number of women students is equal to that of men. Given the present industrial recession, it is difficult to envisage the radical changes that will be necessary if this rate of improvement is to be greatly increased, not least because of the fundamental changes in attitude that will be required. In the meantime, the further education colleges, as one of the prime agencies of educational provision for women and girls, could do much to help by, for example, providing more courses in non-traditional subjects for older women and making girl school-leavers more aware of the training opportunities outside the traditional occupations.

As far as our third category, the handicapped, is concerned, nobody knows how many people have handicaps or how many handicapped people follow further education courses.[32] Certainly, as the Warnock Report has pointed out, it comprises a category which extends beyond the physically handicapped and includes many people who could benefit from further education but are not doing so. Although many colleges have made considerable efforts to provide access for physically handicapped students and to meet their special counselling and teaching needs, a substantial proportion have made little provision.[33] While a few colleges run special courses for the handicapped, aiming to integrate them into society or to enable them to adapt to employment, the majority fit them into their normal classes. A small number of colleges have adopted the questionable policy of linking provision for the physically handicapped with remedial education for the educationally handicapped or under-privileged. In general, it is clear that provision varies considerably from college to college and from region to region, so that in some subjects and in some areas of the country, the handicapped are effectively deprived of the educational opportunities which they need as much as, if not more than, other groups in society.[34]

British society in general and our educational system in particular have for too long been characterized by an insular outlook and a rather smug complacency. Now that we are members of the European Economic Community these attitudes are even more out of date. Moreover, the educational problems that beset us are not unknown across the Channel and we have much to learn from practices in other European countries. Certainly, the truth of this seems to have been borne in upon the Secretary of State: at a recent conference of the ministers of education of the 24 member states of the Organisation for Economic Co-operation and Development (OECD), held in Paris in October 1978, she is quoted as commenting, 'I knew that there were similarities in our problems, but I really did not appreciate until now the extent to which our own experiences in Britain are paralleled in nearly every other country represented here.'[35] If statements of intent are considered to be important, then this conference was an achievement in that it produced a ten-point declaration of policy priorities on which the ministers agreed, though needless to say without any legal commitment to put them into effect. The points are inevitably somewhat anodyne and include such aims as helping the young prepare more effectively for adult life and work by working towards the best possible balance between general and vocational education, stimulating the development of more recurrent educational opportunities for young people and adults, and facilitating the transition of young people to adult life by, among other things, giving them an opportunity to obtain usable vocational qualifications.

While such general statements of intent doubtless serve a useful purpose, they do not necessarily result in the successful implementation of a common policy. For example, the European Economic Community's common policy on vocational training, based on broadly similar principles to those of the OECD, has run into considerable difficulties and officials ascribe the lack of success partly to the fact that there is no methodology to translate abstract principles into concrete action and partly because there has been insufficient distinction between short-term activities such as the exchange of information and long-term ones such as harmonizing practices.[36]

What is more important and useful, therefore, is to acquaint ourselves with developments in other countries which bear directly upon the problems we are currently facing. Of major interest, for example, are the ways in which Western Europe is tackling the problem of educating and training the 16 to 19 age group, at a time when youth unemployment is almost everywhere on the increase. There is reason to believe that education and training are integrated more effectively both in Sweden, where the Upper Secondary school is the main vehicle of vocational training,[37] and West Germany, where part-time day release is compulsory until the age of 18 and where teachers in vocational schools must have at least one year's experience in industry. As we are intending to expand our system of day release and have instituted a small-scale scheme of giving limited industrial experience to secondary school teachers of subjects such as engineering science and physics, we can doubtless learn much from German experience in these matters. As we have seen, another area of major concern to further education where we have much to learn from European practice is adult and recurrent education. In an increasing number of continental countries, the aim is to make adult education part of the overall system of permanent education and, in the present decade, France, West Germany, Norway, Italy and Belgium have all passed legislation concerning the establishment of a pattern of vocational training for adults within a framework of permanent education.[38] As is to be expected, putting the legislation into effect has turned out to be far from easy and, in that respect too, West European experiences are very instructive.[39]

Other issues which must now be considered in their European context include job mobility and the consequent need to ensure comparability of qualifications; the desirability of establishing credit transfer arrangements with other European countries, particularly in respect of joint business and industrial ventures; and the growing number of students who, as part of their course, are on industrial placements in Western Europe. These developments should lead, among other things, to an extension of the presently small-scale exchange of staff between institutions in different countries and a growth in linked research activities. A growing number of further education colleges have established links of one sort or another with other European countries, especially among the polytechnics who, from an early stage, were aware of the need to come to terms with the implications of our membership of the EEC.[40]

Our membership of the European Economic Community is proving helpful to further education in two other ways. First, as part of the EEC's regional and social policy, sums of money are available to sponsor individual projects such as those of particular interest to a specific region which could be hampered or delayed due to lack of funds. One such example is the project based on the Inner London Education Authority and funded by £150,000 of EEC money spread over three years.[41] It involves some 120 young people in various parts of London who are currently taking part in developing linked courses between schools and colleges of further education. There seems no reason why other areas should not capitalize in similar fashion upon EEC funds. Of wider application and eventual importance, however, is the substantial growth in European literature relevant to the concerns of British further education. We have already cited a number of such books and articles which we consider important and we would only add that, to those interested in education and training and youth unemployment, the various European organizations are publishing a growing stream of useful publications.[42]

Meanwhile, in England and Wales, the present decade has witnessed a number of major changes in the provision and validation of courses of further education. For example, the CGLI is moving out of technician education and concentrating on the provision of courses at the craft level and on its Foundation Courses and awards for the Youth Opportunities Programme; the remit of the Technician Education Council has been extended into the field of art and design education and a similar process seems to be happening for agricultural education; the Business Education Council has taken over responsibility for all courses of business education below degree level; and the CNAA has subsumed the role of the former National Council for the Diploma of Art and Design, has moved into the field of Educational Studies and teacher-training, and has taken over responsibility for the Diploma in Management Studies. Whether this administrative rationalization will also make for improved courses, more relevant to the needs of the 1980s, only time will tell.

The administrative framework of further education is also likely to undergo a series of changes, most of which depend upon political decisions. At the time of writing, the future of legislation stemming from the Oakes Report which will create national bodies for the financial management and academic planning of higher education in the public sector is uncertain; a new role for the Regional Advisory Councils is also dependent upon the implementation of the Oakes' recommendations and the re-organization of the administrative structure of teacher education; the National Advisory Council on Education for Industry and Commerce has gone and so far nothing has been put in its place; the Further Education Sub-Committee of the Advisory Committee on the Supply and Training of Teachers, having produced three reports on the training of further education teachers, may or may not continue its existence; and the relationships between the Manpower Services Commission and the DES in the field of education and training are in process of being clarified. These developments are indicative of the multiplicity of levels at which further education operates and the many interests and influences which affect its provision.

As with the schools, responsibility for the provision of further education is placed firmly on the shoulders of the local education authorities by the 1944 Education Act. However, as we have indicated, local control of further education is by no means so clear cut as in the case of the school sector, either as regards financial management or academic planning. As we have seen, the polytechnics and many of the colleges of higher education draw most of their funds from the 'pool', so that in terms of financial management they may be said to lie somewhere between the locally-controlled schools and the 'autonomous' universities. The position in regard to academic planning is equally complex since, although resource allocation is ultimately the responsibility of the local authorities, numerous other bodies such as the RACs, the CNAA, the CGLI, TEC and BEC, not to mention the DES and the college academic boards, all have a hand in course approval and validation. In these circumstances, it is hardly surprising that many polytechnics and other colleges are seeking a greater degree of autonomy. One way to achieve this, would be, in the words of one polytechnic director, 'to lift the polytechnics out of the rut of local control'.

It seems highly unlikely that this will happen, nor would it necessarily be desirable. If the polytechnics were left to their own devices, they would, in the view of Tyrell Burgess and others, lust after false gods by promoting 'academic drift' and generally emulating the universities. Burgess, by contrast, would make the provision of all further education, including higher education, a matter for local authority provision by means of money raised from rates and taxes, like that for the rest of education.[43] By implication, this would appear to remove the necessity for any regional machinery such as the RACs and would place the polytechnics and other colleges unequivocally under the control of the LEAs. However, as we have been at pains to point out, further education is *not* like the rest of the education service, regional machinery of some kind *is* necessary, and the polytechnics are in many

216

ways national institutions, too important to be left to the tender mercies of the LEAs. This is not to argue for cutting them off from contact with the locality or for removing all vestiges of local control. But it is desirable that they should acquire that greater measure of freedom, particularly regarding academic planning and financial management, which they should obtain if, and when, the proposed AFECs come into being. In any case, it is very doubtful if the local authorities have the understanding and expertise to administer further education in its entirety. As we have pointed out, some sort of regional machinery, like the RACs, is essential and it is to be hoped that before too long a government decision to recast the Councils in a manner which is calculated to make them both more efficient and more effective will be forthcoming.

In the course of the last ten years, we have been involved in the somewhat masochistic task of writing three books on the further education system in England and Wales. Of the three, this has undoubtedly proved the most difficult, if the most fascinating, to write. This may be because as our understanding of the sector has grown so we have come to realize that it is not nearly so straightforward as we once thought. More likely, however, it is because the present decade has been a period of considerable growth and development and of ever-increasing complexity. For this reason, we have recast the nature of the book and attempted to concentrate on a critical analysis of the most important issues which today face further education. While drawing attention to areas of concern which have hitherto been neglected, like provision for the 16 to 19 age group and the need for much more research into further education, we have attempted to paint a synoptic picture of further education as it is at present and as it is likely to develop into the 1980s. We would conclude by reiterating our profound conviction that there is great need for someone to take an overall view and to give further education a sense of direction. In our opinion, that someone can only be the DES. As in many other respects, however, the DES needs sound advice, which can only come from informed public debate. One way of stimulating such debate would be to appoint, without delay, a new advisory body to fill the void left by the demise of the National Advisory Council on Education for Industry and Commerce. The membership of this body should span industry, commerce, and the education service, including the universities, and its terms of reference should embrace both advanced and non-advanced further education as well as teacher education. As a result of its deliberations, it will undoubtedly conclude that the time has come for a new framework Education Act which would replace the 1944 Act. In addition to sorting out the legal tangles created by a succession of amending acts over the last 35 years,[44] a new Education Act should realistically

217

reflect the immense growth of further education during that time and help to give it a new sense of purpose.

Appendix 1 Definitions

Further education comprises all forms of post-school education
except the Universities. Much further education is broadly vocational
in purpose but it also includes provision for continued general
education and for cultural and leisure activities. It is normally
sub-divided into advanced further education (AFE) and
non-advanced further education (NAFE).

Advanced further education consists of all courses leading to a final
qualification above Ordinary National Certificate (ONC) or GCE A -
level; these include not only degree and post-graduate work but also the
TEC and BEC Higher Certificates and Diplomas and many other courses
leading to professional and other qualifications such as courses of initial
teacher-training.

Non-advanced further education consists of all courses leading to a
final qualification up to and including Ordinary National Certificates
and Diplomas or GCE A level; these include City and Guilds (CGLI)
courses and TEC and BEC Certificates and Diplomas.

Adult education is provided for both within and without further
education. In further education, it comprises a wide range of general,
non-vocational courses provided by local education authorities. Outside
further education, courses of general education, usually in the
humanities, are provided by extra-mural departments of universities,
by the Workers Educational Association and by some residential
colleges.

Recurrent education has been interpreted in a variety of ways.
However, a broadly acceptable interpretation is that adopted by the
Organisation for Economic Cooperation and Development (OECD),
namely that recurrent education is an alternative mode of educational
opportunity in which education is provided throughout an individual's
lifetime and in alternation with other activities, particularly with work.
Another broader concept does not tie recurrent education to the
principle of organized educational study and periods of work, but
recognizes that these two activities may be concurrent or even

219

synonymous. The term *Continuing education* is sometimes used more or less as a synonym for Recurrent education.

Appendix 2 Reports, circulars and administrative memoranda

Department of Education and Science

1972

Teacher Education and Training (James Report)

Circular	4/72	Education: A Framework for Expansion.
AM	4/72	Report of the Committee of Enquiry into Teacher Education and Training.
AM	6/72	Training for the Future, a Plan for Discussion.
AM	7/72	The Education (No. 2.) Act. Establishments of Further Education other than Colleges of Education.
AM	12/72	Approval of Courses leading to the Diploma in Art and Design.
AM	6/66	(Addendum to No. 4.) Charges for Industrial Training Provided by Colleges of Education.
AM	21/72	Cost Allowances for Further Education and Colleges of Education.

1973

Adult Education: A Plan for Development (Russell Report)

Report of the Joint Advisory Committee on Agricultural Education (*Hudson Report*), NACEIC.

Circular	1/73	Local Government Act 1972. Reorganisation of Local Government: The Education Function.
Circular	7/73	Development of Higher Education in the Non-University Sector.
AM	9/66	(Addendum 5) Charges for Industrial Training provided by Colleges of Further Education.
AM	12/72	(Addendum 1) Approval of Courses leading to the Diploma in Art & Design.
AM	6/73	Report of the Committee of Inquiry into Adult Education in England and Wales.
AM	7/73	Establishment of the Technician Education Council.

221

1974

Circular	6/74	Development of Higher Education in the Non-University Sector: Interim Arrangements for the Control of Advanced Courses.
Circular	7/74	Work Experience.
AM	5/74	Report of the Working Group on Vocational Courses in the Design Technician Areas.
AM	12/74	Report of the Joint Advisory Committee on Agricultural Education.
AM	14/74	Amalgamation of the Council for National Academic Awards and the National Council for Diplomas in Art and Design.

1975

The Training of Teachers for Further Education (Haycocks Report), ACSTT.

Circular	5/75	The Reorganisation of Higher Education in the Non-University Sector: The Further Education Regulations 1975.
Circular	6/75	The Colleges of Education (Compensation) Regulations 1975.
Circular	13/75	Revised Conditions for the Recognition as Efficient of Independent Establishments of Further Education.

1976

Circular	6/76	Government Statement on Unified Vocational Preparation. A Pilot Approach.
Circular	10/76	Approval of Advanced Further Education Courses: Modified Arrangements.
Circular	11/76	Education Act 1976.
AM	11/76	Implementation of the Report of the Joint Planning Group on Links Between the Training Services Agency and the Education Service.

1977

Circular	10/77	Unemployed Young People: The Contribution of the Education Service.
Circular	11/77	The Training of Teachers for Further Education.
AM	4/77	Further Education for Unemployed Young People.
AM	12/77	Links between the Training and Further Education Services.

1978

Report of the Working Group on *The Management of Higher Education in the Maintained Sector* (Oakes Report) Cmnd 7130.

Higher Education into the 1990s.

Report of the Committee of Enquiry into *the Education of Handicapped Children and Young People* (Warnock Report) Cmnd 7212.

Circular	2/78	Tuition Fees in Further Education.
Circular	5/78	Further Education and Public Libraries in Wales.
Circular	14/78	Admission of Overseas Students to Courses of Further Education.
Circular	15/78	Welfare of Overseas Students in Establishments of Further Education.
AM	3/78	Report of the Working Group on the Management of Higher Education in the Maintained Sector.

1979

Three important consultative papers were issued by the DES: *16-18: Education and training for 16-18 year olds*, issued jointly with the Department of Employment, February 1979; *A Better Start in Working Life: Vocational preparation for employed young people in Great Britain*, issued jointly with Departments of Employment and Industry, April 1979; and *Providing educational opportunities for 16-18 year olds*, April 1979.

Management Review of the Department of Education and Science, Report of a Steering Committee, DES, May 1979.

Commercial and Business Studies in the Schools and Colleges of Wales, Welsh Office, HMI Wales, Education Survey T, HMSO, 1979.

The DES also issues *Further Education Circular Letters (FECL)* from time to time, for example, FECL 1/72: T14/75/031, 'Joint Committee for Ordinary National Certificates and Diplomas in Engineering, Ordinary National Diploma in Technology (Engineering)'.

Appendix 3 Sources of information

Abstracts

British Education Index
(4 issues annually) British Library, Bibliographic Services Division,
7 Rathbone St., London, W1P 2AL.

Current Index of Journals in Education
(12 issues)

Higher Education Abstracts
(4 issues) Kingston Polytechnic, Penrhyn Rd., Kingston-upon-Thames,
Surrey, KT1 2EE.

Research Abstracts
Bolton College of Education (Technical), Chadwick St., Bolton, Lancs.

Research into Higher Education Abstracts
(4 issues) SRHE Publications, University of Surrey, Guildford, Surrey,
GU2 5XH.

Resources in Education
(12 issues) Educational Resources Information Center (ERIC), National
Institute of Education, Washington D.C. 20208.

T & D Abstracts
Continuation of *CIRF Abstracts*; publication ended with Vol. 3, 1978.
ILO, CH 1211, Geneva, Switzerland.

Technical Education Abstracts
(4 issues) Information for Education Ltd., Room 302, 19 Abercromby
Square, Liverpool L69 3BX.

Bibliographies

Annotated Bibliography (1968-77)
Technical and Vocational Education
Council of Europe, Council for Cultural Co-operation, Committee for
General and Technical Education, Strasbourg.

A Bibliography of Educational Administration in the United Kingdom
Howell, D.A. NFER Publishing Co. Ltd 1978.

BACIE Bibliography (ongoing)
Vol. 1-4 BACIE Publications 1977.

Orna, Elizabeth, *Thesaurus*
EITB Library and Information Service 1978.

Research Registers and Research Reports

EITB Research Reports

FERA Survey of Research Amongst Members 1976

FEU Annual Report

Current Educational Research Projects Supported by the Department of Education and Science (DES), List 1.

Register of Current Research in Further Education
Brunel FE Monographs 1. Hutchinson Educational 1971.

Register of Current Educational Research Projects (annual)
Funded by Scottish Education Department.

Register of Educational Research in the U.K.
Vol. 1 1973-6, Vol. 2 1976-7, (ongoing)
NFER Publishing Co.

Register of Research in Progress in Adult Education 1976 and 1977
Manchester Monographs, Department of Adult and Higher Education, University of Manchester.

Register of Research into Higher Education
SRHE.

Register of Research into Higher Education in Western Europe
1974-7, SRHE 1977

Research Supported by SSRC
Annual publication complemented by information in SSRC Newsletter (4 issues).

Register of Educational Development Services in Polytechnics
SCEDSIP Standing Conference.

Schools Council Project Profiles and Index
Schools Council Project Information Centre.

Training Research Register
TSD, 162 Regent St., London W1R 6DE

Brunel Monographs 1-6
Hutchinson Educational.

SOURCES OF INFORMATION

SRHE Research Reports
SRHE Publications.

Statistics of Education
Vol. 3 Further Education (annual)
DES, published by HMSO.

Statistics of Education in Wales
(annual) DES, published by HMSO.

Bulletins, Journals and Reports

ACFHE Memoranda and Reports
Association of Colleges for Further and Higher Education.

APT Bulletin
Association of Polytechnic Teachers (monthly).

BACIE Journal
(quarterly) British Association for Commercial and Industrial
Education.

BECNEWS
Business Education Council.

CBI Education and Training Bulletin
(4 issues) (+ Supplements)
Confederation of British Industry.

Coombe Lodge Reports
The Further Education Staff College.

DES Reports on Education
Department of Education and Science.

Education
(weekly)
Councils and Educational Press Ltd.

Education and Training
(11 issues) ABE Publications, 10 Dryden Chambers, 119 Oxford St.,
London W1R 1PA.

EDUCA
A digest for technical and commercial education (3 issues)
Guildford Educational Services Ltd., 164 High St., Guildford, Surrey,
GU1 3HW.

European Training
(3 issues) University of Bradford Management Centre and Durham
University Business School.

Educational Research News
(2 or 3 issues) National Foundation for Educational Research.

Evaluation Newsletter
(2 issues) Joint Committee for Research in Teacher Education (CRITE) and Society for Research in Higher Education (SRHE) publication.

FERA Bulletin
(irregular) Edited by Dr. A.J. Pickup, Research and Development Unit, Garnett College, Roehampton Lane, London SW15 4HR.

Higher Education
(6 issues) An international journal, Elsevier.

Industrial and Commercial Training
(monthly) Wellens Publishing.

Journal of Business Education
(irregular) Faculty of Business, Huddersfield Polytechnic.

Journal of European Industrial Training
MCB Publications Ltd., Bradford, West Yorkshire.

Journal of Further and Higher Education
incorporating Education for Teaching (3 issues)
NATFHE Hamilton House, Mabledon Place, London WC1H 9BH.

Liberal Education
Journal of Association for Liberal Education

MSC Publications
e.g. Annual Report, Annual Review and Plan, Newscheck (12 issues)
Manpower Services Commission.

NASD Journal
(2 or 3 issues) Journal of the National Association for Staff Development.

NATFHE Journal
(9 issues) National Association of Teachers in Further and Higher Education.

OECD Observer
(6 issues) OECD Information Service, 2 rue André Pascal, F75775, Paris.

Staff Development Newsletter
c/o Educational Development Unit
Ealing College of Higher Education, St Mary's Road, Ealing, London W5 5RF.

Studies in Higher Education
(2 issues) SRHE Journal. Carfax Publishing Co., Oxford.

TECNEWS
Technician Education Council.

SOURCES OF INFORMATION

Training and Further Education Consultative Group Bulletins
(irregular) available from DES or TSD.

Trends in Education
(4 issues) DES (HMSO).

Times Educational Supplement
(weekly) Times Newspapers Ltd.

Times Higher Education Supplement
(weekly) Times Newspapers Ltd.

Vocational Aspect of Education
(3 issues) Colleges of Education (Technical)
c/o BCET, Chadwick St., Bolton BL2 1JW.

Appendix 4 Further reading

ASHWIN, CLIVE (ed.), *Art Education: Documents and Policies, 1768-1975*, SRHE 1975.

BRISTOW, ADRIAN, *Inside the Colleges of Further Education*, 2nd ed. 1976, H.M.S.O.

BURGESS, T., *Education After School*, Penguin, 1977.

CURZON, L.B., *Teaching in Further Education*, An outline of Principles and Practice, Cassell, 1976.

DONALDSON, LEX, *Policy and Polytechnics*, Saxon House, 1975.

HENCKE, DAVID, *Colleges in Crisis*, The Reorganisation of Teacher Training 1971-7, Penguin, 1978.

KING, E.G., MOOR, C.H., and MUNDY, J.A., *Post Compulsory Education: The Way Ahead*, Sage Publications, 1975.

KING, RONALD, *Schools and Colleges*, Studies of Post School Education, Routledge & Kegan Paul, 1976.

LANE, MICHAEL, *Design for Degrees*, Macmillan Press, 1975.

LANG, JENNIFER, *City and Guilds of London Institute Centenary 1878-1978*, a historical commentary, CGLI Publications, 1978.

LOCKE, M. and PRATT, J., A Guide to Learning after School, Penguin, 1979.

MACMILLAN, PATRICIA and POWELL, LEN, *An Induction Course for Teaching in Further Education and Industry*, Pitman, 1973.

NEAVE, GUY (ed.), *Research Perspectives on the Transition from School to Work*, Swetz and Zeitlinger, Amsterdam, 1978.

PRATT, J., TRAVERS, T. and BURGESS, T., *Costs and Control in Further Education*, NFER Publishing Co., Ltd., 1978.

RUSSELL, G.J., *Teaching in Further Education*, Pitman, 1972.

RUSSELL, J. and LATCHAM, J. (eds.) *Curriculum Development in Further Education*, F.E. Staff College, Coombe Lodge, 1973.

SPRINGETT, J., *Further Education Outside the Polytechnics*, Association of Colleges for Further and Higher Education, 1975.

WHITBURN, JULIA, MEALING, MAURICE, COX, CAROLINE, *People in Polytechnics*, SRHE, 1976.

Appendix 5 Glossary of abbreviations and addresses

ACACE
Advisory Council for Adult and Continuing Education.

ACFHE
Association of Colleges for Further & Higher Education, at Sheffield
City Polytechnic.

ACRA
The Association of College Registrars and Administrators
Hon. Publications Officer, c/o Churcher's College, Petersfield, Hants.

APC
Association of Principals of Colleges
East Herts College, Turnford, Broxbourne, Herts EN10 6AF.

ACSTT
Advisory Committee on the Supply and Training of Teachers.

APT
Association of Polytechnic Teachers
Throgmorton House, 27 Alphinstone Rd., Southsea, Hants.

BACIE
British Association for Commercial and Industrial Education
16 Park Crescent, Regent's Park, London W1N 4AP.

BEC
Business Education Council, 76 Portland Pl., London W1N 4AA.

CBI
Confederation of British Industry, 21 Tothill St., London SW1H 9LP.

CED
Centre for Information and Advice on Educational Disadvantaged,
11 Anson Rd., Manchester M14 5BY.

CERI
Catering Education Research Institute,
Ealing Technical College, Woodlands Ave., Acton, London W3 9DN.

CGLI
City and Guilds of London Institute
F.E. Department, 46 Britannia Street, London WC1X 9RG.
Publications & Sales Section, 76 Portland Place, London W1N 4AA.

Colleges of Education (Technical)
Bolton College of Education (Technical),
Chadwick St., Bolton BL2 1JW.
Garnett College
Downshire House, Roehampton Lane, London SW15 4HR.
Huddersfield Polytechnic
Holly Bank Rd., Lindley, Huddersfield HD3 3BP.
The Polytechnic Wolverhampton
Faculty of Education, Compton Rd. West, Wolverhampton WU3 9OX.

College of Preceptors
Coppice Row, Theydon Bois, Epping, Essex CM16 7DN.

CDP
Committee of Directors of Polytechnics, 309 Regent St.,
London W1R 7PE.

Coombe Lodge
The Further Education Staff College, Blagdon, Bristol BS18 6RG.

CNAA
Council for National Academic Awards
344-54 Gray's Inn Road, London WC1X 8BP.

DATEC
Design and Art Committee of the Technician Education Council.

EITB
Engineering Industry Training Board
PO Box 176, 54 Clarendon Rd., Watford WD1 1LB.

FERA
Further Education Research Association
Sec. Ann Robinson, Southgate Technical College, High St.,
London N14.

FEU
Further Education Curriculum Review and Development Unit,
Elizabeth House, York Rd., London SE1 7PH.

ITB
Industrial Training Boards (there are 27 in all)
For addresses, see *Personnel and Training Management Yearbook and Directory*, Kogan Page.

ITRU
Industrial Training Research Unit Ltd.,
32 Trumpington St., Cambridge.

Joint Committee for National Certificates and Diplomas
76 Portland Pl., London W1N 4AA.

MSC
Manpower Services Commission
Selkirk House, 166 High Holborn, London WC1V 6PF.

NICEC
National Institution for Careers Education and Counselling
The Polytechnic, Hatfield, Herts.

NATFHE
National Association of Teachers in Further and Higher Education
Hamilton House, Mabledon Pl., London WC1H 9BH.

NEBSS
National Examinations Board in Supervisory Studies.

NFER
National Foundation for Educational Research
The Mere, Upton Park, Slough, Bucks SL1 2DQ.

IPT
Institute of Professional Tutors (originally Association of
Professional Tutors)
Secretary: Leonard Stubbs, South Downs College of Further
Education, College Rd., Purbrook Way, Havant, Hampshire.

RAC
Regional Advisory Councils
For addresses, see *The Education Authorities Directory and Annual.*

REB
Regional Examinations Boards
For addresses, see *The Education Authorities Directory and Annual.*

RMC
Regional Management Centres.

RMCA
Regional Management Centre Association.

RSA
Royal Society of Arts., 6-8 Adam St., Adelphi, WC2N 6EZ.

Rubber and Plastics Processing Industry Training Board,
Brent House, 950 Great Western Road, Brentford, Middx.

Schools Council, 160 Great Portland St., London W1N 6LL.

SCEDSIP
Standing Conference on Educational Development Services in
Polytechnics, c/o Petras, Newcastle upon Tyne Polytechnic, Ellison Pl.,
Newcastle upon Tyne NE1 8ST.

Standing Conference of Principals and Directors of Colleges and
Institutes in Higher Education
Chairman: J.V. Barnett, The College of Ripon & York St John,
Lord Mayor's Walk, York, YO3 7EX.

SCOTBEC
Scottish Business Education Council, 22 Great King St., Edinburgh
EH3 6QH.

SCOTEC
Scottish Technician Education Council,
38 Queen St., Glasgow G1 3DY.

SCRAC
Standing Conference of Regional Advisory Councils.

SIAD
Society of Industrial Artists and Designers
12 Carlton House Terrace, London SW1Y 5AH.

SRHE
Society for Research into Higher Education,
University of Surrey, Guildford, Surrey, GU2 5XH.

Standing Conference of Sixth Form and Tertiary College Principals
Joint Sec.: G.L. Cooksey, Greenhead College, Huddersfield, Yorks.
HD1 3ES.

Tertiary College Panel
Sec.: J.C. Miles MA, Bridgwater, Somerset TA6 5HW.

SSRC
Social Science Research Council,
1 Temple Ave., London EC4Y 0BD.

TEC
Technician Education Council, 76 Portland Pl., London W1.

TOPS
Training Opportunities Scheme of Manpower Services Commission.

TSD
Training Services Division of Manpower Services Commission,
180 High Holborn, London WC1.

UKSC
United Kingdom Standing Conference of Management Heads.

YOP
Youth Opportunities Programme under Special Programme Division
(SPD) of Manpower Services Commission.

References

CHAPTER 2

1 *The Educational System of England and Wales*, DES Booklet, February 1977, p.2.
2 *How the DES is Organised*, DES Booklet, April 1977, p.2.
3 For a summary of the report, see *The Times Higher Education Supplement*, 9 May 1975.
4 See, for example, Lord Crowther-Hunt, 'Long-term planning takes second place', *The Times Higher Education Supplement*, 7 May 1976, p.7.
5 *Policy Making in the DES*, 10th Report from the Expenditure Committee, HMSO, 1976.
6 D. Hencke, *Colleges in Crisis*, Penguin, 1978.
7 As suggested in a paper from the Centre for Institutional Studies, North East London Polytechnic, reviewed in *The Times Higher Educational Supplement*, 13 January 1978.
8 'Functions of a Future NACEIC', NACEIC Minutes, 14 May 1976.
9 D.E. Regan, *Local Government and Education*, George Allen & Unwin, 1977, p.176.
10 D. Mumford, 'A 30-year triumph of hope over experience', *Education*, 5 December 1975, p.iv.
11 John Pratt, Tony Travers and Tyrell Burgess, *Costs and Control in Further Education*, NFER Publishing Co. Ltd., 1978, p.195.
12 D.E. Regan, *op. cit.*, 179.
13 See, for example, 'Significance for universities of regional councils', *The Times Higher Education Supplement*, 7 November 1975.
14 Peter David, 'New Education Bill will implement Oakes Report', *The Times Higher Education Supplement*, 3 November 1978.
15 D.E. Regan, *op. cit.*, p.173.
16 M. Locke in J. Pratt and T. Burgess, *Polytechnics: A Report*, Pitman, 1974, p.168.
17 L.B. Curzon, *Teaching in Further Education: An Outline of Principles and Practice*, Cassell, 1976, p.199.
18 D. Charlton, W. Gent, B. Scammells, *The Administration of Technical Colleges*, Manchester University Press, 1971; L.B. Curzon, *op. cit.*, 192-201; B. Tipton, *Conflict and Change in a*

Technical College, Hutchinson, 1973; and various Reports issued by the Further Education Staff College, Coombe Lodge.

19   *CNAA Annual Report 1977*, p.17.
20   Jennifer Lang, *City and Guilds of London Institute, Centenary 1878-1978*, CGLI, 1978.
21   *The Certificates, Diplomas and Other Awards of the Institute*, A Policy Statement, CGLI, September 1978.
22   *Variety or Chaos*, A Discussion Document, APC, 1978.
23   See, for example, *Glossary of Some Terms in Common Use in Further Education*, ACRA, second edition, 1978.

CHAPTER 3

1   See, for example, 'The 16s-19s — their Education, Training and Employment', Draft Policy Statement, National Association of Teachers in Further and Higher Education, *NATFHE Journal*, May 1977, pp.8-10; and I.F. Roberts, '16-19: The Vital Age Group in FE', *Education and Training*, May 1977, pp.134-6.
2   For a full discussion of student attitudes, see Peggie Sharp, *Students in Full-time Courses in Colleges of Further Education*, Sixth Form Survey, Vol. II, Schools Council, London, 1970.
3   'Examinations at 18+: The N and F Studies', Schools Council Working Paper 60, Evans/Methuen Educational, 1978, Appendix E, 260-4.
4   'Universities and the N and F. Proposals', Standing Conference on University Entrance, Spring 1978, 16.
5   Schools Council Working Paper 45, pp.16-19: *Growth and Response*, 1. 'Curricular Bases', 1972, and 2. 'Examination Structure', 1973. Evans/Methuen Educational.
6   Schools Council, *'Moving towards the CEE'*, 1975, p.2.
7   *Examinations at 18+*, Schools Council Examinations Bulletin, 38, Evans/Methuen Educational, 1978, Chapter IV, pp.252-86.
8   For detailed descriptions of the various forms of provision for the 16 to 19 age group, including tertiary colleges, colleges of further education, sixth form colleges and secondary schools, see Ronald King, *School and Colleges; Studies of Post-Sixteen Education*, Routledge & Kegan Paul, 1976.
9   W. Alexander, *Towards a New Education Act*, Councils of Education Press, 1969.
10   For details, see *1978 Compendium of Sixth Form and Tertiary Colleges*, Greenhead College, Huddersfield, Yorks; and Fred James and John Miles (eds.), *Tertiary Colleges*, Bridgwater College, Somerset, 1978.
11   Judy Dean and Bruce Choppin, *Educational Provision, 16-19*, National Foundation for Educational Research, 1977.
12   'The 16s-19s — their Education, Training and Employment', *op. cit.*, p.9.

REFERENCES

13 See, for example, 'Statement on a Curriculum for Extension of Day Release', NATFHE, 1977, and T. Burgess, *Education After School*, Penguin, 1977.

14 *The Vocational Preparation of Young People: a discussion paper*, Training Services Agency, May 1975.

15 See *Education for the Future*, ATTI, 1970; *Education of the 16-19 Age Group – part-time*, ATTI, 1973; and *Education for the 16-19s*, NACEIC, Papers for discussion in Council, October 1974.

16 Gerry Fowler, 'Agenda for Better Days', *The Times Higher Education Supplement*, 15 April 1977, p.10.

17 DES Administrative Memorandum 12/77, 'Links Between the Training and Further Education Services', 1 August 1977.

18 Josephine Gilbey, 'Unified Vocational Preparation – a progress report', *NATFHE Journal*, December 1977, 8.

19 G. Stanton, *Experience, Reflection, Learning*, FEU, 1978.

20 G. Holland, 'Help where it counts', *The Times Educational Supplement*, 14 April 1978.

21 Mark Jackson, 'Ragged army of trainers take shaky first steps', *The Times Educational Supplement*, 14 April 1978.

22 *Ibid*.

23 G. Holland, *op. cit*.

24 *Ibid*.

25 For a full discussion of the characteristics and advantages of the Tertiary College see 'The Tertiary College', chapter 5, Dean and Choppin, *Education Provision, 16-19, op. cit.*, 47-52.

26 'The 16s-19s; their Education, Training and Employment', NATFHE Draft Policy Statement, July 1977, para. 33.

27 'Moving towards the CEE', Schools Council Statement, April 1975, p.3.

28 NATFHE Draft Policy Statement, *op. cit.*, para. 31.

29 See, for example, L.M. Cantor, *Recurrent Education in the United Kingdom*, S.E.D., October 1977.

30 *Work and Learning*: Proposals for a National Scheme for 16-18 year olds at Work, Third Report of the Study Group on the Education/Training of Young People, Rubber and Plastics Processing Industry Training Board, December 1978.

31 T. Burgess, *Education After School*, Penguin, 1977 and E.J. King, C.H. Moor and J.A. Mundy, *Post Compulsory Education – 2: The Way Ahead*, Sage Publications, 1975.

32 Mark Johnson, 'Whitehall on the brink of a 16-19 age group inquiry', *The Times Educational Supplement*, 3 February, 1978, p.1.

33 *16-18: Education and Training for 16-18 year olds, A consultative paper*, DES/Dept. of Employment, February 1979.

CHAPTER 4

1   Report of the Committee on Technician Courses and Examinations (*Haslegrave Report*), NACEIC, 1969, paras. 149-58.

2   In writing our summary of the work of TEC, in addition to official TEC documents we have drawn principally upon the following articles: D.T. Rees, 'Curriculum Change in Further Education', *Journal of the Faculty of Education*, University College, Cardiff, Vol. 4, No. 3, April 1977, pp.9-18; I.F. Roberts, 'The Technician Education Council: Some Thoughts on TEC as a Curriculum Project', *Education for Teaching*, Autumn 1976, pp.16-28; R. Russell, 'Developments in Further Education, the Technician Education Council', *Industrial Training International*, November 1976, pp.315-7; and P. Santinelli, 'Two part revolution of 1960s comes to fruition', *The Times Higher Education Supplement*, 27 January 1978.

3   I.F. Roberts, 'Time to reappraise the Technician Education Council', *The Times Higher Education Supplement*, 11 June 1976, p.10.

4   J. Mansell, 'TEC: NATFHE Opinion', *NATFHE Journal*, October 1976, pp.8-9.

5   J. MacRory, T. Beaumont and H.T. Taylor, 'Backwards from TEC', *Journal of Further and Higher Education*, Vol. 1, No. 1, Spring, 1977, p.3.

6   *Ibid.*

7   P. Wilby, 'Technicians lost in blackboard jungle', *Sunday Times*, 19 March 1978.

8   K. Ebbutt, 'What is to be done about TEC?', *NATFHE Journal*, March 1977, p.14.

9   'Developments in Teaching, Learning & Research', Trent Polytechnic, No. 10, Spring 1978, p.4.

10 *Ibid.*

11 *TECNEWS*, February 1975.

12 J.R. Rudling, 'Should anything be done about TEC?', *NATFHE Journal*, October 1977.

13 I.F. Roberts, 'The Technician Education Council: Some Thoughts on TEC as a Curriculum Project', *op. cit.*, p.19.

14 J. MacRory *et. al.*, 'Backwards from TEC', *op. cit.*, p.3.

15 *Ibid.*

16 *Ibid.*, p.5.

17 J. Mansell, 'TEC: NATFHE Opinion', *NATFHE Journal*, October 1976, p.8.

18 I.F. Roberts, 'The Technician Council: Some Thoughts on TEC as a Curriculum Project', *op. cit.*, p.24.

19 Dr Harry Law, Director, Preston Polytechnic, quoted in *The Times Higher Education Supplement*, 20 January, 1978.

20 For a description of these and other courses in business education, see L.M. Cantor and I.F. Roberts, *Further Education in England and Wales*, Routledge & Kegan Paul, 1972, 102-26.

REFERENCES

21 For this summary of the work of BEC, we have drawn upon the
    following articles: 'TEC and BEC', *Education*, 18 March 1977,
    pp.i-iv; J. Elliott, 'The shape of business education to come',
    Administrative Accounting, Vol. 30, No. 225, Spring 1976, 57-8;
    and P. Santelli, 'Two part revolution of 1960s comes to fruition',
    op. cit.
22 In a letter to the authors, dated 8 November 1978, from Janet
    Elliott, Deputy Chief Officer of BEC.
23 G. Mace, 'BEC – Which Way Now?', *NATFHE Journal*, August/
    September 1977, p.7.
24 *Ibid.*
25 D. Brace, 'General Studies versus Communication', *Liberal
    Education*, No. 35, 1978, 18-22; and for a discussion of the role of
    general studies in further education, see Cantor and Roberts,
    op. cit., pp.75-9.
26 G. Catchpole, 'Catching the Tide', *Liberal Education*, No. 32,
    1977, p.4.
27 'Assessment for BEC Awards', BEC Circular 4/77, November 1977,
    pp.8-9.
28 G. Mace, *op. cit.*, p.7.
29 BEC National Awards, Course Implementation, Autumn 1977,
    para. 5.1, 11.
30 P. Morris, 'The Proposals of the Business Education Council: A
    Critical Appraisal of BEC as an Exercise in Curriculum
    Development', *Journal of Further and Higher Education*, Vol. 1,
    No. 3, Winter 1977, 6.
31 *Ibid.*
32 Ex. info. Janet Elliott.
33 L.C. Fox, 'The Business Education Council and Distribution',
    Journal of Business Education, Huddersfield Polytechnic, No. 3,
    June 1978, pp.24-9.
34 P. Morris, 'The Proposals of the Business Education Council',
    op. cit., p.13.
35 J. Elliott, 'The shape of business education to come', *op. cit.*,
    p.57.
36 We are indebted for these comments to an unpublished report on
    the development of TEC and BEC courses in a number of East
    Midland colleges by Mrs Lynne Clarke.
37 Haslegrave Report, *op. cit.*, para. 164, p.52.

CHAPTER 5

1 'Higher Education', *Robbins Report*, Cmnd. 2154, HMSO, 1963.
2 See, for example, R. Crossman, *The Diaries of a Cabinet Minister*,
   Vol. I, Hamish Hamilton, 1975, p.326.
3 Cantor and Roberts, *op. cit.*, pp.31-37.
4 *Student Numbers in Higher Education in England and Wales*,

Education Planning Paper No. 2, DES, 1970.
5 For a full and percipient account of this matter and subsequent developments, see David Hencke, *Colleges in Crisis*, Penguin, 1978, pp.45-7.
6 David Hencke, *Colleges in Crisis, op. cit.*, and 'The Government and college reorganisation', *Higher Education Review*, Vol. 9, No. 3, Summer 1977, 7-18; Hugh Harding, 'Harding replies to Hencke over college closures', *Education*, 29 December 1978, pp.631-3 and 'Dull truth transmuted to fool's gold', *Education*, 5 January 1979, pp.11-12; D. Newton, K.E. Shaw and E. Wormald, *Changes in Colleges of Education*, Occasional Papers in Sociology and Education, ATCDE Sociology Section, No. 2, 1975.
7 David Hencke, 'Power of the DES', *The Times Higher Education Supplement*, 18 June 1976, p.11.
8 David Hencke, *Colleges in Crisis, op. cit.*, pp.12-18.
9 'The Management of Non-University Higher Education', *DES Report on Education*, No. 90, May 1977, p.5.
10 *Ibid.*, Table 2, 2.
11 See, for example, E. Robinson, *The New Polytechnics*, Penguin, 1968; T. Burgess and J. Pratt, *Innovation in Higher Education: Technical Education in the United Kingdom*, OECD, 1971; J. Pratt and T. Burgess, *Polytechnics: A Report*, Pitman, 1974; A. Smith, *Many Arts, Many Skills; The Polytechnic Policy and requirements for its fulfilment*, Committee of Directors of Polytechnics; and L. Donaldson, *Policy and the Polytechnics*, Saxon House, 1975.
12 J. Pratt and T. Burgess, *Polytechnics: A Report, op. cit.*
13 T. Burgess, *Education After School, op. cit.*, p.239.
14 J. Pratt and T. Burgess, *Polytechnics: A Report, op. cit.*, pp.23-30.
15 As reported in *The Times Higher Education Supplement*, 20 October 1978.
16 'Lessons of Teesside Collapse', *The Times Higher Education Supplement*, 8 September 1978.
17 A. Suddaby, 'The CNAA: a growing cause for concern', *The Times Higher Education Supplement*, 3 November 1978, p.10.
18 'Report of the Working Group on the Management of Higher Education in the Maintained Sector', *Oakes Report*, Cmnd 7130, March 1978, para. 13.8.
19 L. Donaldson, *Policy and the Polytechnics, op. cit.*, p.200.
20 As reported in *The Times Higher Education Supplement*, 16 June 1972.
21 For example, *Many Arts, Many Skills: The Polytechnic Policy and requirements for its fulfilment, op. cit.*
22 G. Fowler, 'Can Oakes beat the labyrinth that surrounds AFE?', *The Times Higher Education Supplement*, 27 May 1977, p.12.
23 'The Future of Higher Education and the LEA Role', *Coombe Lodge Report*, Vol. 10, No. 12, 1977, p.502.
24 See, for example, Wagner's letter to the editor, *The Times Higher*

Education Supplement, 21 April 1978.

25 G. Fowler, 'Can Oakes beat the labyrinth that surrounds AFE?', *op. cit.*

26 P. David, 'Oakes stirs the local authority pool', *The Times Higher Education Supplement*, 30 December 1977.

27 DES Administrative Memorandum 3/78, 'Report of the Working Group on the Management of Higher Education in the Maintained Sector', 20 March 1978 (Oakes Report), Cmd. 7130.

28 P. Knight, 'The Oakes Report: Ineffective Compromise or Sound Proposals?', *NATFHE Journal*, April 1978, p.10.

29 J. Pratt, T. Travers and T. Burgess, *op. cit.*, pp.226-8.

30 'Oakes: the wrong question is given to the wrong answer', *The Times Higher Education Supplement*, 7 April 1978, p.10.

31 'CNAA must keep its balance', *The Times Higher Education Supplement*, 21 July 1978.

32 T. Burgess, 'Danger lurks in CNAA's new set of regulations', *The Times Higher Education Supplement*, 21 July 1978, p.12.

33 T.R. McConnell, 'The Diploma of Higher Education: Some Dilemmas and Opportunities', *Higher Education Review*, Spring 1977, p.27.

34 'Higher Education into the 1990s: A Discussion Document', DES and SED, February 1978, p.3, para. 9.

CHAPTER 6

1 Sandwich Courses in Art and Design Colleges, Report of London and Home Counties RAC June 1975.

2 For a more detailed description of these courses see Cantor and Roberts, *op. cit.*, pp.132-8.

3 See *Design Education*, (SIAD), No. 6, April 1978, for a description of the foundation courses offered by four different institutions.

4 *Art and Design Education*, A Policy Statement, NATFHE, January 1978.

5 *Design Education*, No. 6, April 1978, p.1.

6 *First Report on Vocational Courses in Art and Design*, IRSCADE, December 1977, para. 6.10.

7 IRSCADE First Report, *op. cit.*

8 'The Structure of Art and Design Education in the Further Education Sector', *Coldstream-Summerson Report*, September 1970.

9 'Vocational Courses in Art and Design', *Gann Report*, HMSO, 1974.

10 Clive Ashwin, 'Art education's artisans', *The Times Higher Education Supplement*, 4 October 1974, p.13.

11 Gordon Lawrence, 'Patterns of Inequality', *The Guardian*, 14 May 1974.

12 See, for example, the Art Institutions Council's observations on the

Gann Report, October 1974.

13 Cited in *The Times Higher Education Supplement*, 11 March 1977, p.2.

14 *Ibid.*, 20 May 1977.

15 *Further Proposals for Art and Design Studies*, DATEC, November 1978.

16 In a letter to the authors dated 18 April 1978.

17 IRSCADE First Report, *op. cit.*, para. 2.8.

18 *Coldstream-Summerson Report, op. cit.*

19 Cantor and Roberts, *op. cit.*, p.143.

20 See, for example, letter from E. Bottomley of Harrow College of Technology and Art in *Design Education*, No. 2, 1976, p.3.

21 *Art and Design Education, op. cit.*, p.9.

22 *Ibid.*

23 *Ibid.*, p.7.

24 'Adult Education: a Plan for Development', *Russell Report*, HMSO, 1973.

25 M. Twyman, cited in *The Times Higher Education Supplement*, 4 October 1974.

26 C. Ashwin, *ibid.*

27 J.E. Blake *et. al.*, 'Report of Art and Design Education Study Conference', *Coombe Lodge Report*, 10 (1), 1977, pp.7-63.

28 For details of full-time and sandwich courses in England and Wales, see *Agricultural Education*, a booklet issued annually by and available from the DES. See also Cantor and Roberts, *op. cit.*, pp.153-9.

29 'Report of the Joint Advisory Committee on Agricultural Education 1973', *(Hudson Report)*, HMSO 1974.

30 *Management Education: Current Developments, Trends and Issues*, British Institute of Management, 1974.

31 Cantor and Roberts, *op. cit.*, pp.116-9.

32 D. Gold, 'Regional Management Centres', *Education and Training*, Vol. 20, No. 7, July-August 1978, p.216.

33 J. Nelson, 'Lesson of RMCs for a policy of "centres of excellence" ', *The Times Higher Education Supplement*, 28 January 1977.

34 P. David, 'Management Centre that knows how to manage itself', *ibid.*, 11 November 1977, p.11.

35 *Ibid.*

36 'First Report on the Supply of Teachers for Management Education', *Nind Report*, National Economic Development Council, HMSO, 1970.

CHAPTER 7

1 WJEC Local Authorities Committee, Minute 2 of Meeting, 29 March 1974.

2 *Teacher Training for the 1980's*, The Polytechnic of Wales,

February 1977.

3   Cited in 'DES accused in reshuffle of Welsh teacher training', *The
    Times Higher Education Supplement*, 29 July 1977.
4   DES *Statistics of Education*, Vol. 3, Further Education, 1975.
5   *Education for 16-19 Age Group*, Report of Conference, 5-7 May
    1978, WJEC.
6   *Principal's Report*, North East Wales Institute of Higher
    Education, 1976-7.
7   *Sixth Form Education in the Schools of Wales*, Education Issues 2,
    Welsh Office, (*Addysg Chweched Dosbarth yn Ysgolion Cymru*,
    Materion Addysg 2, y Swyddfa Gymreig), HMSO, 1978.
8   *Annual Report*, 1977-8, WJEC, Local Authorities Committee
    Appendix, 2.
9   *Geiriadur Termau: Dictionary of Terms*, English/Welsh; Welsh/
    English, University of Wales Press, 1973.
10 For details of establishments and courses in Wales, see *Directory
    of Establishments and Courses for Technical, Agricultural and
    Art Education in Wales*, WJEC, June 1978.
11 *Research Report, 1975-77*, The Polytechnic of Wales.
12 WJEC Technical Education Committee, Minutes of Meeting, 7
    October 1976.
13 K. Porter and J. Hurlow, 'The UCC/UWIST Post Graduate
    Certificate in Education and Certificate in Education (Further
    Education Course)', *Education for Development*, University
    College, Cardiff, Vol. 4, No. 1, April 1976, pp.29-43.
14 Cmnd. 6348, HMSO, November 1975.
15 *Our Changing Democracy: Devolution to Scotland and Wales*,
    Working Party Report, NATFHE Welsh Region, March 1976.
16 Response to Devolution Proposals, NUS Wales, Swansea, March
    1976.
17 Frances Gibb, 'Devolution in Wales', *The Times Higher Education
    Supplement*, 19 November 1976.
18 *Annual Report, 1976-77*, WJEC, Local Authorities Committee
    Appendix, 2.
19 'Further Education and Public Libraries in Wales', *Circular 5/78*,
    DES, *Circular 47/78*, Welsh Office, 31 March 1978.
20 Comments in response to invitation from Welsh Education Office,
    NATFHE Welsh Region, November 1977.
21 Hywel D. Lewis, 'Y Cynulliad a'r Brifysgol', *Y. Faner*, 19 August,
    1977, 18-19; and 'Y Brifysgol a'r Gymru Gyfoes' (Darlith
    Rhydfelen 1978), *Barn*, December/January 1978/9, No. 191/192,
    456-64.
22 Sir Goronwy Daniel, 'Devolution: a chance for educational
    reform?', *The Times Higher Educational Supplement*, 17
    November 1975.
23 *Supplementary Statement on Devolution to Scotland and Wales*,
    Cmnd. 6685, HMSO, August 1976.
24 'Report of the Working Group on the Management of Higher

Education in the Maintained Sector', *Oakes Report*, Chapter XI,
Wales, March 1978.
25 *Annual Report, 1977-78*, Manpower Services Commission, 1978,
p.41.
26 *Ibid.*, p.42.

CHAPTER 8

1 'The Education and Training of Teachers for Further and Higher
Education', Draft Policy Statement, NATFHE, 1978.
2 J. Konrad, 'Towards a United System of Teacher Education',
NATFHE Journal, June/July 1976, p.16.
3 S.C. Stoker, 'One-third of our future', *Education and Training*,
Vol. 20, No. 6, June 1978, p.185.
4 'The Training of Teachers for Further Education', (*Haycocks
Report*), ACSTT, 1975, para. 16.
5 *Ibid.*, para. 27.
6 'The Education and Training of Teachers for Further and Higher
Education', *op. cit.*, para. 4.6.1.
7 *Ibid.*, para. 4.4.
8 'The Training of Full-time Teachers in Further Education', First
Report, London and Home Counties RAC, August 1978.
9 Report of a Seminar on the Haycocks Report, 18 October 1978,
Royal Society of Arts Examination Board.
10 We are grateful to Dr F. Foden, until recently head of the
Department of General Education, Loughborough Technical
College, for making available to us an unpublished paper on the
training of part-time further education teachers.
11 'Entry to Initial Teacher Training Courses in England and Wales',
Circulars 9/78 and 99/78, DES and Welsh Office, 2 August 1978.
12 'Special Educational Needs: Report of the Committee of Enquiry
into the Education of Handicapped Children and Young People',
(*Warnock Report*), Cmnd 7212, HMSO, 1978.
13 See, for example, 'Further Education for Handicapped People,
1978-9', a booklet published by the East Midlands RAC in 1978.
14 G. Tolley, 'Staff Development in Further Education', Paper read to
the annual general meeting of the Association of Colleges in
Further and Higher Education; G.E. Wheeler, 'A Comprehensive
Approach to Staff Development', *Coombe Lodge Report*, Vol. 8,
No. 15, 986-91; and 'Staff Development in Further Education',
Report of Joint Working Party, ACFHE/APTI, 1973.
15 We are indebted to A.S. Addison, FE Teachers Study Group
Organiser, Southern RC, for information on this subject.
16 S.C.C. Stoker, 'One-third of our future', *op. cit.*, p.186.
17 *Staff Development Newsletter*, No. 1, February 1977, p.1.
18 *Haycocks Report, op. cit.*, para. 37.

REFERENCES

CHAPTER 9

1   A. Vernon Ward, *Resources for Educational Research and Development*, NFER, 1973, pp.22-3.
2   Cantor and Roberts, *op. cit.*, chapter 13, 'Research into further education', pp.250-5 and W. van der Eyken, 'Further Education', in Butcher and Pont (ed.), *Education Research in Britain*, Vol. 3, 1973, pp.285-300.
3   Guy Neave (ed.), *Research Perspectives on the Transition from School to Work*, 1978, Swets and Zeitlinger, Amsterdam.
4   W.A. Pirie, 'Identifying Common Skills'. *BACIE J.*, Vol. 30, No. 10, Nov. 1976, pp.185-6 and G. Holland *et. al.*, 'Identifying Common Skills, Part Two', *BACIE J.*, Vol. 31, No. 2, February 1977, pp.29-30.
5   For a review of the research activities of the TSA and ITBs, see Roger Bennet, 'Research into Training and Human Resource Development, 1: The Work of the TSA and the ITBs', *Ind. Training International*, June 1976, pp.184-5; *ibid.*, 2, *Journal of European Ind. Training*, Vol. 1, No. 2, 1977, p.xiii.
6   Rees, Ruth M. *Mathematics in Further Education – Difficulties experienced by craft and technical students*, Brunel Further Education Group, Hutchinson Educational, 1973.
7   *First Policy Statement*, BEC, March 1976, p.20.
8   A.G. Catchpole, 'The Further Education Research Association', *Research into Further Education*, Coombe Lodge Report, Vol. 9, No. 12, 1976, p.414.
9   Judy Dean and Bruce Choppin, *Educational Provision, 16-19*, NFER, 1977.
10 These projects are concerned with Further Education Opportunities for the Physically Handicapped, in conjunction with Hereward College of Further Education, Coventry; and the Development of Assessment Procedures for Blind and Physically Handicapped Further Education Students, at Queen Alexandra and Hethersett Colleges.
11 D.I. McCullum and J.S. Thornton, *Garnett Adult Multi-Aptitude Test*, Garnett College, London, 1978.
12 See, for example, M. Locke, *The Issues in College Government*, Centre for Institutional Studies, NELP, Working Paper No. 8, 1971 and *Financial Provisions in Polytechnic Articles of Government*, NELP Working Paper No. 21, 1972; and J. Pratt, T. Burgess and T. Travers, *Local Government Finance: a Response to the Government's Proposals*, NELP, 1978.
13 M.B. Youngman, R. Oxtoby, J.D. Monk and J. Heywood, *Analysing Jobs: A Case Study of Engineers at Work*, Gower Press, 1978.
14 See, for example, T. Burgess and J. Pratt, *Polytechnic: a Report*, Pitman 1974 and M. Locke, *The constitution of academic boards in polytechnics*, North East London Polytechnic, 1972.

15 I.F. Roberts, 'Education Research in Further Education: A Critical Review', *FERA Bulletin*, No. 15, 1978, p.8. One of the few exceptions is Beryl Tipton, *Conflict and Change in a Technical College*, Hutchinson, 1973.

16 Elizabeth Orna, *Thesaurus*, Engineering Industry Training Board, 1978.

17 Carl Slevin, 'Information in the Net', *The Times Educational Supplement*, 28 April 1978.

18 *Training and Development Abstracts*, ERIC, National Institute of Education, Washington DC, 20208.

19 *16-19, Growth and Response, 1: Curricular bases*, Schools Council Working Paper, No. 45, Evans/Methuen Educational, 1972.

20 *Tomorrow's Managers*, HCIMA Education Committee Consultative Report, August 1974; and D.M. Tyrell, 'The Effective Use of Numbers in Health Service Management', an unpublished Ph.D. thesis, University of Aston, 1976.

21 S.M. Kaneti-Barry, *Engineering Craft Studies: Monitoring a New Syllabus*, NFER, 1974; and NFER Research Information, RI/39.

22 *TEC Mathematics: Is it adding up?*, Conference Papers No. 14, Manchester Polytechnic; and I. McCullum, 'An External Evaluation of some TEC Engineering Course Units', Garnett College, London, 1978.

23 R. Oxtoby, 'The Changing Nature of FE Teacher Training', *NATFHE Journal*, November 1978, p.6.

24 *Certificates, Diplomas and Other Awards of the Institute*, Consultative Document, CGLI, August 1977; and *City and Guilds Broadsheet*, No. 84, October 1978.

25 J. Russell and J. Latcham (joint editors) 'Curriculum Development in Further Education', F.E. Staff College, 1973, revised 1979.

26 F. Fairhurst, 'How Institutes of Higher Education might assist F.E. Colleges in Curriculum Development', *Liberal Education*, No. 32, 1977, pp.34-8.

27 J. Heywood, 'Towards the Classification of Objectives; Training Technologists and Technicians', *International Journal of Electrical Engineering Education*, Vol. 12, 1975, pp.217-33; B.M. James, 'Relating Course Design to Occupational Needs', *The Vocational Aspect of Education*, Vol. XXIX, No. 73, Summer 1977, pp.59-65; and I. Clements, 'The Education and Training of Electrical Technicians: A Case Study', Interim Report, *FERA Bulletin*, No. 12, 1977.

28 'The ILEA Curriculum Development Project in Communication Skills', *FERA Bulletin*, No. 10, p.197.

29 Report of the Sub-Committee on Educational Research in Further Education *Oliver Report*, National Advisory Council on the Training and Supply of Teachers, 1960.

30 'Coombe Lodge Director looks to the Future', *The Times Higher Education Supplement*, 1 July 1977.

31 See, for example, J. Russell, 'Vocational Preparation of the 16-20

year olds – European Perspectives', *FERA Bulletin*, No. 15, 1978, pp.1-3.

CHAPTER 10

1 *The educational system of England and Wales*, DES, *op. cit.*, 29.
2 D. Bethel, 'Polytechnics: Serving the whole community', *The Times Educational Supplement*, 20 October 1978, p.27.
3 R. Pedley, *Towards the Comprehensive University*, Macmillan, 1977; 'Towards a Comprehensive Higher Education System', *NATFHE Journal*, November 1978, p.2; and 'Four Reforms to open up the universities', *The Times Higher Education Supplement*, 29 September 1978.
4 W. Taylor, 'Pros and Cons of keeping the binary system', *The Times Higher Education Supplement*, 20 October 1978.
5 *Ibid.*
6 'Comment', *NATFHE Journal*, No. 5, June 1978, p.2.
7 As reported in *The Times Higher Education Supplement*, 24 November 1978.
8 'Why CNAA must survive', *ibid.*
9 'Oakes is not the millennium', *NATFHE Journal*, No. 5, June 1978, p.2.
10 G. Stanton, *Experience, Reflection, Learning, op. cit.*, p.59.
11 *Ibid.*, p.61.
12 See, for example, *Young People in Transition*, Report of National Union of Teachers' Conference on the education and training of 14 to 19 year-olds, 1978.
13 'Vocational Preparation in Holland', *Educa*, No. 2, October 1978, pp.21-3.
14 A.N. Fairbairn, *The Leicestershire Community Colleges and Centres*, University of Nottingham, Department of Adult Education, 1978.
15 I.F. Roberts, 'School and Further Education: the need for a more effective partnership', Working Paper 3, prepared for NUT Conference, *Young People in Transition, op. cit.*, June 1978.
16 R.D. Williams, 'Whither Adult Education?', *Coombe Lodge Report*, Vol. 19, No. 12, 1977, p.475.
17 L.M. Cantor, *Recurrent Education in the United Kingdom, op. cit.*
18 *Young People in Transition, op. cit.*, p. 18.
19 See, for example, *Work and Learning*, Proposals for a National Scheme for 16-18 year-olds at Work, Rubber and Plastics Processing ITB, December 1978.
20 *Developments in Educational Leave of Absence*, OECD, Paris, 1976.
21 F.M. Bond, 'Making preparation for more part-time students', *The Times Higher Education Supplement*, 3 February 1978, p.14.
22 *Ibid.*

23 'Part-time discrimination', *The Times Higher Education Supplement*, 11 December 1976, p.16.
24 'Employment Problems of Young People from Ethnic Minorities', *Careers Bulletin*, Autumn 1978, p.24.
25 M. Farley, 'Further Education and Ethnic Minorities', *NATFHE Journal*, May 1978, p.10.
26 Jane King, 'Holland: a challenge to us all', *Disadvantage in Education*, Vol. 1, No. 6, September 1977, pp.3-6.
27 M. Farley, *op. cit.*
28 *The Vocational Education of Women*, London and Home Counties RAC, 1976, p.6.
29 'Women in Europe', *European Community*, No. 3, March/April 1976, pp.5-6.
30 A. Walters, 'Why do Girls Under-aspire and Women Under-achieve?', *Technical Journal*, July-September 1974, p.14.
31 *The Vocational Education of Women, op. cit.*, p.7.
32 *Further Education for Handicapped People, 1978-9*, East Midlands RAC, 1978, 2. See also *Disadvantage in Education*, No. 12, March 1979 for a number of articles on the implications of the Warnock Report for the further education sector.
33 P. Bennett, 'Patchy Provision for Handicapped Students', *NATFHE Journal*, October 1978, p.4.
34 *Ibid.*
35 'Paris charter sets target for the west', *The Times Educational Supplement*, 27 October 1978.
36 D.L. Parkes, 'The Educational Work of the EEC', in *16-20: Current Developments in Europe*, Coombe Lodge Report, Vol. 8, No. 15, p.994.
37 Rune Axelsson, 'Vocational Education in the Swedish Upper School: an Evaluation', *Pedagogisk Forskning Uppsala*, No. 1, 1978.
38 Henri Janne, 'Adult Education: school for life', *Forum*, Council of Europe 3/78, p.xiv.
39 Mark Webster, 'Not so permanent education', *The Times Educational Supplement*, 15 April 1978, p.10.
40 See, for example, *Polytechnics and the Implications of EEC Membership: A Report*, Committee of Directors of Polytechnics booklet, 1973.
41 T. Albert, 'Euro-cash builds Putney bridges', *The Times Educational Supplement*, 30 June 1978.
42 See, for example, *Occupational Basic Training 1: Preliminary Definition of a Polyvalent and Cultural Occupational Basic Training*, Council of Europe Doc. CC/EGT(77) 30-E, 1978; and *Youth Employment*, Bulletin of the European Committees, Supplement 4/77, Belgium, 1977.
43 Tyrell Burgess, 'This would be no way to run a public service', *The Times Higher Education Supplement*, 12 May 1978, p.9.
44. G. Fowler, 'Amending the Act', *The Times Educational Supplement*, 1 December 1978.

Index

People, 1978, 170, 212-13
Weitzel, D., 51
Welsh College of Agriculture,
  Aberystwyth, **146-7**
Welsh College of Music and Drama,
  Cardiff, **144-5**
Welsh Joint Education Committee
  (WJEC), 15, 17, 136, 141-2,
  150-5
Welsh Office, 11, **135-6**, 153-5; Report
  on Sixth Form Education, 141;
  *The Management of Higher
  Education in the Maintained
  Sector in Wales*, 1978, 153, 154
West London Institute of Higher
  Education, 109
West Midlands Advisory Council for
  Further Education, 17, 129;
  Regional Curriculum Unit, 189
Wheeler, G.E., 172, 193
White Papers: 1966, *A Plan for
  Polytechnics and Other Colleges*,

86-7, 91-3, 94, 96, 175, 196;
1972, *Education: A Framework for
Expansion*, 1, 2, 21, 87, 91, 112;
1974, *Educational Disadvantage
and the Educational Needs of
Immigrants*, 210; 1975, *Our
Changing Democracy: Devolution
to Scotland and Wales*, 150
Williams, Professor Gareth, 182
Williams, John, 180
Williams, Shirley, 90, 103, 206
Wolverhampton Polytechnic, 159,
  171, 174, 187
Worcester College of Higher
  Education, 172
Workers' Educational Association
  (WEA), 205

Youth Opportunities Programme
  (YOP), 29, 32, **49-52**, 56, 163,
  188, 201
Youthaid, 188